THE MYSTERY WRITER'S ART

THE MYSTERY WRITER'S ART

FRANCIS M. NEVINS, JR., EDITOR

Bowling Green University Popular Press
Bowling Green, Ohio 43403

SOURCES AND ACKNOWLEDGMENTS

"The Contributions of Edgar Allan Poe," by Robert A. W. Lowndes, from *Startling Mystery Stories,* Spring and Summer 1969, as two columns entitled "The Editor's Page"; revised for the present book. Reprinted by permission of Robert A. W. Lowndes, Editor, *Startling Mystery Stories.*

"Poe and the Tradition of the Detective Story," by J. R. Christopher, from *The Armchair Detective,* October 1968, as "Poe and the Detective Story"; revised for the present book. Reprinted by permission of Allen J. Hubin, Editor, *The Armchair Detective,* and J. R. Christopher.

"Who Shall Ever Forget?" by Ellery Queen, from *In the Queens' Parlor,* New York: Simon & Schuster, 1957. Reprinted by permission of Frederic Dannay ("Ellery Queen").

"Sax Rohmer: An Informal Survey," by Robert E. Briney, from *Xero,* No. 10 (May 1963), published by Mr. Richard Lupoff; revised version, *The Rohmer Review,* No. 1 (July 1968), published by Mr. Douglas Rossman; revised again by the author after last publication. Reprinted by permission of Richard A. Lupoff, Editor, *Xero;* Robert E. Briney; Douglas Rossman, Editor, *The Rohmer Review.*

"R. Austin Freeman: The Invention of Inversion," by Norman Donaldson, from *In Search of Dr. Thorndyke,* Bowling Green, Ohio: Bowling Green University Popular Press, 1971. Reprinted by permission of Norman Donaldson.

"Henry Wade," by Charles Shibuk, from *The Armchair Detective,* July and October 1968, as "Henry Wade" and "Henry Wade Revisited"; revised for the present book. Reprinted by permission of Allen J. Hubin, Editor, *The*

Armchair Detective, and Charles Shibuk.

"The Poetics of the Private-Eye: The Novels of Dashiell Hammett," by Robert I. Edenbaum, from *Tough Guy Writers of the Thirties,* edited by David Madden. Copyright © 1968 by Southern Illinois University Press. Reprinted by permission of Southern Illinois University Press.

"The Drury Lane Quartet," by Francis M. Nevins, Jr., from a section in Part Two of Mr. Nevins' series *Royal Bloodline: The Biography of the Queen Canon,* in *The Queen Canon Bibliophile,* January 1969; slightly revised for the present volume. Reprinted by permission of Rev. Robert E. Washer, Editor, *The Queen Canon Bibliophile,* and Francis M. Nevins, Jr.

"The Firm of Cool and Lam," by Frank E. Robbins, from *The Michigan Alumnus Quarterly Review* (now *The Michigan Quarterly Review*), 59 (Spring 1953), pp. 222-228. Reprinted by permission of Sheridan Baker, Editor, *The Michigan Quarterly Review.*

"Hitchcock's *Psycho,*" by Robin Wood, from *Hitchcock's Films,* London: A Zwemmer Ltd., 1965; revised ed., London: The Tantivy Press, 1969. Reprinted by permission of Robin Wood and Peter Cowie, Editor, The Tantivy Press.

"High and Low," by Donald Richie, from *The Films of Akira Kurosawa,* University of California Press, 1965. Reprinted by permission of University of California Press.

"The *Black Mask* School," by Philip Durham, from *Tough Guy Writers of the Thirties,* edited by David Madden. Copyright © 1968 by Southern Illinois Press. Reprinted by permission of Southern Illinois University Press.

"The Grandest Game in the World," by John Dickson Carr, from *Ellery Queen's Mystery Magazine,* March 1963. Reprinted by permission of John Dickson Carr and Frederic Dannay for *Ellery Queen's Mystery Magazine.*

"Detection and the Literary Art," by Jacques Barzun, from *The Delights of Detection,* ed. Jacques Barzun, Criterion Press, 1960. Reprinted by permission of Jacques Barzun.

"The Janus Resolution," by Frank D. McSherry, Jr., from *The Armchair Detective,* October 1968, as "A New Category of the Mystery Story"; revised for the present volume. Reprinted by permission of Allen J. Hubin, Editor, *The Armchair Detective,* and Frank D. McSherry, Jr.

"An Essay on Locked Rooms," by Donald A. Yates, from *The Michigan Alumnus Quarterly Review* (now *The Michigan Quarterly Review*), Spring 1957, as "The Locked Room"; revised for the present book, published (as revised) in *The Armchair Detective,* January 1970, as "The Locked House: An Essay on Locked Rooms." Reprinted by permission of Sheridan Baker, Editor, *The Michigan Quarterly Review*; Allen J. Hubin, Editor, *The Armchair Detective*; Donald A. Yates.

"The Detective As Metaphor in the Nineteenth Century," by Elliot L. Gilbert, from *Journal of Popular Culture*, Winter 1967. Reprinted by permission of Ray B. Browne, Editor, *Journal of Popular Culture*, and Elliot L. Gilbert.

"The Writer as Detective Hero," by Ross Macdonald, from *Essays: Classic and Contemporary*, edited by Richard W. Lid, published by J. B. Lippincott Company; entire selection *as printed in R. W. Lid's Essays: Classic and Contemporary*. Reprinted by permission of Harold Ober Associates, Inc. Copyright © 1964 by *Show Magazine*, Hartford Publications, Inc.

"The Detective Story as Historical Source," by William O. Aydelotte, from *Yale Review*, XXXIX, 1949-50; text revised for anthology. Reprinted by permission of Mary Price, Managing Editor, *The Yale Review*, and William O. Aydelotte.

"The Shape of Crimes to Come," by Frank D. McSherry, Jr. Never previously published. Printed by permission of Frank D. McSherry, Jr.

"Six Mystery Movies and Their Makers," by William K. Everson. From his notes for the New School of Social Research and the Theodore Huff film society. Printed by permission of William K. Everson.

COVER DESIGNED BY FRANK D. MCSHERRY, JR.

For Ray Hall

CONTENTS

Introduction

PART I. APPRECIATIONS

The Contributions of Edgar Allan Poe   1
    Robert A. W. Lowndes
Poe and the Tradition of the Detective Story   19
    J. R. Christopher
Who Shall Ever Forget?   37
    Ellery Queen
Sax Rohmer: An Informal Survey   42
    Robert E. Briney
R. Austin Freeman: The Invention of Inversion   79
    Norman Donaldson
Henry Wade   88
    Charles Shibuk
The Poetics of the Private Eye: The Novels of
          Dashiell Hammett   98
    Robert I. Edenbaum
The Drury Lane Quartet   122
    Francis M. Nevins, Jr.
The Firm of Cool and Lam   136
    Frank E. Robbins
Hitchcock's *Psycho*   149
    Robin Wood
High and Low   162
    Donald Richie
Six Mystery Movies and Their Makers   180
    William K. Everson

PART II. TAXONOMY

The *Black Mask* School   *Chandler*   197
    Philip Durham
The Grandest Game in the World   227
    John Dickson Carr
Detection and the Literary Art   248
    Jacques Barzun
The Janus Resolution   263
    Frank D. McSherry, Jr.

An Essay on Locked Rooms   272
    Donald A. Yates

PART III. SPECULATION AND CRITIQUE

The Detective as Metaphor in the Nineteenth Century   285
    Elliot L. Gilbert
The Writer as Detective Hero   295
    Ross Macdonald
The Detective Story as a Historical Source   306
    William O. Aydelotte
The Shape of Crimes to Come   326
    Frank D. McSherry, Jr.

INTRODUCTION

The object of this book is simply to bring together some of the best writing of recent years on the almost inexhaustible but critically neglected subject of crime fiction. The authors of the essays collected here include top-flight mystery writers, professors, editors, literary and film critics, and some of the most knowledgeable and articulate readers alive. Their perspectives are varied but their competence and commitment to the genre are alike.

There is only a tiny handful of anthologies dealing with crime fiction, the greatest being Howard Haycraft's loving and monumental *The Art of the Mystery Story* (Simon & Schuster, 1946). Since its appearance, several noteworthy developments in the field have occurred, of which three at least are reflected in certain essays in the present book: a greater stress on the work of individual authors rather than on the structure and characteristics of the genre; exploration of the common frontier shared by the mystery story and science fiction; and a recognition of the crime film as a near or fully equal partner to written crime fiction. The factors underlying these trends are not difficult to pin down: the number of first-rate mystery writers who have completed enough work to be judged as an organic whole is far greater today than in 1946; science fiction at its best has matured virtually into an art form over the intervening years; and the explosion of film-consciousness during the Sixties has made us look at today's (and yesterday's) mystery movies with a new vision.

A fourth trend is presupposed by this book as a whole—the quality of attention being paid to the genre has risen perceptibly over the past few years, and hopefully will continue to rise. One

reason for this development is that today at long last mystery
fiction has its own journals, specifically devoted to the study of
the genre in all its aspects. You will find these periodicals referred
to in the notes and credits hereafter, but I would like to point out
the first, best and most frequently cited of all, and the one in
which more of the following pieces first appeared than in any
other source. It is *The Armchair Detective,* an impossible-to-
praise-too-highly quarterly edited by Allen J. Hubin, mystery
critic of the *New York Times.* Without Mr. Hubin's incredible
labors in the field, the entire movement of critical interest in the
genre would lack its center, its focus, in a very real but non-
military sense its command post. What politicians have promised,
he has done; he has brought us together.

I would like to express my deepest thanks to Mr. Hubin; to
all of the contributors to this volume, both for their essays and
for the countless other ways in which they helped put the book in
shape; to Ray Browne, my editor, for giving me complete
autonomy and unstinting support; and to my wife Muriel, who
kept quiet as a rabbit during the times of frustration.

Francis M. Nevins, Jr.
East Brunswick, New Jersey
November 14, 1970

PART I

APPRECIATIONS

† There has been a tendency in recent years—for example, in A.E. Murch's The Development of the Detective Novel *(1958)— to stress the forerunners of Poe (whom we might call the great-uncles of the detective story) and to play down Poe's monumental achievement of taking the elements he found in the work of his predecessors, adding concepts of his own, and fusing the whole into the genre that is the subject of this book. Without denying the importance of Poe's historical antecedents, Mr. Lowndes in the following essay reaffirms the individual and collective importance of the personal contributions of that demon-haunted man who forged a new genre of fiction—a type of story which proclaims, in Hegel's words, that "Pure reason, incapable of any limitation, is the deity itself."*

The Contributions of Edgar Allan Poe
by Robert A.W. Lowndes

Just how far back in time the mystery tale goes is a moot question, and the question of how far back goes the tale wherein a mystery is solved by the use of reason, rather than magic or divination, is also open. The Book of Daniel contains two episodes which make very respectable detective stories: "Bel and the Dragon" and "Susanna." However, these two stories, as far as we know, were not written as fiction or understood by their readers to be fiction. We must come far forward in time from those days, to the nineteenth century to be exact, to find the beginnings of what we now consider the detective story, wherein a fictional character solves a fictional mystery through the use of inductive and deductive reasoning—ratiocination, as this operation was called

1

in the early nineteenth century. Such a story might indeed include thrilling events and action, but in no way does the solution of the mystery depend upon action. The detective may need to take steps in order to achieve justice, but the physical action derives from the solution to the mystery, at which the detective has arrived either by a combination of inspecting the premises and listening to or reading reports, or on the basis of reports alone, without ever having stirred from his chair.

The date to remember is April 1841 (in those days magazines were not dated ahead), and the publication to honor is *Graham's Magazine,* published in Philadelphia. It was here that readers saw "The Murders in the Rue Morgue," by an author who was already well known to followers of magazines: Edgar Allan Poe. This was the first of three tales of ratiocination devolving about a character named C. Auguste Dupin, whom Ellery Queen justly honors as "the world's first fictional detective in a modern sense." A little more than a year and a half later, the second Dupin tale, "The Mystery of Marie Rogêt," appeared as a three-part serial in *The Ladies' Companion,* November and December 1842 and February 1843. (Remember that one-month hiatus; it will become important later.) The final story, "The Purloined Letter," appeared in *The Gift,* late in 1844. An examination of these three tales will indicate the range of Poe's inventions in the detective story.

The first thousand or so words of "The Murders in the Rue Morgue" are devoted to an introductory essay on analysis. Some sort of introductory material preceding what can properly be called the start of a story was common apparatus for 19th century authors; but most of Poe's stories (as opposed to pieces which are sometimes included among the "tales" but are little more than essays or whimsies) either start at once or begin after no more than a paragraph or two of introduction. This preliminary essay, then, is unusual for Poe. Whether he employed it for his own benefit (feeling his way, as it were, in a new type of story), whether he felt that the reader needed this introduction in order to comprehend or sympathize with what the author was doing, or whether it represents a combination of the two previous suggestions, is something I'll gladly leave to the experts. Having read it with care, I can assure you that today's reader does not need it at all. There is nothing in it that is not accomplished better in the course of the story, once the story starts. The introduction ends with this brief paragraph: "The narrative which follows will appear to the reader somewhat in the light of a commentary upon the propositions just advanced."

Now the story begins, with the introduction of Monsieur C. Auguste Dupin. "This young gentleman was of an excellent, indeed of an illustrious family, but, by a variety of untoward events, had been reduced to such poverty that the energy of his character succumbed beneath it, and he ceased to bestir himself in the world, or to care for the retrieval of his fortunes." Our narrator meets Dupin in an obscure library where both are in search of the same "very rare and very remarkable" volume. They find they are kindred souls in a sufficient number of ways so that they decide to share quarters, so long as our narrator stays in Paris. ". . . and as my worldly circumstances were somewhat less embarrassed than his own, I was permitted to be at the expense of renting, and furnishing in a style which suited the rather fantastic gloom of our common temper, a time-eaten and grotesque mansion, long deserted through superstitions into which we did not inquire, and tottering to its fall in a retired and desolate portion of the Faubourg St. Germain."

We see at once that the world's first private detective is an unusual person of unusual tastes and temperament; with Poe, it could hardly be otherwise. "Had the routine of our life at this place been known to the world, we should have been regarded as madmen—although, perhaps, as madmen of a harmless nature." My own feeling is that this represents more of the author's characteristic gestures—his routine manner of describing an intelligent and educated gentleman with whom he hoped to capture the readers' attention—than carefully thought-out harmony between story and character. The pair leave their quarters only at night, while "At the first dawn of the morning we closed all the massy shutters of our old building; lighted a couple of tapers which, strongly perfumed, threw out only the ghastliest and feeblest of rayś. By the aid of these we then busied our souls in dreams—reading, writing, or conversing, until warned by the clock of the advent of the true Darkness. Then we sallied forth into the streets, . . . seeking, amid the wild lights and shadows of the populous city, that infinity of mental excitement which quiet observation can afford." Apparently this was before eyestrain was invented.

Nonetheless, despite the fact that the original portrait of Dupin is overdone (and later must be modified so that he can accomplish what he must accomplish), this very opening had tremendous influence upon subsequent authors of detective fiction. Sherlock Holmes, Father Brown, Hercule Poirot, Philo Vance, Sir Henry Merrivale, and Nero Wolfe—to list but a few—are all, to one degree or another, bizarre characters. And Dr. Doyle found that he had to modify a great deal of the description of Holmes' limitations as well as some of his habits (as presented in *A Study in Scarlet)* in order to fit him into later stories.

Poe goes on for slightly more than 800 words about the weird living style of the narrator and Dupin, then launches an episode wherein Dupin demonstrates his skill in induction and deduction, startling the narrator with a comment which would seem to indicate that Dupin could read his thoughts. Sherlock Holmes, you will remember, startled Dr. Watson at their first meeting, and Watson later compares Holmes to Dupin. Whereupon: "Sherlock Holmes rose and lit his pipe. 'No doubt you think that you are complimenting me in comparing me to Dupin,' he observed. 'Now, in my opinion, Dupin was a very inferior fellow. That trick of his of breaking in on his friends' thoughts after a quarter of an hour's silence is really very showy and superficial. He had some analytical genius, no doubt; but he was by no means such a phenomenon as Poe seemed to imagine.'" *(A Study in Scarlet,* Chapter II.)

But as Michael Harrison notes in his essay on Dupin ("Dupin: The Reality Behind the Fiction," in *The Exploits of the Chevalier Dupin,* Mycroft & Moran 1968), Doyle is really drawing a red herring across the reader's path, hoping thus to distract him from the size of the debt he actually owes to Poe and, in this first Holmes story, to "The Murders in the Rue Morgue" in particular. As Harrison indicates, Doyle was just beginning at that time, and was worried about being dismissed as a mere imitator of Poe; had he started writing about Sherlock Holmes after he was well established, he might have been more generous. (Later in *A Study in Scarlet*, Holmes tells Watson that his is a unique profession: the world's first consulting detective.   For after all, Dupin was a fictional character.)

It is not until after the thought-reading episode that we get to the crime: Dupin and the narrator see an account "Extraordinary Murders" in the evening paper. However, the material preceding this point and dealing with the first meeting between the narrator and Dupin is not superfluous, however awkward some of the attempts to make Dupin himself seem extraordinary. The two friends follow the newspaper accounts for a time, then when the arrest of a particular person is announced, Dupin asks the narrator's opinions. He replies: "I could merely agree with all Paris in considering them an insoluble mystery. I saw no means by which it would be possible to trace the murderer."

We shall see later on in the story that the narrator, while not adept at ratiocination to anything like the extent of Dupin, is nonetheless able to observe and to ask intelligent questions. The difference between Dupin and the narrator in these tales is nowhere near the difference between Holmes and Watson. Of course our detective must be ahead of his Boswell (otherwise the story might as well be written from the viewpoint of the detective himself); but the difference between Dupin and the narrator in Poe's tales, and between Holmes and Watson, is particularly interesting. Poe was writing for readers who were on the whole far better educated and addicted to thought than the general public for which Doyle wrote. The magazines to which Poe contributed were read by the "gentle" class, and only incidentally here and there by members of the general populace. But in late 19th-century England, the popular magazines, though priced for the most part beyond the means of the lower classes (the so-called penny dreadfuls were for them), had a much broader circulation. It was not only Doyle's need to show but also the reader's need to see how extraordinary Holmes was that required Watson to be rather lazy-minded and decidedly slow on the uptake—outside of his profession, that is.

The beautiful thing about Holmes' line "You know my methods, Watson" is that Watson really did know Holmes' methods, but he didn't know he knew them. He employed them constantly as a doctor, but it never occurred to him to use them outside the practice of medicine.

Whether consciously or not, Doyle used a technique which was perfectly appropriate for his general readership. He makes Watson a little denser than the reasonably well informed and alert reader, so that while the reader is perhaps rarely able to beat the great detective to the solution of the mystery, at least he's better than Watson. In respect to acumen, later authors have made their narrators pretty much either the Watson or the colleague-of-Dupin sort: Agatha Christie's Captain Hastings, whom she dropped after awhile for good reason, is more stupid than Watson (although he improves a bit after his marriage), and Archie Goodwin, while not up to Nero Wolfe's level, is at least as intelligent as the companion of Dupin.

Both Sherlock Holmes and Hercule Poirot said that their Boswells inspired genius, and we must suspect that one reason these sleuths are so fond of their companions is that the two masters appear so brilliant by comparison; in his heart each of the detectives realizes that he isn't as wonderful as his "friend and colleague" thinks he is. On the other hand, while Nero Wolfe has a certain fondness for Goodwin, he keeps Archie around because Archie is alert, intelligent and useful, more like the Poe than the Doyle type of narrator.

After the newspaper accounts of "The Murders in the Rue Morgue" comes a discussion of the police and their limitations. "The Parisian police, so much extolled for *acumen,* are cunning, but no more. There is no method in their proceedings, beyond the method of the moment. . . .The results attained by them are not unfrequently surprising, but, for the most part, are brought about by simple diligence and activity. When these qualities are unavailing, their schemes fail."

There is in these tales a certain amount of competition and rivalry between Dupin and G———, the Prefect of Police, but neither is really contemptuous of the other. Dupin respects the police on their level of competence, and acknowledges readily that they can do better than he on *most* crimes; for most crimes are very ordinary affairs, perpetrated by people with little imagination, and thus readily susceptible to diligence and cunning. But when the police are up against the extraordinary crime, the criminal with both intelligence and imagination, their methods are often inadequate. Poe does not lean heavily on exalting Dupin by presenting G——— and the police as imbeciles.

Sherlock Holmes, on the other hand, is usually at loggerheads with Scotland Yard, and rarely has a good word for Lestrade and the others. They, quite humanly, resent Holmes' airs (in addition to his very presence which is itself something of an insult to them); but they cannot always withhold a grudging respect for him, and eventually Scotland Yard men will mourn his apparent death.

Agatha Christie plays it both ways. Poirot already has the respect of the police on both sides of the Channel before the time of the first case that Captain Hastings records (*The Mysterious Affair at Styles*), but at times he has difficulty with a particular police detective (like Giraud in *Murder on the Links*) who considers him a conceited has-been. Miss Marple never has trouble with the police: to criticize them would be out of character for her. Willard Huntington Wright (S.S. Van Dine) wrote *The Benson Murder Case* as a burlesque, so the police are utter idiots. Philo Vance is a close friend of District Attorney Markham, and after one brief misunderstanding wins the respect of Sergeant Heath. As Wright began to find that he enjoyed writing murder mysteries he became less satirical, but I don't recall that the police ever go beyond the simplest level of competence in the series. Nero Wolfe and Archie Goodwin are in an endless feud with police authorities, who are constantly trying to get Wolfe's license revoked. Sir Henry Merrivale is a clown as well as a genius, but in general John Dickson Carr/Carter Dickson leans more toward Poe's rather than Doyle's method of handling the police. Father Brown, as a priest, renders unto Caesar that which is Caesar's.

But all the outstanding detectives of fiction who appear in a series of novels follow Poe in one respect: the murder or mystery is almost always an extraordinary one, not susceptible to the usual routine of diligence and cunning which at its best results in the solution of most crimes. Admittedly I have just presented a judgment disguised as a definition: I define outstanding fictional detectives as those who appear in cases of extraordinary crimes, requiring the methods of a Dupin, a Holmes, a Poirot or a Father Brown. My definition excludes crime stories where the only extraordinary element is the amount of violence, stupidity and sordidness that can be strung out before a simple and uninteresting "mystery" is solved. (Blood and horror are not barred *ipso facto:* "The Murders in the Rue Morgue" is as gruesome as any of the mindless gangster epics.)

To return to "The Murders," Dupin draws different conclusions than did the police from the facts available, one such conclusion being that there is something to be observed at the scene of the crime which the police did not notice. We do not know yet whether something right under their eyes escaped them, or whether they failed to look for something which hardly anyone would have noticed. These are two different possibilities, and Poe and his followers employed them both singly and in combination.

Another important element we find here is that it becomes necessary for the detective to observe at firsthand. (As we shall see, Dupin will solve a later case without stirring from his chair.) In the short story form we often find detectives who arrive at their solutions by sheer ratiocination, such as Miss Marple in *The Tuesday Club Murders* and a number of stories collected in other volumes; but in her novel-length cases she is required to move around a bit. Sherlock Holmes, for all his pipe-smoking and armchair deductions, is highly active in chasing down clues. Poirot scorns legwork that a police detective can do just as well, gets others to do most of the sniffing, and relies upon his gray cells—after, of course, getting everyone involved to talk at length about all sorts of matters seemingly unrelated to the crime. Father Brown goes around to a certain extent but is more of a Dupin than a Holmes. Nero Wolfe tries to give us the impression that he never leaves his brownstone, but it is astonishing how frequently he actually does go out; nonetheless his is the "gray cells" method, with Archie and subordinate private detectives such as Saul Panzer gathering the needed information preparatory to the climactic session in Wolfe's office.

When Dupin personally investigates the scene of the murders in the Rue Morgue, he discovers what he was looking for: a method of entering the murder room which was not considered possible. He knows now what he seeks as well as the type of person he seeks, and arranges for the person to come to him rather than going out to look for the party. There is a private confrontation and a confession, and Dupin's report to the police results in the release of the man who had been arrested and charged with the crime.

What was unique about "The Murders in the Rue Morgue"? Let us recapitulate some of the many elements in it that would be carried forward, or at least onward, by Poe's successors.

1.   C. Auguste Dupin is a private citizen, neither presently nor formerly a policeman, nor associated with the police in their work.

2.   Dupin is an eccentric, with a genius for induction and deduction as applied to human behavior.

3.   Dupin has not made a special study of crime and criminal methods beyond the extent to which an ordinary well-read person of his time would have done so.

4.   We see Dupin through the eyes of a close friend and associate, whose capabilities are above average, but lesser than Dupin's.

5.   Dupin is attracted by the extraordinary features of the crime in the Rue Morgue; ordinary crimes do not interest him.

6.   The case is a locked-room mystery.

7.   Several important clues are presented squarely to the reader in the initial accounts of the crime that Dupin and the narrator read in the papers. The number of clues is not important; what is important is that the reader is given a fair chance to see an essential part of the truth before the detective reveals it.

8.   But even if the reader follows these clues to a logical conclusion, the crime still appears to be impossible.

9.   Dupin has apparently reached a tentative conclusion from reading the newspaper accounts. However, if this conclusion is correct, the police have overlooked something that is there to be seen.

10.   Dupin arranges to examine the scene of the crime with the consent of the police. Relations between him and the Prefect show mutual respect and reasonable amity.

11.   Dupin considers police methods adequate for most crimes, which are committed by people with very little imagination. He is interested only in the unusual cases, for which routine methods are inadequate. He acknowledges that the police can do better in the routine cases than can he.

12.   Dupin is spurred to solve the riddle of the Rue Morgue by the fact that a person of whose innocence he is certain has been arrested and charged with the murders.

13.   Dupin satisfies himself by an examination of the scene of the crime that his hypothesis is correct. The reader is shown the evidence, and, if astute, now knows essentially as much as Dupin does.

14.   Dupin does not at once present his findings to the police, but sets a trap for the person he seeks.

15.   Dupin does not turn this party over to the police after he has heard the entire story, a good deal of which he has deduced.

16.   Dupin presents the police with just enough data to insure the release of the wrongly arrested gentleman.

17.   Even if the astute reader has solved the puzzle in essence before Dupin reveals the whole truth, there are aspects of the final summation which are likely to surprise, and the summing-up is therefore rewarding to read. (My opinion is that in a well-done puzzle detective story, even the most alert and ingenious reader never figures out the whole truth as revealed at the end.)

18.   There are no subplots in the story.

19.   Dupin and the narrator neither run into danger nor are threatened with violence.

20. "The Murders in the Rue Morgue" is a short story. A writer before Poe's time would probably have made the same material into a long novel, filling it out with extraneous matter. Poe's story, however, contains nothing inessential except the introduction, which was necessary in this pioneering instance.

Had Poe never written another Dupin story, "The Murders in the Rue Morgue" would still be a monument for everyone today who loves the puzzle type of mystery tale, wherein the puzzle is solved by reason rather than physical violence, and the reader is given the clues he needs to solve the puzzle himself if he is astute enough. But in fact Poe did write more than one Dupin story; so let us look at what he did in the second story, "The Mystery of Marie Rogêt."

This, I am told, is the least popular of the three tales, although I should think that the person who enjoys true crime stories as I enjoy mystery-puzzle fiction would find it the best of the three. A young girl named Mary Cecilia Rogers had been murdered in the vicinity of New York. At the time Poe wrote his second Dupin tale, the crime had not been solved. So, fascinated by his own theories of ratiocination, Poe set out again to do something which (to my knowledge) had never been done in fiction before. He essayed to solve not a crime that had taken place in the dim past but a still-unsolved mystery of the present—one which might even be solved between the time his story was being printed and the time it came to the reader's attention. Poe was risking disaster for his theories.

For what Poe did was to take the Mary Rogers case and transpose each separate element of it, using nothing more than newspaper accounts. As the brief introduction to the tale states in part: "The 'Mystery of Marie Rogêt' was composed at a distance from the scene of the atrocity, and with no other means of investigation than the newspapers afforded. Thus much escaped the writer of which he could have availed himself had he been on the spot and visited the localities."

Mary Rogers became Marie Rogêt, the essential facts of the real murder were duplicated in detail and the inessential facts were paralleled. Poe both draws the reader's attention to what he is really doing and disguises his objective in the brief introduction, where he speaks of coincidences which may seem almost supernatural but which actually are quite natural in the light of what he terms the "Calculus of Probabilities." And, he says, a prime recent example of such coincidence is the case of Mary Cecilia Rogers; for, *mirabile dictu,* a nearly exact parallel took place in Paris, "about two years after the atrocity in the Rue Morgue." And its solution was one of the most brilliant exploits of the narrator's friend, C. Auguste Dupin.

The crime is not extraordinary, but rather common and sordid. Why then does Dupin bother with the Marie Rogêt case? "The first intelligence of the murder was brought us by G—, in person. . . . He had been piqued by the failure of all his endeavors to ferret out the assassins. His reputation—so he said with a peculiarly Parisian air—was at stake. Even his honor was concerned. The eyes of the public were upon him; and there was really no sacrifice which he would not be willing to make for the development of the mystery. . . ."

Dupin gets his information from the police, from newspaper accounts, and from editorials in the papers. He makes no investigation of the scene of the crime, and he proposes his solution from the armchair. At the end of Dupin's solution appears the following paragraph, placed in square brackets.

"For reasons which we shall not specify, but which to many readers will appear obvious, we have taken the liberty of here omitting, from the MSS. placed in our hands, such portion as details the *following up* of the apparently slight clew obtained by Dupin. We feel it advisable only to state, in brief, that the result desired was brought to pass; and that the Prefect fulfilled punctually, although with reluctance, the terms of his compact with the Chevalier. . . .—*Eds.*

The "Eds." is generally taken as referring to the editors of *The*

Ladies' Companion, in which "Marie Rogêt" was originally published; I cannot but wonder, though, whether the paragraph did
not appear in Poe's own original manuscript. Since the Mary
Rogers case was still open, surely Poe would have realized that,
assuming his solution correct, revelation of the details whereby the
essential clues should be followed up might serve to insure the
culprit's escape.

An interesting feature of "Marie Rogêt" is that Poe therein
punctures common notions about the behavior of corpses under
water; this element too has been widely followed by subsequent
authors. Of course, the question whether Dupin's certainties as to
the facts are actually any less fallacious or superstitious than the
opinions he is puncturing remains moot. New superstitions drive
out old ones, and the notion that what drives out an old superstition cannot possibly be superstition itself is among the greatest
of superstitions.

Poe, as noted above, took a considerable risk in publishing
this story; for not only did he lack the advantage of examining the
locale himself, but he was in danger of being misled by the sort of
sloppy reporting that one frequently finds in the papers at any
time in the history of journalism. Nevertheless, we are assured in a
footnote to the story as it appears in book form that "the confes-
sions of *two* persons (one of them the Madame Deluc of the
narrative) made, at different periods, long subsequent to the publication, confirmed, in full, not only the general conclusion, but
absolutely *all* the chief hypothetical details by which that conclusion was attained."

On the basis of this note, most readers of "Marie Rogêt" have
accepted Poe's claim that he solved the actual murder of Mary
Cecilia Rogers. But new light has recently been shed on this subject by John Walsh in his book *Poe the Detective* (Rutgers University Press, 1968). A former newspaperman, Mr. Walsh searched
through the files of newspapers published in New York and New
Jersey in 1841/42—i.e., Poe's own source material—and familiar-
ized himself with the area of New York City where Mary Rogers
lived and worked. Contemporary maps and woodcuts of the

Hoboken-Weehawken area gave further assistance, so that it was possible for him to come up with nearly as much material as Poe had, as well as some that Poe did not have. Walsh then made a close examination of Poe's story in the light of known or probable events in the author's life during 1841-42, and compared the original magazine version of the story's final sections with the version later reprinted in hard covers, with numerous footnotes added. His conclusion is that Poe's claim to have solved the case in his story amounts not to a triumph of ratiocination but of flummery. The footnotes added to the hardcover reprint, plus a few ingenious alterations (both additions and deletions) in the text of the reprint, have given a misleading impression for well over a century.

At least that is Mr. Walsh's thesis, and the late Prof. Thomas Ollive Mabbott, who wrote the Introduction to *Poe the Detective*, found it convincing; as I do myself, mainly for the following reasons. (1) The issue of *The Ladies' Companion* which carried part three of the story was not January 1843 but February 1843. The first two installments appeared in the issues of November and December 1842, and there was a January 1843 issue; why then was Poe's final installment held up a month? Walsh's researches indicate that fresh material in the Mary Rogers case which threatened to refute Poe's solution came to light just around the time the final installment of "Marie Rogêt" was due to be printed. The most likely theory seems to be that publication was held up so that Poe could do a quick revision incorporating the newly discovered material. (2) Although Poe's original manuscript cannot be found, two slightly different texts exist. In his book Walsh prints the text we are familiar with, plus the alterations (the additions and deletions), so that we can see where the two versions differ, and correlate the variant texts with the footnotes which made Poe's claim so convincing to both readers and scholars up to the present time. (3) Walsh confirms my suspicion that Poe himself wrote the bracketed paragraph quoted above, which is signed "*Eds.*" in the hardcover text. (Which raises the question, which never before occurred to me, Watson that I am: might not Poe have written *all* the footnotes?)

But regardless of whether or not it solved the actual murder of Mary Rogers, "The Mystery of Marie Rogêt" gives us some more firsts for Poe.

21. Dupin is the first fictional private detective to appear in a series of stories.

22. The police come to Dupin, imploring his help.

23. Dupin solves the mystery upon data brought to him, without leaving his quarters, thereby becoming the first armchair detective.

24. Dupin questions no one other than the Prefect, and solves the case solely on official data and newspaper accounts.

25. In this second appearance, Dupin is no longer presented as a bizarre character but only as a slightly eccentric fellow.

26. Dupin presents the police with data enabling them to apprehend the culprit, but takes no part himself in following up his deductions.

27. In the course of discussing the case, Dupin undertakes to explode popular notions on matters often connected with crime.

"The Purloined Letter," last of the Dupin series, is easily the best in a number of ways, but not in all ways. It is the best written, judged by the modern taste. "The Murders in the Rue Morgue" could not help but arouse suspicion that it was merely an invention to illustrate Poe's theory of analysis rather than an episode in the career of C. Auguste Dupin. An equal suspicion of ulterior motives lies behind "The Mystery of Marie Rogêt": Poe is so full of enthusiasms and messages, so quick with fables which "prove" his contentions! But "The Purloined Letter" has no such flaws; it starts at once, in Dupin's quarters, one autumn evening.

By a most interesting coincidence, the narrator and Dupin have just been discussing the two previous cases when Monsieur G—, the Prefect of Police, enters. What is more, he enters at the end of the very first paragraph. The game is afoot, as a spiritual son of Dupin will say.

In several pages of animated dialogue, we learn that the Prefect's problem is a stolen letter for which all search thus far has been futile but which must be recovered. Dupin says he can only suggest that the Prefect and his men search once again, even more thoroughly, the premises where the letter must be hidden.

> "I have no better advice to give you," said Dupin. "You have, of course, an accurate description of the letter?"
>
> "Oh, yes!"—And here the Prefect, producing a memorandum-book, proceeded to read aloud a minute account of the internal, and especially of the external, appearance of the missing document. Soon after finishing the perusal of this description, he took his departure, more entirely depressed in spirits than I had ever known the good gentleman before.

It is generally contended that the reader has no fair chance to solve the mystery of the letter's hiding-place; and so far as the precise spot is concerned, I would agree. But it seems to me that the reader is given a fair enough opportunity to grasp the principle of concealment that is the point of the story.

A month passes, then the Prefect drops around to Dupin's quarters again, and admits that he is completely stumped. He again searched the premises of the man who stole the letter, as Dupin suggested, but to no avail. (There is no doubt who the culprit is, nor is there anything to be gained by arresting the man, for a royal scandal will ensue if the existence of the letter becomes known.)

Dupin asks if there is a reward for the return of the letter, and the prefect replies: ". . .I wouldn't mind giving my individual check for fifty thousand francs to anyone who could obtain me the letter. The fact is, it is becoming of more and more importance every day; and the reward has been lately doubled. If it were trebled, however, I could do no more than I have done."

After a little badinage, wherein the Prefect repeats that he would *really* give fifty thousand francs to anyone who could aid him in the matter, Dupin gets up, produces his checkbook, and replies: "In that case,. . . you may as well fill me up a check for the amount mentioned. When you have signed it, I will hand you the letter."

After the Prefect has signed the check, Dupin, "unlocking an *escritoire,* took thence a letter and gave it to the Prefect. This functionary grasped it in a perfect agony of joy, opened it with a trembling hand, cast a rapid glance at its contents, and then, scrambling and struggling to the door, rushed at length unceremoniously from the room and from the house, without having uttered a syllable since Dupin had requested him to fill up the check." And herewith G— exits from the series, for he does not return to learn how Dupin obtained the letter or where it had been hidden. Several pages of question and answer between the narrator and Dupin fill us in.

From this dialogue we learn something of Dupin's past, of the days prior to those misfortunes that left him in the rather sorry condition in which the narrator first met him in "The Murders in the Rue Morgue." Dupin's narration shows him taking action for once, and rather dangerous action; however, he had deduced in advance how to look for the letter, and that, of course, is the answer to the riddle. Although it has become astonishingly easy to locate the letter, recovering it is another matter, and Dupin resorts to assistance to create a diversion just long enough so that he can substitute a facsimile for the letter.

Although Dupin's explanation covers more pages than were taken to come to the delivery of the letter to the Prefect, Poe continues to hold the reader's interest. The pace slows a little, as it must when an illustrated lecture is being given; but the slow-down is more than compensated for by the suspense and the revelation of Dupin's character. Although it is actually somewhat longer than it appears to be, "The Purloined Letter" remains a remarkably swift-moving short story. From it we may add the following features to our list.

28. New facets of Dupin's character are revealed.

29. An element of humor (the practical joke on the Prefect) is worked in without appearing strained.

30. Dupin has a personal score to settle with the culprit.

31. The essential problem is not how to reveal but how to help officially conceal the existence of a crime.

32. Since the health of the state is involved, "The Purloined Letter" is a cloak-and-dagger story of intrigue in addition to being a genuine puzzle mystery.

My list of elements that subsequent authors derived directly or indirectly from Poe's Dupin stories comes to 32. It is a sizeable list, and I know of no subsequent author who has added half so much again to the list. Even if some of the elements can be traced back to writers predating Poe, he was the first to put them all together in a shorter total of words than you will find in any of the best novels that came after him.

MORE ON AUTHOR AND SUBJECT

Robert A. W. Lowndes was born in 1916 and grew up in Rhode Island and Connecticut. He has spent most of his working life as editor and manager of a wide variety of pulp magazines, but has also found time over the years to publish four science fiction novels and innumerable short stories and articles of his own. Since he has been avidly reading science fiction, weird fiction, and detective stories since high school, it is fitting that among the magazines he is presently associated with are Magazine of Horror, Weird Terror Tales, *and* Startling Mystery Stories. *He is a member of both the Baker Street Irregulars and the Praed Street Irregulars; and if anyone should start a society of Rue Dunôt Irregulars, the essay you have just read will certainly entitle him to charter membership.*

For more on the subject of Poe, simply turn to the next essay.

† Since Poe in "The Murders in the Rue Morgue" dealt with the divergent but overlapping accounts of witnesses to the same events, it is not inappropriate that we next consider Prof. Christopher's account of Poe's contributions, which also overlaps but diverges from Mr. Lowndes' essay. Without neglecting to state his own view of Poe's substantive achievements, Christopher puts greater emphasis on the tradition Poe founded, how it was carried forward, and what others have said about different aspects of that tradition.

Poe and the Tradition of the Detective Story
by J. R. Christopher

Edgar Allan Poe (1809-1849) is generally credited with creating the detective story. Like all such historical truths, this is a half truth. Puzzle stories and mystery stories existed before Poe. "The Story of Bel" in the *Apocrypha* is a clear example. There is a locked room from which the food-sacrifices to the idol Bel have been vanishing; the prophet Daniel sprinkles flour on the floor to find out who has been taking the food and from whence he or they come (it turns out not to be Bel). Probably the fullest literature of the detective-story type before Poe is the long series of short stories and novels about the Chinese judges or magistrates of about 1000 A.D., written down four hundred or more years later. But besides these and other early parallels, the detective story as we

19

know it had to wait until there were professional detectives in the West, and these did not appear until the eighteenth century. In England the capture of criminals was originally the function of a group of professionals known as the Bow Street Runners. Fictional use of the Runners was occasional: a couple appear in *Oliver Twist*, for example. More recently, John Dickson Carr's *The Demoniacs* (Harper, 1962), set in 1757, has a Bow Street Runner as its hero, and Sir John Fielding, the blind Metropolitan magistrate who presided at Bow Street, appears in a central role.[1]

More influential than the fictional cases of Bow Street which appeared in nineteenth-century England was a parallel occurrence across the Channel: François Eugène Vidocq, thief, vagabond, jail-breaker, and finally thief-catcher, issued his fictionalized *Mémoires de Vidocq* in 1828-9. Poe was acquainted with this work, and he deliberately set up his C. Auguste Dupin as an amateur who speaks slightingly of his countryman Vidocq[2] and who is far abler than his contemporary G——, the Prefect of the Parisian police. Here is born the amateur-professional struggle (or private detective-police struggle) which has remained basic down to the current Nero Wolfe-Inspector Cramer encounters.

The first detective story, like the first novel, is hard to find; but the point of crediting "The Murders in the Rue Morgue" (1841) with being first is more valid than most. For in that tale Poe began most of the traditional features of the detective story. For example, there is a nameless narrator, almost as imperceptive as Dr. Watson, who chronicles his first meeting with Dupin, their sharing of a house, and the detective problem; Sir Arthur Conan Doyle followed this pattern, sans Gothicism, for his first Sherlock Holmes story, *A Study in Scarlet* (1887). Poe also started, and Doyle continued, the convention of the detective being able to follow his companion's thoughts by means of his minor actions; Holmes depreciated this device of Dupin in *A Study in Scarlet* but used it himself in "The Resident Patient." In addition, Poe began other conventions: the eccentric detective (Dupin prefers night to day), the locked-room puzzle (the police break into a room where minutes before a woman was screaming, and find her murdered, with the windows

shut and the door locked from the inside), and the unjustly suspected or arrested person (in this story, a bank clerk). Perhaps Poe here
also created the scientific detective, since Dupin from a tuft of
hair and a span of fingerprints deduces a non-human killer, then
checks his deduction against a textbook from his shelves. Of all
these conventions, two have been especially significant: the
eccentric detective (exemplified today by Rex Stout's Nero Wolfe,
who among other idiosyncrasies grows orchids on the roof of his
New York brownstone), and the locked-room puzzle (on which
John Dickson Carr built his reputation).[3]

Poe's second detective story, "The Mystery of Marie Rogêt"
(1842-3), is the least popular of his three stories about Dupin, but
it is of equal generic importance with the first. The simple fact
that it is a second Dupin story establishes the series detective, and
prefigures the four novels and five books of short stories about
Sherlock Holmes, and the fifty-one Father Brown stories by G. K.
Chesterton. Secondly, Dupin here functions as the armchair detective, never leaving his rooms, never seeing the people involved as
he makes his deductions; the most famous work in this tradition is
Baroness Orczy's series of short stories about The Old Man in the
Corner. Third, "Marie Rogêt" is based on an unsolved case which
Poe read about in the newspapers, the 1841 murder of the New
York City cigar girl Mary Cecilia Rogers.[4] There are several mystery
novels which are based on actual crimes, but few in which factual
unsolved crimes are solved fictionally, the most common probably
being the stories about the Jack the Ripper murders, such as Ellery
Queen's *A Study in Terror* (Lancer, 1965). Finally, mention
should be made of the realism of "Marie Rogêt" as contrasted
with the unusual, outré atmosphere of the first Dupin story, even
though "Marie Rogêt" is a far cry from today's police procedural
story.

The third and final case for Dupin is "The Purloined Letter"
(1844). It is the most popular of the three cases, probably because
it does not depend on a series of outrageous circumstances as does
the first (a rusted nail, a sailor chasing his orangutan through the
streets of Paris), and it is not as long and newspaperish as the

second. On the other hand, it is not a fair detective story in the sense that the reader has an equal chance with the detective to solve the case; for, aside from a few very general hints of the direction in which the solution lies, the reader does not know that there is a letter out in the open in Minister D——'s rooms until Dupin tells the narrator how he solved the case and retrieved the stolen letter, which was returned to (presumably) the Queen of France. There are five conventions which first appeared in this story: (1) the concept of psychological detection; (2) the ultra-obvious concealment (brilliantly exemplified in John Dickson Carr's 1950 short story "The Gentleman from Paris," which is set in 1849 and features Poe himself as its detective);[5] (3) the staged diversion (which Doyle borrowed for "A Scandal in Bohemia"); (4) the detective's long and condescending explanation at the end of the story; and (5) the involvement of the detective in state affairs (another concept which Doyle carried forward in the Sherlock Holmes saga, particularly in "The Adventure of the Second Stain," which also concerns a stolen document of political importance).

"The Purloined Letter" as a story of psychological detection has a number of ramifications. Dupin, using the analogy of the boy who judges the intelligence of his fellows in their game of "even and odd," explains that the detective must put himself in the mind of his opponent. This psychological identification may be the forerunner of Father Brown's empathetic knowledge of the criminal mind, and is the basis of the traditional master detective's belief that the police are good only for obvious types of cases. Further, the concept of the psychological union of opposites relates "The Purloined Letter" to those Poe stories, such as "William Wilson," which deal with doubles. Indeed one literary critic has carried this relationship so far as to insist that "The Purloined Letter" is not a detective story but a psychological romance about the struggle of the ego and the shadow—to use Jung's term for the two sides of the same personality—over the anima (or over a letter to her, although the envelope offers interesting psychoanalytical possibilities). The critic's case is overstated, but it may help to explain the popularity of this story. Another aspect of "doubleness" may unite Dupin to the Minister D——; Howard Haycraft in *Murder for Pleasure* (1941) has suggested that the two characters were based on André Dupin (1783-1865), a statesman and writer on French criminal procedure, and his brother Francois Dupin (1784-1873), an author of mathematical and economic treatises.

Before we bid adieu to the Chevalier, it should be mentioned that Dupin has recently inspired a series of pastiches by Michael Harrison, originally published in *Ellery Queen's Mystery Magazine* and collected, with an Introduction by Queen, in *The Exploits of the Chevalier Dupin* (Mycroft & Moran, 1968).   Two of these pastiches were published in magazine form in 1966, one hundred and twenty-five years after the appearance of Poe's first Dupin story; two are locked-room puzzles, fittingly since Poe created the form in "The Murders in the Rue Morgue"; and one is a stolen-documents case, like the final Dupin tale by Poe. Harrison's book is not the only volume of detective pastiches ever published——*The Exploits of Sherlock Holmes* by Adrian Conan Doyle and John Dickson Carr comes to mind——but very few such volumes have appeared. (Should one say that very few fictional detectives have been so exploited?)

But perhaps when we leave Dupin we also leave our subject of Poe and the detective story tradition. For Haycraft in *Murder for Pleasure* stated that he considers the three Dupin stories the only detective stories that Poe wrote, and based his conclusion on the fact that in the two other Poe tales often regarded as detective stories, evidence is withheld from the reader until after the solution is reached. But as we have already seen, evidence is also withheld in "The Purloined Letter"; and indeed this is also true of "The Murders in the Rue Morgue." Admittedly the first Dupin story, described by Ellery Queen as having "the evidence fully presented to the reader," is fairer than "The Purloined Letter." It certainly presents the testimony of the witnesses fairly. But the room's windows and the lightning rod are not described until Dupin begins his explanation, halfway through the story; further, the tuft of hair and the greasy hair-ribbon are not mentioned until Dupin produces them in the course of his explanation. And as for "Marie Rogêt," John Walsh's masterly *Poe the Detective*, referred to earlier, shows clearly how unfair to the reader Poe was in that tale. Thus we can hardly follow Haycraft in his elimination of the remaining stories for not playing fair, since on this basis we would have no Poe stories at all to discuss here. Let us then proceed to what Queen for one calls the fourth Poe detective story.

"'Thou Art the Man'" (1844) is a poor story, told in a jocular tone which does not come off effectively;[6] but several of its detective patterns are of interest. These are (1) the use of the least likely person as the murderer (although Poe exaggerates this device for humorous effect by naming the murderer Goodfellow, devotees of Agatha Christie will know what subtle changes can be rung on this theme); (2) as Anthony Boucher has pointed out, "the to this day much rarer device of the . . .Least Suspected Detective—a device brilliantly exploited by Q. Patrick, whereby the reader, up to the last moment, has no notion who is the murderer *or* who is going to denounce him" (Boucher himself used this device in his 1939 novel *The Case of the Crumpled Knave);* (3) the planting of false clues (a concept carried to its logical climax in Queen's "The Adventure of the Glass-Domed Clock"); (4) the confession produced by psychological third degree (as in Queen's "The Adventure of the Mad Tea-Party"); and (5) detection by an anonymous investigator (which probably reached its culmination in Cornell Woolrich's "One Drop of Blood," wherein both the detective and the criminal are nameless).

"'Thou Art the Man'" also features an apparent supernatural occurrence that is later explained logically—an approach stemming from the Gothic novels of Ann Radcliffe and frequently used in our own time by John Dickson Carr. The hearing for Pennifeather, his trial, and the explanation of *cui bono* (how many nephews in mysteries since Pennifeather have been accused of killing their uncles?) foreshadow the present-day legal mystery, although Poe himself never used a lawyer-detective. The small-town setting of "'Thou Art the Man'" may bring to mind the Notlaw, Wyoming of Dorothy Gardiner's Sheriff Moss Magill stories or the Farrington, Montana of Margaret Scherf's novels about Rev. Martin Buell. Another point is that the detective of "'Thou Art the Man'" is also the narrator; although Holmes also narrated a few of his own cases, such as "The Adventure of the Lion's Mane," the difficulties of keeping up the suspense in a puzzle story when the solver of the puzzle is relating his own thoughts limited the use of this first-person approach until, with Hammett's Continental Op and Chandler's Philip Marlowe, the hard-boiled private eye story and the puzzle story coalesced. Finally, and climactically, as both Ellery Queen and Anthony Boucher have pointed out, "'Thou Art the Man'" is *not*, as Howard Haycraft alleged, unfair to the reader. In Boucher's words: "Mr. Haycraft's statement [in *Murder for Pleasure*] that 'the all-important factor of the bullet which passed *through* the horse' is concealed from the reader needs no disproof beyond a rereading of paragraph six: '. . .a pistol-shot, that had gone clean through and through the poor animal's chest. . .'" And, as Queen has said: "Had Poe never written 'The Murders in the Rue Morgue,' 'The Mystery of Marie Rogêt,' and 'The Purloined Letter' —had he written only 'Thou Art the Man'—critics the world over would be mashing one another in the rush to acclaim it literature's first detective story and a herculean *tour de force*."[7] Thus Poe's story must be considered a forerunner of the Golden Age of fair-play mysteries in the 1920's and '30's.

A far more famous Poe tale, "The Gold-Bug" (1843), has been considered a detective story by Dorothy L. Sayers in her Introduction to the first *Omnibus of Crime* and by A..E. Murch in her *The Development of the Detective Novel* (London: Peter Owen, 1958; New York: Kennikat Press, 1968). The tale is certainly not much of a puzzle, but nonetheless has several devices which have been used by later writers. For instance, there is the search for buried treasure, which hardly seems a detective motif until one remembers that Ellery Queen solved a riddle to find a pirate treasure in "The Adventure of the Needle's Eye." It must be confessed that he embarked on the case of Captain Kidd's treasure with a relish ". . .suitable to a small boy in his first hot pursuit of Mr. Legrand's golden *scarabaeus*. . ." Queen writes; and both Queen's and Legrand's resurrected treasures are found by means of high-placed eyes, and both consist of coins and jewelry loosened from its settings. A far more basic detective device of "The Gold-Bug" is the cipher which Legrand solved; another substitution cipher appears in Doyle's "The Adventure of the Dancing Men," and a more complicated if far shorter such cipher may be found in Anthony Boucher's "The Numbers Man," which also features an anonymous detective. Legrand's refusal to share his knowledge with his assistants is matched by the reticence of many well-known sleuths, such as Nero Wolfe. "He. . .can't stand it to have anyone keep up with him at any time on any track. . . . I admit that even under ideal circumstances it wouldn't happen very often, but it would ruin a good meal for him if it ever happened at all," Archie Goodwin writes of his employer in "Instead of Evidence," Legrand's excuse for his similar behavior is that his anonymous Boswell believes him crazy.

A recent novel squarely in the tradition of "The Gold-Bug" is John Dickson Carr's *Dark of the Moon* (Harper, 1967). Both authors employ the setting of Charleston, South Carolina, and in both stories most of the events take place on a nearby island. Carr uses James Island for this purpose, but he has Dr. Gideon Fell make a visit to Sullivan's Island, where Poe served in the army.

> Dr. Fell gaped like an idiot, the cigar slipping through his fingers.
> "Sullivan's Island? This it can't be!"
> "Why not?"
> "These wide, swept streets and trim villas? This air of suburban prosperity a-doze? Forgive me," bumbled Dr. Fell, groping as though for sanity, "if my notions of the island are derived soley from Edgar Allan Poe, *The Gold Bug,* and that wild, desolate spot where they dug up Captain Kidd's treasure."

Dr. Fell and his companions also visit the museum at Fort Moultrie and look at a photograph of Poe as a soldier. But there is more resemblance between the stories than just setting. Henry Maynard in Carr's novel spends time at calculations, as William Legrand ciphered strange figures; mysterious messages appear on a blackboard in *Dark of the Moon,* as Legrand worked out a message on his slate; Dr. Fell peers at Fort Sumter through binoculars, as Legrand peered at a skull through a telescope. There is a love-affair in Carr's novel which in one way resembles Poe's marriage, and a method of murder that is analogous to Jupiter's dropping the Gold-Bug through an eye of the skull.

The five stories I have discussed have been regarded by many reputable critics as the foundations of the detective-story genre. However, two other tales have some claim to be added to the list. One is "A Tale of the Ragged Mountains" (1844), which Anthony Boucher suggested is, like Thomas Burke's "The Hands of Mr. Ottermole," a detective story with only the reader as detective.[8] Boucher argued that the evidence offered in Poe's story by Dr. Templeton to support Bedloe's psychic vision is falsified evidence; that although the portrait of Oldeb with its "scarcely visible" date, and the "freshly written" manuscript about Oldeb's adventure in India, are produced to verify the vision, in reality Dr. Templeton planted the vision in Bedloe hypnotically after himself preparing this "evidence," in order that the narrator would not investigate further when Bedloe died by a sangsue fastened to his temple (an "accident" in many ways resembling the snake-like arrow which killed Oldeb). If Boucher is right, then besides writing a story in which the reader is the detective (which, according to Ellery Queen, Dashiell Hammett also did in "His Brother's Keeper"), Poe here also wrote the first mystery in which false evidence is planted by hypnotic suggestion (a device carried on by Cornell Woolrich in "Nightmare"). It should also be noted in passing that Bedlo(e) and Oldeb are another pair of Poe's doubles, and that their names come very close to being anagrams of the word.

The final tale with possible connections to the detective genre is Poe's "The Man of the Crowd" (1840), reprinted by Ellery Queen with a critical afterword in his anthology *Poetic Justice* (New American Library, 1967). Queen points out that the story's anonymous narrator begins as an armchair detective, deducing the occupations of passers-by from their appearances (much as Sherlock and Mycroft Holmes in "The Greek Interpreter" deduced the biographies of the people who passed the windows of the Diogenes Club). Queen's second contention is that Poe's narrator becomes an active detective, almost a private eye, when he shadows the "old man" who "is the type and genius of deep crime," dogging his footsteps while wearing "caoutchouc over-shoes," which, says Queen, is Poe's name for gumshoes. Queen admits that the detective fails in finding out about the old man, but contends that there is no rule of the genre that requires the detective to be always successful (he could but did not cite Holmes' failure in "The Yellow Face" at this point). Although Poe's narrator is detective-like in his approach to others, the main difficulty with reading this story as detective fiction is that the old man is so obviously a walking symbol, and the narrator is not much better. The narrator says that he has recently been ill, but manages to keep awake, most of the time shadowing the old man, for twenty-four hours. Not only does the old man fail to realize he is being shadowed (near the end of the story the narrator stands directly in front of him and yet is not seen), but also the old man continually searches for places where people are, where the crowd is, as if he took his animation, his life, from them—or as if he is simply a symbol of the social or public life. Did Poe, the introvert, think a symbolic extrovert naturally "the type and genius of deep crime?"

We have considered seven stories and the tradition they created through device, episode and character in later detective stories, and I have listed approximately twenty-five of these traditional elements, or perhaps more, depending on where the reader divides some of them. Despite the rich variety of detective fiction over the century and a quarter since Poe wrote, the inspiration for the genre was Poe's, and a large number of the traditions lead back to him. So all honor (as far as the Calculus of Probabilities allows) be unto Poe, the father of the detective story tradition.

NOTES

[1]In 1829 Sir Robert Peel, for whom London's Bobbies are named, reformed the entire English police system, and created Scotland Yard. Again, the best fictional account of the Yard's first days is by John Dickson Carr, in *Fire, Burn!* (Harper, 1957).

[2]In *A Study in Scarlet* Sherlock Holmes speaks identically of both Vidocq and Dupin.

[3]The most important critical discussions of locked-room theory appear in Chapter XVII of Carr's *The Three Coffins* (1935), Chapter 13 of Clayton Rawson's *Death from a Top Hat* (1938), and Chapter 14 of H.H. Holmes' (Anthony Boucher's) *Nine Times Nine* (1940).

[4]One reason this is not a popular story is that it consists of newspaper paragraphs followed by Dupin's comments; another reason is its obscure ending, which was probably dictated by historic reasons, though not the reasons given in the story. John Walsh in *Poe the Detective* (Rutgers University Press, 1968) argues persuasively that after completing the story Poe was forced by new revelations in the newspapers to revise the ending so as to make it ambiguous.

[5]A further note on the ultra-obvious concealment: both the Poe and the Carr story deal with hidden papers,but there have been other uses of the concept. Chesterton's "The Invisible Man," Thomas Burke's "The Hands of Mr. Ottermole" and Ellery Queen's "The Adventure of the Tell-Tale Bottle" all play with the idea of the murderer himself being so obvious that he is ignored. And Carter Dickson's (John Dickson Carr's) Colonel March story "Hot Money" deals with a piece of furniture too obvious to be checked by trained investigators as a hiding place for stolen goods.

[6]On this point Anthony Boucher has commented: "There's an unanswerable matter of taste involved here; but I think it's possible to take a different view. . . . In 'Thou Art the Man' Poe discovered that even murder can be treated with casual irony; and this story can be considered the forerunner of such important modern writers (who have also been accused occasionally of unpleasant flippancy) as Edwin Greenwood, Richard Hull and Francis Iles."

[7]Interestingly enough, although the passing of the bullet through the horse's body in "'Thou Art the Man'" is exactly paralleled by the passing of the bullet through the man's body in Queen's "The Adventure of the Invisible Lover," Queen has stated that he had not read Poe's story before he duplicated Poe's plot device, which was one of the earliest uses of ballistics in a mystery.

[8]I disagree that Burke's story contains no internal detective; there is one, but he is murdered at the end of the story.

POE AND THE DETECTIVE STORY:
A SELECTIVE BIBLIOGRAPHY OF THE CRITICISM

Bandy, W.T. "Who Was Monsieur Dupin?" *PMLA*, LXXIX:4:i (September, 1964), 509-510.
   The author sums up some critical views of the origin of Dupin's name: Killis Campbell, in *The Mind of Poe and Other Studies* (1933), suggests the family name of "George Sand"; Arthur Hobson Quinn, in *Edgar Allan Poe: A Critical Biography* (1941), suggests Marie Dupin, a character in "Marie Laurent" by J.M.B., a (fictional?) continuation of Vidocq's memoirs; and T.O. Mabbott, in his edition of *The Selected Poetry and Prose of Edgar Allan Poe* (1951), suggests André Marie Jean Jacques Dupin (if I understand Bandy). Although Bandy does not mention *Murder for Pleasure*, Haycraft agrees with Mabbott; Harrison (see below) picks André's younger brother, François. (George Sand, advocated by Campbell, was also a relative of the Dupin brothers.) At any rate, Bandy goes on to reprint a letter to Poe, from the Griswold papers in the Boston Public Library, in which S. Maupin tells the terms under which C. Auguste Dubouchet could be hired to teach French in Richmond. Bandy suggests "C. Auguste Du(bouchet)+(Mau)pin". The letter is dated September 30, 1840, and the first Dupin story was published in April, 1841.

Barzun, Jacques (ed.). *The Delights of Detection.* New York: Criterion Books, 1961.
   In this anthology Barzun reprints William Leggett's "The Rifle" (1830), in which (says Barzun) for the first time in American fiction, crime was brought home to a culprit by means of ballistics. In this sense, the story prefigures Poe's "'Thou Art the Man'" (1840) which has often been cited as the first use of ballistics. Murphy (see below) points out an actual case, midway between the two stories, which might also have influenced Poe's tale.

Benton, Richard P. "'The Mystery of Marie Rogêt'—A Defense," *Studies in Short Fiction,* VI:2 (Winter, 1969), 144-151.
   Containing a very useful summary of the criticism of this story in book-length studies of Poe, this essay follows Dorothy Sayers in defending "The Mystery of Marie Rogêt," although Benton goes so far as to suggest that it is the best of the Dupin stories. Sayers pointed to the fact that therein Poe created the armchair detective tradition, but Benton takes a more general approach, arguing that the story belongs to the intellectual tradition in prose fiction which Northrop Frye called the "anatomy," that it pits the intellectual against the Jacksonian mass mind (the police and the newspapers), and that it contains insight into murderous psychology. As part of a rebuttal, Benton indicates a few minor flaws in the other two Dupin stories.

Blanch, Robert J. "The Background of Poe's 'Gold Bug,'" *English Record* (New York State English Council), XVI:iv (April, 1966), 44-48.
   This essay suggests that the characters and general plot involving buried treasure were based on Washington Irving's "Wolfert Webber, or

Golden Dreams" in *Tales of a Traveller;* other suggestions about the setting of "The Gold-Bug" (based on Poe's experiences on Sullivan's Island
while in the army) and its cryptogram (part of Poe's interests at the time)
follow standard biographical works.

Bonaparte, Marie. *The Life and Works of Edgar Allan Poe: A Psycho-Analytic
   Interpretation.* Foreword by Sigmund Freud. Translated by John Red-
   ker. London: Imago Publishing Co., Ltd., 1949.
      Chapters are devoted to "The Gold-Bug," "The Man of the
   Crowd," and "The Murders in the Rue Morgue." The dominant theme
   of the first Dupin story is found to be the archetypal murder of the
   mother.

Boucher, Anthony (ed.). *Great American Detective Stories.* Cleveland and
   New York: World Publishing Co., 1945.
      Boucher reprints Poe's "'Thou Art the Man'" (pp. 295-307), with
   an editorial afterword (pp. 307-308) in which he points out that the
   story is a fair-play puzzle. He also argues that what most commentators
   term the unpleasantly jocular tone of the story was in fact a deliberate
   attempt by Poe to treat the subject of murder with casual irony. It
   should be noted that, like virtually every other critic prior to the 1961
   reprinting of Leggett's "The Rifle" by Barzun (see above), Boucher
   credited Poe in this story with "the first use of ballistic clues" in fiction.

Boucher, Anthony. Untitled note on Poe's "A Tale of the Ragged Mountains,"
   The Magazine of Fantasy and Science Fiction, 14:3/82 (March, 1958),
   86. Reprinted with additional comment (not wholly serious) by Ellery
   Queen, *Ellery Queen's Mystery Magazine,* 45:2/255 (February, 1965),
   96-98.
      Boucher argues that "A Tale of the Ragged Mountains" is a detec-
   tive story in which the only detective is the reader. For details of his
   argument, see my essay above.

Christopher, J. R. "Poe and the Detective Story," *The Armchair Detective,*
   II:1 (October, 1968), 49-51.
      The first version of the present essay, covering only the three
   Dupin stories, "'Thou Art the Man,'" and "A Tale of the Ragged Mountains." Letters concerning the essay appear in the same magazine, II:
   2 (January, 1969), 131-132.

Davidson, Edward H. *Poe: A Critical Study.* Cambridge: The Belknap Press
   of Harvard University Press, 1957.
      An interesting philosophical   interpretation of Poe's detective
   stories appears on pp. 213-222.

Diskin, Patrick. "Poe, LeFanu, and the Sealed Room Mystery," *Notes and
   Queries,* O.S.CCXI/N.S. XIII:9 (September, 1966), 337-339.
      The main part of this note is concerned with Poe's possible use of
   Joseph Sheridan LeFanu's "Passage in the Secret History of an Irish
   Countess" (*Dublin University Magazine,* November 1838) as a basis for

"The Murders in the Rue Morgue." After pointing out a number of striking parallels in the locked rooms and the characters created by Poe and LeFanu, Diskin refers to other sources from which Poe may have borrowed: Sir Walter Scott's *Count Robert of Paris* (the orang-outang), LeFanu's "The Fortunes of Sir Robert Ardagh" (the lock of hair clutched by the dead person), and J.C. Mangan's "The Thirty Flasks" (the train of mental associations started in the street and ending with shoes).

Falk, Doris V. "Poe and the Power of Animal Magnetism," *PMLA,* 84:3 (May 1969), 536-546.

Designed in part as an answer to Lind's essay (listed below), the article discusses Poe's "The Facts in the Case of M. Valdemar," "A Tale of the Ragged Mountains," and "Mesmeric Revelation." Although the first and last stories do not concern this study, the author's comment about "Valdemar" should be noted: "Poe plays the 'mystery' game fairly—the clues to the outcome are all there but neither the narrator nor the reader sees them at first" (p. 539). As Miss Falk understands "A Tale of the Ragged Mountains," Bedloe, after his death as Oldeb, is re-animated and kept alive by the animal magnetism which already existed, although unconsciously, between Templeton and Oldeb.

Harrison, Michael. "Dupin: The Reality Behind the Fictions," an introductory essay (pp. 3-14) in his *The Exploits of the Chevalier Dupin.* Sauk City, Wisconsin: Mycroft and Moran, 1968.

Harrison presents a fascinating argument that Poe based his detective's name on that of F.-P. Charles Dupin, Chevalier of the Order of St. Louis. He also presents much evidence indicating that Poe's foster father and this Dupin were probably acquainted at a time when both men, along with Poe himself, were in England.

Hawkins, John. "Poe's 'The Murders in the Rue Morgue,'" *Explicator,* XXIII: 6(February, 1965), Item 49.

This note analyzes the story in terms of the opening contrast between draughts (checkers) and chess; Hawkins contends that both the story and the Rue Morgue plot resemble a draughts game, and that at the end Dupin is the draughts-player and the Prefect the chess-player.

Haycraft, Howard. *Murder for Pleasure: The Life and Times of the Detective Story.* New York: D. Appleton-Century Company, 1941. Reprinted without substantial change, New York: Biblo and Tannen, 1968.

The first chapter, "Time: 1841—Place: America" (pp. 1-27), is devoted to Poe's three stories about Dupin. A list of twelve conventions of the detective story which Poe established appears on p. 12. The resemblance between Poe's "'Thou Art the Man'" and Ellery Queen's "The Adventure of the Invisible Lover," mentioned in the essay above, is referred to on p. 10n. Haycraft speculates that the name Dupin may have been borrowed from André Marie Jean Jacques Dupin; Harrison (listed above) contends that the name is based on André's younger brother François, and Bandy (listed above) argues for an entirely different theory.

Lind, Sidney E. "Poe and Mesmerism," *PMLA*, LXII:4 (December, 1947), 1077-1094.

The author discusses "A Tale of the Ragged Mountains," "Mesmeric Revelation," and "The Facts in the Case of M. Valdemar." Only the first story (discussed on pp. 1079-1085) concerns this study. The author explains the usual interpretation of the story (that of metempsychosis, Oldeb's psyche being transferred to Bedloe), then offers his own interpretation: that while Dr. Templeton believes in metempsychosis, he has actually implanted the story in Bedloe's mind at a distance (which could be done according to mesmeric theory of the time) by writing down the account of Oldeb's death.

Murch, A. E. *The Development of the Detective Novel*. London: Peter Owen, 1958; Port Washington, New York: Kennikat Press, 1968.

In Chapter IV, "The Short Detective Story: Edgar Allan Poe" (pp. 67-83), the author discusses the three Dupin stories, "The Gold-Bug," and "'Thou Art the Man.'" Later in the book (pp. 178-180) Miss Murch compares Dupin and Sherlock Holmes, and Poe and Conan Doyle. Although her treatment of 20th-century authors is spotty and of poor quality, the material on Poe, Doyle and their predecessors seems very good.

Murphy, George D. "A Source for Ballistics in Poe," *American Notes and Queries*, IV:7 (March, 1966), 99.

The author suggests that Poe's idea of the identifiable bullet in "'Thou Art the Man'" (1844) was based on an actual case in England in 1835: ". . .Henry Goddard, one of London's famed Bow Street Runners, . . .traced an irregularly shaped bullet taken from the victim's body to a pair of correspondingly irregular moulds owned by his assassin."

Queen, Ellery (ed.). *Ellery Queen's Mystery Magazine*, 14:72 (November, 1949).

This issue, published on the anniversary of Poe's death (October 7), is a centennial commemoration. Of special interest here is the reprinting in this issue (pp. 77-80) of Edward D. Radin's "The Mystery of Mary Rogers." The author briefly summarizes the New York murder on which Poe based "The Mystery of Marie Rogêt," giving both the "police theory" and Poe's but not attempting to decide between them. Radin makes several errors of fact, and does not raise the question of an abortion. Walsh, Wimsatt and Worthen (listed below) deal at greater length with the Mary Rogers problem.

Queen, Ellery. *In the Queens' Parlor, and Other Leaves from the Editors' Notebook*. New York: Simon and Schuster, 1957. Reprinted without alteration, New York: Biblo and Tannen, 1969.

Although many of the essays and notes in this volume mention Poe in passing, there are six sections that are especially important. "Leaf 4: With the Author's Compliments" contains a subsection, "The Crown Jewels of Detectivedom," which discusses presentation copies of books, including (pp. 16-17) the two inscribed volumes of Poe's stories. "Leaf 6: Something Rich and Strange" (pp. 23-24) quotes Poe's and Doyle's statements about detection and impossibilities. "Leaf 23: A Ghost Haunting America" (pp. 78-80) is Queen's fullest discussion of Poe's contributions to the detective story in the three Dupin tales and "'Thou Art the Man.'" "Leaf 26: A Far Cry from Julius Africanus" (pp. 99-100) discusses the frequency of use of letters of the alphabet as given by Poe in "The Gold-Bug" and Doyle in "The Adventure of the Dancing Men," among others. "Leaf 42: Poe-tic License," dealing with some poets who have written detective stories (with emphasis, of course, on Poe), foreshadows Queen's later anthology *Poetic Justice* (listed below). "L'Envoi" (p. 180) is a final tribute to Poe.

Queen, Ellery. "Introduction," to Michael Harrison's *The Exploits of the Chevalier Dupin.* Sauk City, Wiconsin: Mycroft and Moran, 1968.
        Queen's introduction (pp. ix-xi) discusses Poe's contributions to the detective story in the three Dupin tales and "'Thou Art the Man,'" covering the same ground and sometimes using the same words as in "A Ghost Haunting America" in *In the Queens' Parlor.*

Queen, Ellery (ed.). *Poetic Justice: 23 Stories of Crime, Mystery, and Detection by World-Famous Poets from Geoffrey Chaucer to Dylan Thomas.* New York: The New American Library, 1967.
        Queen here reprints (pp. 69-78) Poe's "The Man of the Crowd," discussed in my essay above. Queen's introduction (pp. 67-69) emphasizes Poe as a poet, and his critical afterword (pp. 78-81) considers the tale as a detective story.

Quinn, Patrick F. *The French Face of Edgar Poe.*• Carbondale: Southern Illinois University Press, 1957.
        The author analyzes (pp. 224-228) the Watson-narrator in Poe's detective stories from Poe's psychology rather than on the detective's technical usefulness as did Sayers (listed below). He discusses (pp. 230-232) "The Man of the Crowd," but not as a detective story.

Sayers, Dorothy L. "Introduction" to *Great Short Stories of Detection, Mystery, and Horror* (London: Gollancz, 1928), published in the United States as the first *Omnibus of Crime* (New York: Payson and Clarke, 1929). This introduction has been reprinted as "Detective Fiction: Origins and Development" in A.S. Burack (ed.), *Writing Detective and Mystery Fiction* (Boston: The Writer, Inc., 1945) and as "The Omnibus of Crime (1928-29)" in Howard Haycraft (ed.), *The Art of the Mystery Story* (New York: Simon and Schuster, 1946).
        Sayers' essay covers far more than Poe's stories, but she does discuss in detail the three Dupin tales, "'Thou Art the Man,'" and "The Gold-Bug."

Thompson, G.R. "Is Poe's 'A Tale of the Ragged Mountains' a Hoax?", *Studies in Short Fiction,* VI:4 (Summer, 1969), 454-460.
        The reader of the story "will find that under the supernatural tale lies, first, a 'scientific' explanation of the apparently supernatural

events, which leads, second, to a very different 'psychological' explanation of the events, and to, third, an insinuated burlesque. . . of a Gothic novel by Charles Brockden Brown" (p. 455). The scientific explanation is based on Lind's article on mesmerism (listed above; Falk's answer to Lind, also listed above, appeared too late to be considered by Thompson). The psychological explanation advanced by Thompson, resembling somewhat the reading by Boucher (listed above), is that Templeton, after believing Bedloe to be the revived Oldeb, psychotically re-kills him. The insinuated burlesque is of Brown's *Edgar Huntley.*

Walsh, John. *Poe the Detective: The Curious Circumstances Behind "The Mystery of Marie Roget."* New Brunswick, New Jersey: Rutgers University Press, 1968.
    This is probably the definitive study of "The Mystery of Marie Roget" and its historic and artistic background. Walsh includes the text of the story, indicating the changes Poe made from its magazine form when he reprinted it in his *Tales,* and explaining in great detail why Poe came to believe these changes were necessary.

Wimsatt, Jr., W.K. "Poe and the Mystery of Mary Rogers," *PMLA,* LVI:1 (March, 1941), 230-248.
    This essay, providing much of the basic information about Poe's revisions of his story and about the probability that Mary Rogers died from the results of an abortion, has been superseded in most details by Walsh's book (listed above).

Wimsatt, Jr., W.K. "Mary Rogers, John Anderson, and Others," *American Literature,* 21:4 (January, 1950), 482-484.
    In a brief discussion of Worthen's essay (listed below), Wimsatt provides further evidence for the theory that Mary Rogers died during an abortion. Walsh (listed above) sums up all of this material, although he does not agree with the theory of an earlier abortion.

Worthen, S.C. "Poe and the Beautiful Cigar Girl," *American Literature,* 20:3 (November, 1948), 305-312.
    This essay studies the evidence of John Anderson's connection with Mary Rogers in light of the case of "Laura V. Appleton v. The New York Life Insurance Company and Frederick A. Hammond" (1891-2). The evidence, suggesting that Anderson arranged an abortion for the girl, is summed up in Walsh's book.

MORE ON AUTHOR AND SUBJECT

Joe Christopher received his Ph.D. from the University of Oklahoma, his dissertation being on "The Romances of C. S. Lewis," and is Associate Professor of English at Tarleton State College, Stephenville, Texas. He is a joint devotee of mysteries and of science fiction, and has published commentary in both areas. Besides the above essay and his Lewis dissertation, he recently co-authored a monumental bibliography of the late Anthony Boucher, which was published serially in The Armchair Detective. *He is married and has three lovely children, with all of whom your august editor has played horsie.*

If anyone wants to read more on Poe after he has finished all items listed in Prof. Christopher's bibliography, he is a scholar indeed.

†No one doubts that the greatest figure ever created in the Dupin tradition is Sherlock Holmes; but the Master, and Conan Doyle who gave him life, are so well-known to millions of readers, and so well-celebrated in millions of words, that an editor searching for something "different" faces an almost infinite embarrassment of riches. Finally the thought came: why not the discovery of Holmes by the creator of Holmes' "logical successor?" Happily Ellery Queen was willing . . .

Who Shall Ever Forget?
by Ellery Queen

This is one of the Queens speaking. . . . As a boy my reading habits were pure and innocent. I confess now that I never read a Nick Carter until I was past voting age. My literary childhood consisted of Horatio Alger, Tom Swift, the Viking legends, the multi-colored Lang fairy books, Frank Merriwell, Baseball Joe, the Rover Boys, Tarzan, The Three Musketeers, Jules Verne, Peck's Bad Boy, and—yes, the Oz stories. I can reread the Oz books today—and I often do. Somehow the detection of crime failed to cross my path in all those happy days, except in the movies—remember "The Exploits of Elaine" with Arnold Daly as Professor Craig Kennedy, Creighton Hale as Walter Jameson, Pearl White as Elaine, and the

sinister Sheldon Lewis as The Clutching Hand? The closest I might
have come to fictional blood and thunder in those golden sum-
mers was *Tom Sawyer, Detective*—I say "might have come" because oddly enough I have no recollection of *Tom Sawyer, Detective* as part of my boyhood reading.

When I was twelve years old, my family moved from upstate
New York to New York City, and for a time we lived with my
grandfather in Brooklyn. It was in my grandfather's house, in the
winter of 1917, that I first met Sherlock Holmes. Oh, unforgettable day!

I was ill in bed when the great moment occurred. In those
far-off days I was afflicted periodically with an abscess of the left
ear. It came year after year, with almost astronomical regularity—
and always, I recall, during the week of school exams. My grandfather had an old turnip of a watch that he used to place flat
against my left ear, and it always astounded him to learn that I
couldn't hear the tick of his Big Ben even after having had my ear
lanced.

I was lying in bed, in a cubbyhole of a room, on just such a
day as Dr. Watson has so often described—a "bleak and windy" day
with the fingers of winter scratching at the windowpane. One of
my aunts walked in and handed me a book she had borrowed from
the nearby public library.

It was *The Adventures of Sherlock Holmes*.

I opened the book with no knowledge that I stood—rather, I
sat—on the brink of my fate. I had no inkling, no premonition,
that in another minute my life's work would be born. My first
glance was disheartening. I saw the frontispiece of the Harper
edition—a picture of a rather innocuous man in dress coat and
striped trousers holding the arm of a young woman in bridal gown.
A love story, I said to myself—for surely this unattractive couple
were in a church and about to be married. The quotation under
the illustration—"The gentleman in the pew handed it up to her"—
was not encouraging. In fact, there was nothing in that ill-chosen
frontispiece by Sidney Paget to make a twelve-year-old boy sit up
and take notice—especially with his left ear in agony.

Only an unknown and unknowable sixth sense prompted me to turn to the table of contents—and then the world brightened. The first story—*A Scandal in Bohemia*—seemed to hold little red-blooded promise, but the next story was, and always will be, a milestone.

A strange rushing thrill challenged the pain in my ear. *The Red Headed League!* What a combination of simple words to skewer themselves into the brain of a hungry boy! I glanced down quickly—*The Man with the Twisted Lip*—*The Adventure of the Speckled Band*—and I was lost! Ecstatically, everlastingly lost!

I started on the first page of *A Scandal in Bohemia* and truly the game was afoot. The unbearable pain in my ear—vanished! The abyss of melancholy into which only a twelve-year-old boy can sink—forgotten!

I finished *The Adventures* that night. I wasn't sad—I was glad. It wasn't the end—it was the beginning. I had knocked fearlessly on the door to a new world and I had been admitted. There was a long road ahead—even longer than I realized. That night, as I closed the book, I felt that I had read one of the greatest books ever written. And today I marvel how true and tempered was my twelve-year-old critical sense. For in the mature smugness of my present literary judgment, I still consider *The Adventures of Sherlock Holmes* one of the world's masterworks.

I could not have slept much that night. If I slept at all, I merely passed from one dream world to another—with the wide-awake dream infinitely more wondrous. I remember when morning came—how symbolically the sun shone through my window. I leaped from bed, dressed, and with that great wad of yellow-stained cotton still in my ear, stole out of the house and made my shaky way to the public library. Of course it was too early for the library to be open, but I sat on the steps and waited. And though I waited hours, it seemed only minutes until a prim old lady came and unlocked the front door.

But alas, I had no card. Yes, I might fill out the form, and take it home, and have my parents sign it, and then after three days—three days? three eternities!—I could call and pick up my card.

I begged, I pleaded—and there must have been something irresistible in my voice and in my eyes. Thank you now, Miss Librarian-of-Those-Days! These thanks are long overdue. For that gentle-hearted old lady broke all the rules of librarydom and gave me a card—and told me with a twinkle in her eyes where I could find books by a man named Doyle.

I rushed to the stacks. My first reaction was one of horrible and devastating disappointment. Yes, there were books by a Doyle on the shelves—but so few of them! I had expected a whole libraryful—rows and rows of Sherlock all waiting patiently for my "coming of age."

I found three precious volumes. I bundled them under my arm, had them stamped, and fled home. Back in bed I started to read—*A Study in Scarlet, The Memoirs* (with a frontispiece that almost frightened me to death), *The Hound of the Baskervilles.* They were food and drink and medicine—and all the Queen's horses and all the Queen's men couldn't put Ellery together again.

But my doom had been signed, sealed, and delivered in *The Adventures.* The books which followed merely broadened the picture, filled in the indelible details. For who can ever forget that tall, excessively lean man with his razorlike face and hawk's-bill of a nose. . .or his mouse-colored dressing gown and amber-stemmed pipe. . .or the way he paced up and down that legendary room at 221B Baker Street, quickly, eagerly, his head sunk upon his chest . . .or the way he examined the scene of a crime, sometimes on all fours, his nose to the ground. . . .

Who could ever forget that gaunt, dynamic figure and his incisive speech. . .or the mysterious Victorian household appliance called a gasogene. . .or the Persian slipper in which the Master kept his tobacco and the coal scuttle in which he kept his cigars. . .or the patriotic bullet pocks on the wall and the scraping violin which produced such weird melodies. . .or the hypodermic syringe—what a shock that was to my fledgling sensibilities!. . .or the ghostly hansom cab that loomed out of the London mist—with a twelve-year-old boy clinging by some miracle of literary gymnastics to its back as it rattled off to perilous adventure. . . .

Yes, who shall ever forget?

MORE ON AUTHOR AND SUBJECT

Anyone who is unaware of the almost godlike stature in the mystery field of the name Ellery Queen, or who does not know that Queen "is" Frederic Dannay and Manfred B. Lee, has probably picked up this book by mistake. Such a browser may profitably begin research on Queen with Anthony Boucher's pamphlet Ellery Queen: A Double Profile *(Little, Brown, 1951), and update it with the excellent unsigned article "A Case of Double Identity" in* MD Magazine *for December 1967.*

Mr. Dannay, who wrote the above account of that well-nigh religious experience of his youth when he first met Mr. Holmes, has set down many reminiscences of his boyhood in Elmira, New York [for example, in the Introduction to Queen's suppressed anthology The Misadventures of Sherlock Holmes *(Little, Brown, 1944) where the preceding account first appeared]. His published reminiscences culminated in a novel,* The Golden Summer *(Little, Brown, 1953), under the byline of Daniel Nathan, in which he evoked the peace of a vanished time and recreated the child who was the father of the man he had become. This novel, which Mr. Dannay wrote alone, is nevertheless directly relevant to Ellery Queen's life and work (and to the above memoir), and will amply repay whatever amount of effort needed to hunt down a copy.*

The literature on Holmes, of course, is as voluminous as the literature on Hamlet, and any good work in the field will lead you to a host of others.

†If detective fiction is "the romance of reason," it is well to remember that there is also a romance of unreason; and one of its most celebrated practitioners was the gentleman who created that fiend incarnate, Dr. Fu Manchu. If Poe created Dupin to hedge against the night-side of his soul, what are we to make of the fact that the following definitive survey of Sax Rohmer was written by a professor of mathematics?

Sax Rohmer: An Informal Survey
by Robert E. Briney

The name "Fu Manchu" has long since been absorbed into the popular vocabulary. As a synonym for old-time Oriental villainy, the name is recognized—and used—by people who probably have never heard of the man responsible for it: Sax Rohmer.

In addition to the chronicles of Dr. Fu Manchu, Rohmer wrote some three dozen other books, populated with a variety of memorable characters, sinister and otherwise. There is much in this body of work to interest the *aficionado* of mystery, as well as the devotee of fantasy and the supernatural. The best of Rohmer's stories display, in addition to their full quota of action and suspense, a seemingly boundless inventiveness of exotic detail and a genuine atmosphere of strangeness and menace.

42

The present survey is intended as a guide both to the high spots, which will repay investigation, and to the shallows, where only the hardened enthusiast need venture.

"I Couldn't Keep Track of the Money.
I Just Gave Up and Spent It."

"Sax Rohmer" was the pseudonym adopted by the British writer Arthur Sarsfield Ward when he embarked on a full-time writing career. Ward was born in 1883, in or near Birmingham in the English Midlands. (He himself claimed not to know the precise date or location.) Both parents were Irish: his father, William Ward, was a civil engineer from County Wicklow and his mother, Margaret, was from Athlone. The elder Ward's profession had led the family to settle in England. Ward's urge to write developed at an early age, along with an interest in Ancient Egypt and other exotic times and places that was to color virtually all of his writing. His early stories were markedly unsuccessful. In fact, editorial disinterest was so pronounced that at one stage he resorted to the use of colored stationery and odd-sized envelopes to make his submissions more noticeable. By his late teens, he had accumulated enough "editorial regrets" to paper an entire wall of his room.

After completing his formal schooling, Ward tried for a Civil Service appointment in the Middle East, but failed to pass the examination. He thereupon followed his father's prescription for a sensible career and became a teller in the London branch of a Hong Kong banking house. There he became friendly with another teller, a young man by the name of Pelham Grenville Wodehouse. The latter was also a budding author, and in fact had already had one book published. In 1903 Wodehouse left his job, having discovered that his earnings from free-lance writing amounted to more than his salary from the bank. Shortly thereafter, Ward also in 1903 abandoned the world of finance, though his literary success was still to take considerable time to arrive. His first

published story appeared in *Pearson's Magazine* in 1904, when
Ward was twenty-one years old. Four or five other stories were
published during the next two years. One of them led a publisher
to propose a series of stories involving the same central character.
The idea seems to have engendered a mild panic in Ward. He
immediately gave up his nascent literary career and left England,
paying the first of many visits to the Continent.

When he returned, it was neither to banking nor to free-lance
writing. The well-known Irish editor, T.P. O'Connor, a friend of
his mother's family, opened the way to a job in Fleet Street, and
Ward became a newspaper reporter. This career too was notable
more for brevity than for distinction. Ward's active imagination
and his impatience with the prosaic were as evident in his newspaper work as in everything else he did. His interviews with dull
people were livened up to the point where the subjects complained.
"It's hard to say now whether I walked or was thrown out of
Fleet Street," he said many years later.

Ward's lively attention now turned in one direction after
another. He took up the study of art. He studied at several
schools, with the intention of becoming a black-and-white illus-
trator, but apparently lost interest in this endeavor after having
one or two drawings published. He made a first assault on the
theater world by concocting, with the help of three friends, a one-
act play for the variety stage. The play got as far as a "trial week,"
but was then jettisoned. He dabbled in chemistry, in an attempt
to perfect a new variety of mothball, and again success eluded him.

During this period Ward developed a wide circle of acquaintances in the theater and music-hall world. One of these acquaintances was the girl he later married, the actress and variety performer Rose Elizabeth Knox, sister of the comedian Teddy Knox.
Two other friends were the comedians Little Tich (Harry Relph)
and George Robey. For the latter, Ward wrote a large number of
comedy songs and routines. (In a *New Yorker* interview in 1947
he was able to quote one of these songs from memory.) This
writing for the stage, together with a number of free-lance newspaper articles, led Ward back to his first love, a literary career.

He rented an office in Limehouse, adopted the made-up name "Sax Rohmer," and once again bombarded editorial offices with stories.

The break came when Newman Flower purchased his first serial, *The Sins of Séverac Bablon,* for the newly-founded *Cassell's Magazine.* Thereafter, a steady stream of books and stories flowed from his pen. (Literally: he seldom if ever used a typewriter, but wrote his stories in longhand, in tiny and barely-decipherable handwriting.) His books were an immediate popular success, and most of them went through numerous editions both in England and in the U.S., as well as in foreign-language translations.

In addition to books, Rohmer wrote several plays. Three of these were produced in London during the 1920s. The first and most successful was a "musical adventure" called *Round in Fifty,* which opened at the London Hippodrome on March 16, 1922. Hiding behind the somewhat obscure title was an adaptation of Jules Verne's *Around the World in Eighty Days.* Rohmer wrote the script in collaboration with Julian and Lauri Wylie (the producers of the show), and most of the music was composed by the popular songwriters Herman Finck and James Tate. After the sudden death of the latter, Rohmer was called upon to contribute both music and lyrics for some of the songs. The leading part, that of Phileas Fogg's spendthrift son (replacing the Passepartout role in the novel) was played by George Robey. Robey later recalled *Round in Fifty* as his favorite among all the musical revues in which he appeared. The show was popular with audiences as well, and ran for 471 consecutive performances.

Rohmer's next theatrical effort was *The Eye of Siva,* a mystery play in three acts, which opened at the New Theater on August 8, 1923. The central character was a detective, Paul Harley, who also figured in one of Rohmer's series of short stories and novels. The part was played by the distinguished actor Arthur Wontner, who some years later would appear in the role of Sherlock Holmes in a succession of British films. The play featured a great deal of elaborate scenery and special effects, and the cast included a live female leopard. The play was moderately successful, and ran for about two months.

The third theatrical venture was less of a success. *Secret Egypt*, which opened at the "Q" Theater on August 4, 1928, lasted less than a week. (In spite of the title, the play bears no relation to any of the stories in the book *Tales of Secret Egypt*.)

The success of his books brought Rohmer relative financial security, threatened from time to time by his natural improvidence and an unwise choice of business associates. In the mid-1950s he estimated that he had made close to two million dollars from the Fu Manchu books alone. Small wonder that in signing his name he customarily wrote the S of Sax as a dollar sign . . .

Among other things, a steady income allowed Rohmer to indulge his love of travel. He travelled extensively in Europe, in Egypt and the Near East, in the West Indies, and in the eastern United States. He lived, at various times, in London and in the Surrey countryside, in Funchal, Madeira, in Jamaica, and in Manhattan. Most of these locations turned up sooner or later in his books. Around 1950 he and his wife settled permanently in New York.

In the spring of 1959, Rohmer was one of the many people stricken during the epidemic of Asiatic flu. He recovered sufficiently to be able to set out, with his wife, on a trip to England. However, by the time their ship reached England, his condition had turned for the worse. After arriving in London, he was confined to bed. Finally, he was admitted to University College Hospital, where he lingered, virtually in a coma, until his death on June 1, 1959. He was 76 years of age.

"Seek Not My Ashes. I Am the Lord of the Fires!"

Even as the installments of *Séverac Bablon* were appearing in print, another character was taking shape in Rohmer's mind:

the Satanic genius, Dr. Fu-Manchu. Fu-Manchu was not the first Oriental arch-criminal in fiction, but he epitomized the breed to such an extent that earlier representatives are all but forgotten. Later examples, from such pulp magazine imitations as Dr. Yen Sin and Wu Fang to Ian Fleming's Dr. No, seem only pale imitations of Rohmer's "Devil Doctor."

The exploits of Fu-Manchu and his battles with his would-be Nemesis, Nayland Smith of Scotland Yard, are chronicled in thirteen books and three short stories which span almost the whole of Rohmer's literary career. The first book to carry the Rohmer byline was *The Mystery of Dr. Fu-Manchu*, published in England in June, 1913, and issued later that year in the United States as *The Insidious Dr. Fu-Manchu*; Rohmer's last book was *Emperor Fu Manchu*, published less than two months before the author's death. In the intervening years the "evil yellow doctor" was featured not only in books but in comic strips, in radio and television serials, and in several motion pictures. (In one of the latter, Boris Karloff gave a memorable performance as Fu Manchu.) In 1947, Rohmer wrote a play about Fu Manchu, in which he wanted Basil Rathbone to star (because, as he said, Rathbone was "appropriately tall, cold, and suave, and masterful even in pyjamas"). The play was never produced, but later formed the basis for the novel *Shadow of Fu Manchu*. The three Fu Manchu short stories themselves are little more than footnotes to the saga.

The Fu-Manchu history was originally intended to consist of only three books. These first appeared as a series of related short stories in *Collier's Weekly*: the ten episodes of the first book in the Spring of 1913, those of *The Return of Dr. Fu-Manchu* between November 1914 and December 1915, and the nine episodes of *The Hand of Fu-Manchu* between April 1916 and June 1917. Each of the twenty-nine stories follows one of three patterns: Nayland Smith and his companion Dr. Petrie, who narrates the stories, are either a) menaced by one of Fu-Manchu's exotic death-traps, b) captured by his agents, or c) engaged in trying to foil a murderous attempt on the life of someone who Knows Too Much. In about half of the episodes the protagonists triumph either by good luck or by their own efforts; in the rest they are aided by the beautiful Kâramanèh, one of Fu-Manchu's company who has fallen in love with Petrie.

The stories are populated by dacoits and Thugs[1] and less nameable creatures, and are overflowing with mysterious poisons, mutated insects, and other death-dealing agencies bearing such names as "The Zayat Kiss," "The Coughing Horror," and "The Flower of Silence." The locale is pre-World War I London and its surrounding countryside. (These stories are as firmly wedded to their period as the Sherlock Holmes stories are to the late Victorian era.) And over everything broods the shadow of the seemingly omnipresent and omniscient Dr. Fu-Manchu.

At the end of each of the three books, Fu-Manchu is apparently killed—trapped in a burning house in the first, shot through the head (by Kâramanèh) in the second. The third death was, at the time, intended to be permanent. Fu-Manchu had been disowned and sentenced to death by the Si-Fan, the secret organization which he had employed to further his own plans for conquest. The Si-Fan was broken up by Scotland Yard, and in an attempt to flee the country by sea Fu-Manchu was caught by a storm in the English Channel, shipwrecked, and presumably drowned. Petrie married Kâramanèh and retired to Egypt, and Nayland Smith set off in pursuit of less colorful and undoubtedly less dangerous foes.

Three of Smith's "extracurricular" cases are recounted in minor short stories. Here Smith is even more of a stick-figure than he appears in the Fu-Manchu books. It is clear that much of his stature in the latter is merely a reflection of the quality of his opponent: a man who has survived against such a foe as the Doctor, and who is held in such esteem by him, *must* have unusual capabilities, even though there is little solid evidence of them in the books. In effect, we are taking Fu-Manchu's word for Smith's abilities. That we are willing to do so is a measure of Rohmer's success in realizing his chief villain.

The Doctor was allowed to rest (with one exception, to be noted later) for thirteen years.[2] During this period seventeen other books by Rohmer were published and three of his plays were produced on the London stage. With the serialization of *Daughter of Fu Manchu* in 1930, it became clear that drowning at sea had been no more fatal to the durable Oriental than had his earlier "deaths." In this book, Fu Manchu's daughter Fah Lo Suee has set about reviving and reorganizing the Si-Fan. She causes so much trouble that at last Fu Manchu himself, old and lame, emerges from retirement to join forces with Nayland Smith and bring about her downfall. The renewed taste of power stimulates the Doctor's own ambitions, and in *The Mask of Fu Manchu* he is once again scheming for world domination in the old familiar way. He has also managed to grow younger, with the help of an elixir developed in his secret laboratories. This book and the previous one are set mainly in the Near East, and are narrated by a young archaeologist named Shan Greville. Petrie and Inspector Weymouth, from the earlier books, play subsidiary roles.

In *Fu Manchu's Bride* the Doctor's activities move to the French Riviera. He is experimenting with hybrid insects and with new strains of plague germs, which he tries out on unsuspecting human subjects. Petrie, who has acquired a considerable reputation as an expert on tropical diseases, is called in by the French authorities to investigate the plague. He soon learns all too much about it from first-hand experience. The book is narrated by Alan Sterling, the son of an old friend of Petrie, and an orchid hunter by profession. The damsel in distress, who fortunately never quite manages to deserve the appellation in the book's title, is named Fleurette. She turns out to be the long-lost daughter of Petrie and Kâramanèh, kidnapped by Fu Manchu when she was a baby. Sterling and Fleurette are featured again in *The Trail of Fu Manchu*. Here Fu Manchu becomes particularly fiendish. He operates a large blast-furnace in a cavern under Limehouse, where he uses human bodies as fuel in an alchemical process for making gold. One of the bodies he feeds to the furnace is that of his rebellious daughter, Fah Lo Suee. (But fear not, she is as durable as he is!) In *President Fu Manchu* the scene shifts to the New World; the plot is a faint foreshadowing of Richard Condon's *The Manchurian Candidate*. At the end of the book, Fu Manchu is again "killed"—swept over Niagara Falls in a small boat. This in no way inhibits his appearance in the next volume, *The Drums of Fu Manchu,* which is set in England, Paris, and Venice. This is one of the weaker books in the series, and seems in part nothing more than a mechanical reprise of earlier adventures. Indeed, the opening scene of *Drums* is virtually a copy of that of *The Insidious Dr. Fu-Manchu.* In place of Petrie as narrator we have Bart Kerrigan, a journalist. His love-interest is a latter-day Kâramanèh named Ardatha. These two are also the featured players in *The Island of Fu Manchu.* (The Doctor never relinquishes control over one of his beautiful victims after only a single book. . .) Here the locale shifts to Haiti, and zombies and voodoo rites are added to the more traditional ingredients of Fu Manchu's arsenal. The infusion of new blood, as it were, has a revitalizing effect on quality. *Bride, Trail,* and *Island* provide some of the most exciting and most readily enjoyable parts of the entire series. The old shadows-in-the-fog mood has been replaced by a more cosmopolitan and at the same time more fantastic atmosphere. The writing is smoother, the pace faster, the exotic locales and weird inventions more plentiful and more vividly described than in the previous books. The elaborate biological laboratory on the Riviera and the cavern-world beneath Haiti are a far cry from the dingy Chinatown haunts of the first three books in the series.

Fu Manchu hibernated during the war years, but returned in 1948 in *Shadow of Fu Manchu.* Having mellowed somewhat in his old age (of one hundred plus), he is now fighting on the side of the good guys: "My mission is to save the world from the leprosy of Communism." His methods, however, have not changed. He is still served by dacoits and zombies and beautiful but love-starved girls, and still uses the poisoned darts (tipped with "B.W. 63, of which I had a little left") with which he tried to kill Nayland Smith at their first meeting in the Burmese jungle more than thirty-five years earlier. On the whole, the book is routine, although the writing is livelier than usual, and there are touches of humor. Some of the latter is unintentional, as when Fu Manchu instructs a hypnotized girl, "Tonight you will seduce him with your hair. The rest I shall leave to him. . .."

It is easy to believe that by this time Rohmer had become heartily tired of his most famous creation. Nine years passed before the Doctor appeared again in print. *Re-Enter Fu Manchu*, published as a Gold Medal Original paperback in the U.S. and in hard covers in England, is a weary re-telling of the typical Fu Manchu plot. The action moves (but just barely) from London to Cairo to New York, and the "hero" stands around doing nothing except complain that he is doing nothing, and staring in stupefaction when practically everyone turns out to be someone else in disguise. The final Fu Manchu book, *Emperor Fu Manchu,* is unlike the others both in style and in atmosphere. Parts of it resemble an unsuccessful pastiche of previous stories. The principal defect of the book is that present-day Communist China, where much of the action takes place, is an unsuitable locale for the kind of story-book Oriental menace which was one of the charms of the earlier books. The Cold Men—Fu Manchu's army of zombies—inspire no dread, and the Doctor himself has been reduced to the two extreme postures of quiet menace and maniacal rage. It is a poor quietus for so honorable a villain; in the words of Nayland Smith, "an assassin, a torturer, the most dangerous criminal the law has ever known; but always an aristocrat."

"Are You Admiring My Justly Celebrated Legs?"

On any list of "the worst of Sax Rohmer" *The Emperor of America* would come very near the top. In places it verges on self-parody. It was written in the familiar form of a series of related short stories (stretching through nine and a half months in *Collier's*), simply placed end-to-end for the book version. Each story ends with a suitable punchline ("Unless I am greatly mistaken," Roscoe replied, "M. Pascal is *Head Centre!*"), and the first few paragraphs of the following chapter are devoted to setting a new scene, reintroducing the characters, and summarizing the plot situation. The latter does not change all that much during the course of the book, and Rohmer was able to carry over short passages virtually intact from one episode to the next.

The forces of law and order are represented by Commander Drake Roscoe of the U.S. Navy (almost a dead ringer for Nayland Smith) and Dr. Stopford, a ship's doctor on the Cunard line (fashioned from the same mold as Dr. Petrie, even to the apparent lack of a first name). Opposing them is an elaborate subversive organization known as The Zones. Head Centre, one of its controlling officers, turns out to be an ex-Governor of New York and current Presidential candidate, although the mastermind, Great Head Centre, is a mere duchess with delusions of grandeur. The goal of The Zones is the overthrow of the United States government and the establishment of an American Empire. Comparison with Fu Manchu and the Si-Fan is inevitable. However, there is no Oriental touch here. The minions of Great Head Centre are not Chinamen or dacoits, but representatives of most of the non-Anglo-Saxon races in the Western world.

The concoction is topped off with dialogue in pure comic-book-British. ("Cheery ho," Stopford murmured. "Failin' dalliance with the fair, there's nothing I enjoy more than a spot of danger.") There is one memorable scene—the trip through the caverns underneath Manhattan in the company of mad Tom Flynn—but it is scarcely worth suffering through the rest of the book.

The Emperor of America was published in 1929. Some twenty years later, in his last series of books, Rohmer resurrected Drake Roscoe (now an American Secret Service agent) to battle against the Order of Our Lady, the inevitable secret organization threatening world peace. The Order is the creation of Marquise Sumuru, otherwise known as The Madonna, and is dedicated to "purging the world of ugliness, and destroying the rule of brute force." This is to be accomplished by placing women in control of everything—especially men. ("Women were designed by their Creator to be not men's mistresses but their masters.") Sumuru's main weapon in this crusade is sex, and for those important men whose control she cannot trust to any of the lesser Sisters of the Order, she reserves the ultimate refinement of this weapon: herself. For some reason never made clear, she includes Roscoe in this select group, so that when, in the concluding pages of *Sumuru*, he bursts into her hideout, he finds her waiting for him. (She has been whiling away the time with her favorite diversion—skinny-dipping in her penthouse pool with a pet barracuda named Satan.) There is a quick tumble among the mink rugs, and when reinforcements arrive a short time later, they find the apartment empty.

When next encountered, in *The Fire Goddess*, Roscoe is known only as Drakos, a faithful but not-too-satisfied member of the Order of Our Lady. The locale this time is Jamaica, where Sumuru has to contend not only with the local police and an Inspector from Scotland Yard, but also with a rebellion in her own ranks. One of her disciples, Sister Melisande, has revived old voodoo practices and employed them to usurp Our Lady's authority. In the end, Sumuru deals with the recalcitrant Sister by having her body turned into a chryselephantine statue and presented as a gift to the people of the island. More by accident than design, Roscoe manages to betray Sumuru. She is forced to flee Jamaica, and he is released from his bondage.

However, he never learns. In the next book, *Return of Sumuru*, he invades Our Lady's Egyptian headquarters to rescue the daughter of an American millionaire, whom Sumuru has kidnapped. He succeeds in this objective, but in the process he falls in love with Sister Dolores, Sumuru's second-in-command. The book ends as he leaves the rescued girl and her lover, and prepares to rejoin the Order. It seems that his reception is somewhat less than satisfactory, for the final book, *Sinister Madonna*, opens with Roscoe, near death from having been beaten and tortured, babbling in delirium in a hospital room. He recovers, physically at least, and there is some foofaraw as he foils Sumuru's attempts to obtain the legendary Seal of Solomon. At the end of the book he again departs to rejoin Dolores and the Order. This is the last we hear of either of them, or of Sumuru.

The preceding summary omits the first book in the Sumuru series, *Nude in Mink*. This book takes place in England, and does not involve Roscoe. The plots of all five books are roughly the same, and they can be read in any order with little loss of continuity. Of them all, only *The Fire Goddess* has enough inventiveness or intriguing detail to make a lasting impression.

"I Speak All Kinds of English.
Tell Me Which Kind You Prefer."

Neither Nayland Smith nor Drake Roscoe is in any sense a detective. (The villainies they encounter are seldom subtle enough to require any detection.) Rohmer did, however, create several fictional detectives. In his first novel, *The Sins of Séverac Bablon,* Rohmer makes reference to "the three great practical investigators of the world." The greatest of these, M. Victor Lemage of the Paris Sûreté, appears in person in the latter half of the book, while a second is merely mentioned by name: Mr. Brinsley Monro of Dearborn Street, Chicago. The third member of the trio, Mr. Paul Harley of Chancery Lane, performs some off-stage investigations in the book; he was later featured in a series of novels and short stories.

The first of Rohmer's detectives to have a book of his own was Gaston Max, also of the Paris Sûreté. Max is a younger version of Lemage; it is as if Rohmer regretted the latter's retirement at the end of *Séverac Bablon* and decided to let him continue his career under another name. Like Lemage and all of Rohmer's other detectives, Max is a master of disguise and mimicry, and makes heavy use of both skills in his pursuit of criminals. Max's first appearance was in *The Yellow Claw* (serialized in *Lippincott's Magazine* in 1915 and published in book form in the same year). The malefactor in this novel is a mysterious "Mr. King," agent of a Sublime Order which is suspiciously like the Si-Fan. In Max's second adventure, *The Golden Scorpion,* the villain is revealed at the end to be an agent of Fu Manchu himself, and the latter makes a brief anonymous appearance in the book.

Like Fu Manchu, Max was allowed to rest during the 1920's. He reappeared in 1930 in *The Day the World Ended.* This is one of the relatively small number of Rohmer's books in which the fantastic or science-fictional element is dominant. The action takes place in and near the Black Forest in Germany, whither reporter Brian Woodville has been sent to investigate rumors of an outbreak of vampirism: bodies of men and animals drained of blood, and huge bat-like creatures seen flying over the country-side at night. Woodville is warned by a disembodied voice to leave the area. He himself sees one of the flying creatures, watching it land and disappear among the tombs in the local cemetery. He investigates the ruined castle of Felsenweir, and finds its crumbling walls patrolled by seven-foot men in armor—and at this point the plot comes tumbling back (almost) to earth. Gaston Max makes his appearance, by the simple expedient of removing the disguise behind which he has been hiding for seventy-five pages, and reveals that the weird goings-on are not supernatural in nature but are the work of a genuine Mad Scientist, complete with death-ray, Buck Rogers-type flying suits, and plans to conquer and/or destroy the world. Happily, this more mundane explanation does nothing to diminish the excitement and suspense of the book.

After this adventure, Max retires for another thirteen years, returning for the last time in *Seven Sins* to track down a Nazi spy ring in wartime London. His investigations this time are compli-cated by a titled Englishman who dabbles in the occult, and by an impossibly all-American-boyish Air Force lieutenant ("Put up your hands, because I am going to thrash you until I am tired"), but with the help of half a dozen well-chosen disguises, he emerges victorious.

The Tongs which are lacking in the Chinatown episodes of the Fu Manchu and Gaston Max books are present in full force in the stories involving Daniel "Red" Kerry, Chief Inspector (later Superintendent) of the C.I.D. The two short stories "The Daughter of Huang Chow" and "Kerry's Kid," from *Tales of Chinatown*, and the novels *Dope* and *Yellow Shadows*, are set in London's Limehouse, and are replete with opium dens, Tong wars, dope smuggling, and white slavery. Rohmer may not have invented the notion of the "wily Chinee," but these books epitomize the idea. Perhaps the sinister, fog-shrouded Limehouse of which he writes never existed, but it takes on vivid life in the pages of these stories. Rohmer's xenophobia is unusually obtrusive, and Chief Inspector Kerry is a cold and unpleasant character, but even these defects cannot entirely destroy the appeal of the stories.

"I Have Triumphed Over Auguste Dupin."

Paul Harley was a closer approximation to the traditional fictional detective. He was a private investigator whose services were sought not only by individuals but also by the Government. He maintained a suite of offices in Chancery Lane, staffed with a private secretary and a typist, decorated with Oriental artifacts and an engraved portrait of Edgar Allan Poe, and supplied with secret exits and a fully-equipped theatrical dressing room wherein he assumed and discarded his numerous disguises. In conversations with his friend Malcolm Knox, who accompanied him on several of his cases, he compared himself half-facetiously to C. Auguste Dupin. He was selective in his choice of client ("I have intimated to that distressed nobleman. . . that a laundry is the proper place to take his dirty linen"), but any touch of the strange or abnormal was certain to catch his attention.

Some years after serving as an off-stage presence in *The Sins of Séverac Bablon*, Harley appeared in a succession of short stories. Three of these (*Collier's*, 1920) formed part of a connected sequence which was included in the collection *Tales of Chinatown*. His best known cases are recounted in the novels *Bat Wing* and

Fire-Tongue. The former is essentially a straightforward and fairly good murder mystery. Sandwiched in the middle of it is an episode with strong fantasy elements, centering around West Indian voodoo. As John Dickson Carr was later to do in such books as *He Who Whispers,* Rohmer threw in this fantasy episode as a red herring; the mystery turns out to have an entirely rational solution. In *Fire-Tongue,* the better of the two novels, Harley is involved with a sect of Indian fire-worshippers on the loose in England. He also appeared in a short novel, "The Black Mandarin" (*Collier's,* 1922; included in *Tales of East and West*), set in the same Chinatown locale as three of the early short stories. The play *The Eye of Siva* (1923) is also part of the Harley canon, and there are a number of other short stories featuring Harley. One of the earliest of them, "The Red Mist," was included as an advertising device in certain British editions of the book *The Quest of the Sacred Slipper.* (That novel itself does not involve Harley.) Three further "investigations of Paul Harley" were included in *Salute to Bazarada and Other Stories.* One of these, "Skull Face," is the result of self-plagiarism on Rohmer's part. It is a rewritten version of an earlier story, "The Man with the Shaven Skull," with the locale and the characters' names changed. The mystery is why the author bothered.

Predictably enough, in view of his interest in occult subjects, Rohmer at one time turned his hand to the creation of a psychic detective. The result is one of his most satisfying books, *The Dream Detective,* published in England in 1920 and in the United States five years later. It consists of ten episodes in which Moris Klaw employs his method of "odic photography" to investigate cases of haunting, possession, and other occult phenomena, as well as a couple of ordinary murders. Klaw is one of Rohmer's most fascinating characters: tall and stoop-shouldered, "a very old man who carries his many years lightly, or a younger man prematurely aged; none can say which." He poses as an antiquarian, and keeps a musty curio shop near Wapping Old Stairs. The shop is cluttered with broken statuary and old books, and inhabited by canaries, white rats, a pet owl, and at times by hedgehogs and armadilloes.

The door is guarded by a parrot who invariably reacts to the arrival of visitors with the cry "Moris Klaw! Moris Klaw! The Devil's come for you!" Klaw lives in the back of the shop, sharing a small apartment with his beautiful daughter, Isis. Klaw's true identity and personality are things on which no two of his acquaintances agree, for he is adept at assuming many roles. Although his cases are less well known than those of such confrères as John Silence, Carnacki the Ghost-Finder, and Jules de Grandin, they are no less fascinating. "The Headless Mummies" is an amusing crime story, and "The Veil of Isis" is an eerily effective fantasy.

The last of Rohmer's family of detectives to appear in book form was Major Mohammed Ibrahim Brian Barûk, an Anglo-Egyptian. The ten short stories about Barûk, collected in 1944 under the title *Bimbâshi Barûk of Egypt*, are equally divided between detective stories with an English setting and stories of espionage and international intrigue in the Near East. Of either type, they are smoothly written, entertaining, and forgettable.

One other of Rohmer's series characters deserves notice, if only because of the number of stories in which he appears. He is Bernard De Treville—adventurer, Secret Service agent, and tracker-down of lost treasures. Between 1937 and 1945, sixteen short stories featuring De Treville were published in *This Week* magazine. Many of them are variations on the same theme—the search for a stolen jewel or other valuable item hidden in an unusual place—which may explain why they have never been collected in book form. Several of them, such as "The Mystery of the Paneled Room" and "The Secret of the Ruins," have appeared more than once in anthologies.

"Watch Out for the Devil at Your Elbow. . ."

Sax Rohmer's first novel, *The Sins of Séverac Bablon*, is a peculiar affair. What attractions it once had have largely been eroded by the years, and it now appears heavy-handed and crudely written. It was serialized in *Cassell's Magazine* in 1912, before the first Fu Manchu stories were published, but did not appear in book form until 1914. Although it remained in print in England into the mid-1930s, it was not published in the U.S. until 1967, when a limited edition was made available to collectors.

Séverac Bablon was a descendant of the Royal House of Israel, the pure line of descent having been preserved in secret since the break-up of the Kingdom after the time of Solomon. He could command the allegiance of (most of) the world's eight million Jews. In appearance he was young, dark, and handsome. He was given to smoking opium cigarettes, which he carefully left burning in ashtrays as "calling cards." He was filled with noble ideals—or at any rate, one noble ideal—but aside from this he appears now to have been cut from the same pattern as Rohmer's other Oriental villains. He possessed enormous wealth and secret influence, was attended by deferential Arab servitors, and had hordes of silent henchmen who climbed up the sides of buildings and used an eerie minor-key whistle as their signal. Bablon was also, judging by his actions, slightly simple-minded.

Bablon has been described by Rohmer as a Jewish Robin Hood. His victims were always rich, miserly Jews. Sometimes he robbed them outright; more often, by trickery, threats, or black-mail, he forced them to donate vast sums to charities and "worthy projects." As he at one point stated his purpose to one of his victims:

> "You are found guilty, Israel Hagar, of dragging through the mire of greed a name once honored among nations. It is such as you that have earned for the Jewish people a repute it ill deserves. You have suc-ceeded in staining [the Jewish name]. I have a mission. It is to erase that stain."

One of Bablon's worthy projects was the building of an airfleet for Britain. Another involved alleviating the suffering of the poor and unemployed by going out into the slum sections of London and throwing handfuls of gold coins into the crowds (thereby starting riots in which several people were injured). But perhaps his greatest achievement was the prevention of the First World War: by frightening and blackmailing the Jewish financiers involved, he prevented a loan to Germany with which that country had intended to wage war on Britain. "For this will be forgotten all my errors, forgiven all my sins!"

The following item, which appeared in many U.S. newspapers in 1936, provides an ironic footnote to the book:

Sax Rohmer Tells Germany He's Irish, Not Jew

London, Feb 13 — The banning of Sax Rohmer's books in Germany, supposedly on the ground that Rohmer is a Jew, will be protested by the writer, who turns out to be a good Irishman. His full name is Arthur Sarsfield Ward and he has full-blooded Irish parents on both sides.

Before sailing at Southampton today for New York, he said: "The only explanation I and my agents can think of for the Germans banning my books is that they think I am a Jew, and that, of course, is ridiculous. Naturally, I am protesting against the banning and have asked the authorities, through my agents, to explain."

A few short years later, Rohmer's books proudly carried on the copyright page the notice that his books had been banned by the Gestapo in 1936. . .

The Sins of Séverac Bablon retains today mostly curiosity value. Had it been written entirely in the style of a thriller, in which vein Rohmer from the first showed considerable facility, it would have fared better. Instead, the book continually attempted to treat in a serious manner an essentially ludicrous theme. This combined with a pervasive infelicity of style ("Zoe Oppner entered the room, regally carrying her small head") to produce an almost total debacle.

The Orchard of Tears is an entirely different matter. It is the closest that Rohmer ever came to writing a "serious" novel. It is a near-fantasy, but is written in a quiet and restrained style. All the occult forces and Unseen Powers are kept firmly in the background.

The protagonist is Paul Mario, a successful poet and playwright who, after years of meditation and study of ancient manuscripts, has built up certain Egyptian and other pre-Christian teachings into a religio-philosophical system for the modern world. This system bears more than a slight resemblance to Theosophy, and includes everything from "the Hermetic concept of God and Creation" to a belief in reincarnation. Mario is doubtful about publishing his philosophy, but is urged to do so by an influential neighbor, a financier named Jules Thessaly. The publication of "The Gates," the first section of Mario's manuscript, has widespread consequences not only in literary and political circles throughout the world, but also on the populace at large. (Unfortunately we are only told about these consequences at second hand; they are never shown or described in detail.) These consequences cause Mario to doubt the wisdom of publishing further sections of his book. He comes to realize that he has "given life to something which has lain dormant, occult, for untold ages," that he has created a thing which already has outgrown his control. He begins to suspect that Thessaly may have urged publication of the book precisely for the purpose of unleashing this unspecified occult force.

There is a wandering sub-plot concerning a young artist named Flamby Duveen, Mario's protégé. As the book progresses, her life and Mario's become more and more intertwined, and the situation builds up to a genuinely tragic ending.

The novel is full of unrelieved anti-German sentiment, which is natural, considering that it was published less than three weeks before the Armistice in 1918. Aside from this, the overall impression is one of restraint. Never again did Rohmer exercise such discipline over his imagination.

In fact, with the publication of *The Quest of the Sacred Slipper* a year later, it was loose and in full flight again. This one is about the Hashishin, the ancient Order of Assassins, who are sent to England to punish in bloody fashion the theft from Mecca of a slipper believed to have been worn by Mohammed. The story of the attempts to regain the sacred relic makes a suspenseful Oriental thriller.

Thrills, together with virtually everything else of interest, are conspicuously missing from *Moon of Madness*. This is an inane love story, combined with a tale of Communist agents (vintage 1927) plotting evil doings in Madeira and London. It has a witless heroine, sinister South Americans, compromising letters, a couple of cryptograms, coincidences galore, and a cast of inert clods.

She Who Sleeps offers a distinct contrast. It revolves around a perfect fantasy situation: in an ancient Egyptian manuscript is found the record of a young captive princess in the court of Seti I, who was placed in a state of suspended animation and entombed, to awake in a later age as a living advertisement of the greatness of Seti and his kingdom. The manuscript not only gives the location of the princess' tomb and the recipe for awakening her from her age-long sleep, but also contains codicils added at intervals during a three-hundred-year period following the entombment, recording several trial awakenings. Guided by this manuscript, millionaire Egyptologist John Cumberland sets out to uncover the tomb of Zalithea, "She Who Sleeps But Who Will Awaken." The tomb is discovered and opened, the ancient reawakening ritual is performed, and Zalithea awakens. . .

Unfortunately, *She Who Sleeps* is not a fantasy. Zalithea and her tomb turn out to be part of an elaborate hoax, and the story which opened on a note of supernatural mystery and continued in the unreal atmosphere of a fantasy ends on a thoroughly mundane level. However, this does not detract in the least from the effectiveness of the middle portion of the book, which describes the excavation of the tomb and the awakening of Zalithea. This entire episode is brought to life in vivid and meticulous detail,

pleasantly leavened with humor. There is, for example, the pro-
lem of how to obtain a passport for a girl whose legal guardians
have been dead for three thousand years. . .

Despite the let-down at the end, this remains one of Rohmer's
best books. The annoying elements of his style are at a minimum
and the virtues at a maximum.

Although *Yu'an Hee See Laughs* opens in the midst of fog-
shrouded Limehouse, the action quickly shifts to warmer climes:
via Paris and Marseilles to Port Said, and finally to a small island
in the Red Sea, off the coast of Yemen. It is to this island that the
Marquis Yu'an Hee See has summoned his criminal employees from
all over Europe and the Orient for some unspecified large-scale
operation; and it is to this island that several of these employees
have been traced by Scotland Yard inspector Dawson Haig. His
suspicions having first been aroused by the Marquis' activities in
fencing stolen goods in London, Haig soon learns that much more
is involved: narcotics smuggling, and both black and white slave
traffic. But even these are only sidelines, and the real purpose
behind the gathering in the Red Sea remains a secret until too late.

Yu'an Hee See is known to his employees as "Mr. King," the
same alias used by the never-identified mastermind in *The Yellow
Claw*; however, there is no overt connection between the two
books. Rohmer may have been trying to start a new series to rival
the Fu Manchu books: Yu'an is referred to as "perhaps the most
evil man in the civilized world." He is certainly a far more vicious
and unpleasant creation than Fu Manchu. However, even though
he escapes unscathed at the end of the book, he never reappears in
any further stories.

The book has possibly the most annoying heroine in the
Rohmer *opera,* even more tiresome than Nanette in *Moon of Madness.* She has been provided with such idiotic dialogue that the
moment she opens her mouth one becomes impatient for the
villains to come along and shut her up.

There are similarities in locale and plot situations between
Yu'an Hee See Laughs and the novel *White Velvet.* In the latter,
Rohmer attempted a more serious work than his usual thriller, and

succeeded in creating characters who were not exotic stereotypes or mere bundles of eccentricities. The first half of the book centers around The Kofmanns, a vaudeville troupe performing at the Folies Egyptiennès in Port Said. The troupe consists of Pa Kofmann, the domineering but slow-witted head of the family, who cannot understand why the customers would rather ogle the girls in the chorus than watch him lift weights; Ma Kofmann, colorless, quiet, and hardworking, who alone of the family does not hate or despise Pa; "Little Miss" Sally, their granddaughter, an accomplished acrobat, dancer, and mimic at the age of seven; and Musette (née Elizabeth Morton), a husky-voiced singer whom Pa hired when she was stranded and out of work and who is kept busy dodging his heavy-handed advances. These, and other members of the family, are brought vividly and interestingly to life. However, habit proved too strong for Rohmer, and he set his characters down in the midst of a melodramatic tangle of narcotics smugglers and Secret Service agents, kidnapping and murder. Musette falls in love with Lawrence Tabrer, who is on the trail of the kingpin of a drug syndicate. The latter is known only as "Snow Rat." One of the syndicate members persuades Tabrer that Musette is a member of the gang and has tried to have him killed; at the same time, Musette is tricked into believing that Tabrer has deserted her. She leaves the Kofmanns and goes off to Istanbul. The latter half of the book chronicles her adventures there, where she plays a part in the eventual break-up of the syndicate. The revelation of the true identity of "Snow Rat" is no surprise to any mildly attentive reader, but it gives the concluding scenes of the book an enjoyably ironic flavor. The Near Eastern atmosphere is evoked with uncommon skill and economy, and the book contains some of Rohmer's best writing.

The last Rohmer novel to be serialized in *Collier's,* and the last of Rohmer's books to appear in hard covers in the United States, was *Hangover House.* Like *Shadow of Fu Manchu,* this book originated as a stage play, but was never produced. It is a fair detective novel in the classic English tradition: an assorted cast of characters assembles in a fog-bound country house, and very quickly one of their number turns up in a pool of blood, stabbed with a silver dagger. Enter Scotland Yard, and the deduction is on. Apparently out of a sense of obligation to his readers, Rohmer included in the cast a mysterious Egyptian, who pops up occasionally to quote bad proverbs and give advice. He is quite properly ignored by everybody. A startling moment occurs halfway through the book, when the corpse suddenly decides to get up and walk around (promptly to expire once more of a heart attack). Even this is explained in a relatively reasonable manner at the dénouement.

The Moon Is Red was the last of Rohmer's non-series novels. It was published only in England, in 1954. The American publishers who have so far ignored it have missed a bet. It is certainly one of the best of Rohmer's later novels. The locale is the east coast of Florida, and the framework is that of a detective novel. Simultaneously with the escape from the Ringbarn Circus of an intractable male gorilla, there occurs the first of a series of brutal murders. The escaped gorilla is the natural suspect, until it is learned that two similar murders had occurred months earlier in Paris and London. The first victim was the estranged wife of a Parisian acrobat named Gene Marat; Marat was in London at the time of the second killing, and is now in Florida. All the victims were young, beautiful, red-haired women; all had been strangled and then savagely stripped and beaten; all had been found in rooms locked from the inside, and having windows accessible only to some abnormally acrobatic creature. Around the bodies were strewn shreds of paper and clothing, torn by strong teeth. And the killings all occurred on nights when the moon was full. . .

At this point the reader crosses his fingers and begins hoping that the ending will not be a disappointment. It isn't. Several wild hints in the early part of the book, which seem at the time to be red herrings, turn out to be all too pertinent. The ending fully lives up to expectations.

". . . At This Moment I Am Among the Dead."

It is appropriate to discuss Rohmer's sole non-fiction book, *The Romance of Sorcery*, in connection with his fantasy novels. Here are found many of the occult and supernatural impedimenta which later turn up in fictional form: the legendary Egyptian *Book of Thoth*, the elemental spirits, the Theosophical beliefs, Cagliostro's experiments in sorcery. . . It is obvious that the book was written by a believer. There are ritual gestures in the direction of impartiality ("If I have formed any opinion on this matter, I will not state it here") and even skepticism, but one feels that they are not meant to convince, and they do not. In addition to a rambling and diffuse history of sorcery, there are biographical chapters devoted to five noted practitioners of the art: Apollonius of Tyana, Nostradamus, Dr. John Dee, Cagliostro, and Madame Blavatsky. (Many of these same persons figure in the excellent volume *Spirits, Stars and Spells* by L. Sprague de Camp and Catherine C. de Camp.[3] It is amusing and instructive to compare the treatments in the two books.) Rohmer's prose in this book has a fake-scholarly stateliness which slides frequently into pomposity. Many impressively convoluted passages turn out on closer examination to be virtually without meaning. But in spite of such drawbacks in content and style, the book does have value, both as entertainment and as a compendium of anecdotes and quotations from obscure sources.

Rohmer's first fantasy novel, *Brood of the Witch Queen*, made its appearance in 1914, the same year as *The Romance of Sorcery*. Three serial versions appeared simultaneously, in British, Canadian, and U.S. magazines. The book editions were delayed until 1918 in Britain and 1924 in the U.S. The novel divides readily into nine episodes, each centered around one particular bit of ancient Egyptian sorcery at work in the modern world. The third of these episodes is virtually unconnected with the remainder of the book, and constitutes in its own right an excellent tale of vampirism. In the rest of the episodes Antony Ferrara, a young man of mysterious antecedents, employs ancient witchcraft to murder his adoptive father, the Egyptologist Sir Michael Ferrara, and attempts to gain control of the latter's estate. He is opposed by Sir Michael's life-long friend Dr. Bruce Cairn, and the latter's son. The Cairns are the only people who know of Ferrara's sorcerous activities, and even though they have witnessed his experiments in anthropomancy and even less pleasant arts, they have no legal proof with which to enlist the aid of the law. It is ultimately left to Dr. Cairn to use his own knowledge of arcane matters to defeat the fire elemental which Ferrara sends against him, and to bring about the sorcerer's destruction.

Brood of the Witch Queen is probably the best known of Rohmer's books outside of the Fu Manchu series and, in spite of the recent appearance of a paperback edition, the one most eagerly sought in second-hand book stores. It is unlike many of Rohmer's later books in that the supernatural is accepted on its own terms, and there is no attempt to explain it away as hoax, coincidence, or the product of as-yet-unknown scientific principles. The book remains today as suspenseful and exciting as when it was first published.

The Green Eyes of Bâst was Rohmer's contribution to the literature of the were-animal. It begins as newspaperman Jack Addison finds himself followed to his home one evening by a shadowy figure, and watched through the window by a pair of enormous glittering cat-like eyes. When the grounds are examined the next morning, the only signs of the nocturnal visitor are several deep imprints of a woman's high-heeled shoes. This is Addison's introduction to Nahémah, the cat-woman. She is not a were-cat in the traditional sense, but a teratological sport whose feline tendencies and attributes become dominant only at certain times of the year (corresponding to the Sothic month of Phanoi, sacred to the Egyptian cat-headed goddess Bâst). Nahémah is engaged in terrorizing (and decimating) the Coverly family, for which she has conceived a deep hatred. Her guardian, a mad-scientist-type named Dr. Damar Greefe, is forced to aid her in this program. He is finally done in when Nahémah goes wild and escapes his control, but before the end he manages to deliver a three-chapter dying confession which reveals the secret of Nahémah's birth and the reason for her vendetta against the Coverlys. (A quotation from Éliphas Levi in *The Romance of Sorcery* explains Rohmer's apt choice of her name.) The fantastic elements of the plot are partially rationalized away, and the concluding chapters do not live up to the promise of the early part of the book.

There are interesting similarities between Rohmer's novel *Grey Face* and Barré Lyndon's play *The Man in Half Moon Street*. The central figure in both works is a man who has succeeded in renewing his youth and prolonging his life beyond the normal span with the help of certain glandular secretions taken from young, healthy, and usually unwilling donors. Lyndon developed about this figure a suspenseful melodrama, with few further ramifications to the plot. For Rohmer, however, a mere elixir of youth was not nearly enough to fill a book. His Professor Hadrian von Gühl is, in a quite literal sense, a spiritual successor to Cagliostro—a successful alchemist, an occult Adept, and a flamboyant criminal mastermind. He has the secret of manufacturing gold and of growing jewels of gigantic size, with one of which he is able to control people's minds at a distance. Another of his toys is a "temporal eavesdropper," with which he can hear and reproduce any conversation or sound out of the past.

A more disciplined or more restrained writer might have turned this accumulation of improbabilities into a coherent book. As it stands, however, *Grey Face* is confused, disjointed, full of loose ends—and utterly fascinating to read.

In *The Bat Flies Low* the fantastic element concerns the secret of producing cheap power and light, a secret recorded in the *Book of Thoth* and guarded through the ages by an ancient Order having its headquarters at the Temple of Light, hidden in the deserts of Upper Egypt. The manuscript containing the secret is stolen from the Temple and sold to Lincoln Hayes, president of a large utilities company in the United States. The First Prophet traces the manuscript to New York and manages to steal it back before it has been fully translated. The document shuttles back and forth between New York and Egypt, changing hands a few more times, and the process it describes is finally put into practice. And:

> "In the darkest hours of a very dark night, there appeared an unnatural dawn. Seismic instruments all over the world registered an earthquake in the West. Towering buildings in New York rocked on their foundations. . ."

In spite of this impressive climax, the book seems both slow-moving and dull. The rapid-fire inventiveness and furious action, which in other books often served to distract attention from the "funny hat" characterizations, are missing here, and nothing substantial has taken their place.

"My Man,. . . Reclothe Your Indecently Nude Person."

Two of Rohmer's volumes of short stories have already been discussed: *The Dream Detective* and *Bimbâshi Barûk of Egypt*. Each of these is a collection of stories centered around a single leading character. A third volume of the same type is *The Exploits of Captain O'Hagan*. This was Rohmer's first short story collection, published in England in 1916. (A limited facsimile edition was published in the U.S. in 1968.) The stories are full of labored humor and show their age badly. Captain the Honourable Bernard O'Hagan, V.C., D.S.O., as his calling card modestly identifies him, is a demented Irishman who stalks about London in a satin-lined cape, staring rudely through his monocle and interfering in other people's business. In his first "exploit" he befriends a young lady song-writer, comments on what an unusual name she has for a person of the lower classes, beats up her fiancé (who he decides is not good enough for her), and at gun-point forces a lecherous publisher to purchase her songs. She, poor thing, is pathetically grateful. O'Hagan, "never for a moment presuming upon his superiority of blood," kisses her hand, claps her father patronizingly on the back, and strides on to further triumphs.

The other short story collections are more bearable. The next to appear was *Tales of Secret Egypt*. Of the twelve stories included, six concern the enigmatic *Imám* Abû Tabâh. The narrator of these stories is a dealer in bogus Egyptian antiques. His schemes for turning a dishonest profit invariably land him in trouble—witness the affairs of "The Death-Ring of Sneferu" and "The Whispering Mummy"—from which he is extricated with engaging insouciance by the *imám*. The remaining stories include two fine fantasies, "Lord of the Jackals" and "In the Valley of the Sorceress," and an amusing Arabian Nights tall tale called "Pomegranate Flower."

The third collection, *The Haunting of Low Fennel*, appeared under this name only in England. However, six of its seven stories were reprinted in the American edition of *Tales of East and West* in 1933. Of the three fantasies included, "The Curse of a Thousand Kisses" is the best and the most widely known; it has been reprinted at least half a dozen times in magazines and anthologies. One of the other stories, "The Master of Hollow Grange," is an excellent borderline horror story. The one story in the collection which has not been reprinted is "The Blue Monkey," a brief and not very believable murder mystery. It is worth mention only because it is the first of the three stories in which Nayland Smith appears without his usual enemy, Fu Manchu. Although not referred to by name, Smith and Dr. Petrie, who narrates the story, are readily recognizable.

Rohmer's best short story collection is probably *Tales of Chinatown*. Six of its ten stories form a loosely connected sequence; two of these have "Red" Kerry as the protagonist and three others involve Paul Harley. All are good, the best being "The Daughter of Huang Chow." The remaining stories are even more memorable. "Tchériapin" is an excellent fantasy, possibly the best story that Rohmer ever wrote; certainly it is the most widely reprinted of all his stories. "The Hand of the Mandarin Quong" and "The Dance of the Veils" are highly effective exotic tales.

The British and American editions of *Tales of East and West* are quite different books. The British edition appeared first, in 1932, and contained ten stories. Among them are the two Nayland Smith short stories "Mark of the Monkey" and "The Turkish Yataghan." In the former, Smith and Petrie visit Devonshire for a short holiday (to recuperate after the events of *The Hand of Fu-Manchu*) and encounter a murderer who dispatches his victims with a poisonous fungus (of Oriental origin, of course). In the latter story, the narrator of *The Daughter of Fu Manchu* and *The Mask of Fu Manchu* returns to London's Chinatown for a nostalgic visit, accompanied by Smith, who is now Assistant Commisioner of Police. The two men are immediately involved in a murder investigation. The murder turns out to be a quite ordinary crime of passion, and is solved in off-hand fashion by Smith. Another story in the collection is "The M'Villin," a lively historical adventure. This is the only one of Rohmer's very early stories to be preserved in book form. It appeared in *Pearson's Magazine* in 1906 under the byline A. Sarsfield Ward.

The U.S. edition of *Tales of East and West* was published by Doubleday for The Crime Club in 1933. It contains thirteen stories, five of them (including the Paul Harley short novel "The Black Mandarin") from the British edition and six others reprinted from *The Haunting of Low Fennel*. Two additional stories from *Collier's* are included.

Rohmer's last short story collection was *Salute to Bazarada and Other Stories*. This is another of the titles published only in England, and is probably the rarest of all the author's books. The title story is a "novel" cobbled together out of six short stories which were published in *Collier's* in 1937-8. The central character is a stage magician and adventurer named Bazarada. (The book is dedicated to "my friend, Harry Houdini.") Both Bazarada and his adventures are unmemorable. As has already been noted, *Salute* also contains three Paul Harley stories. The remaining two stories are "Sheba's Love-Pearls" and an excellent "mood" story, "Limehouse Rhapsody."

In addition to the stories which are included in the various collections, Rohmer wrote an undetermined number of stories that have appeared only in magazines and newspapers. Some of these are very good: ghost stories like "Affair of Honor" from *This Week* and "The Broken Blade" from *Blue Book,* and mood-pieces and character studies such as "Jamaican Rose" from *This Week* (which was rewritten and included as an episode in the Sumuru novel, *The Fire Goddess*), "Midnight Rendezvous" from *Collier's,* and "Narky" from *Ellery Queen's Mystery Magazine.* An enterprising publisher may yet give these stories, and others like them, a deserved home in book form.[4]

NOTES

[1]"The doctor's servants, by the way, are usually brown, not yellow, are naked to the waist, hairy, and have a silent tread." —H. Douglas Thomson, *Masters of Mystery* (1931).

[2]It was during this interval that he lost the hyphen from his name.

[3]Canaveral Press, 1966.

[4]Since this writing Ace Books has done just that. See *The Secret of Holm Peel* in the following checklist.

CHRONOLOGICAL CHECKLIST OF THE BOOKS OF SAX ROHMER

The Mystery of Dr. Fu-Manchu	London: Methuen	1913
as *The Insidious Dr. Fu-Manchu*	N.Y.: McBride, Nast	1913
The Sins of Séverac Bablon	London: Cassell	1914
	N.Y.: Bookfinger	1967
The Romance of Sorcery	London: Methuen	1914
abridged edition	N.Y.: E.P. Dutton	1924
The Yellow Claw	N.Y.: McBride, Nast	1915
	London: Methuen	1915

The Devil Doctor	London: Methuen	1916
as *The Return of Dr. Fu-Manchu*	N.Y.: McBride, Nast	1916
The Exploits of Captain O'Hagan	London: Jarrolds	1916
	N.Y.: Bookfinger	1968

[He Patronises Pamela, He Clears the Course for True Love,
        He Meets the Leopard Lady, He Buries an Old Love,
        He Deals with Don Juan, He Honours the Grand Duke]

The Si-Fan Mysteries	London: Methuen	1917
as *The Hand of Fu-Manchu*	N.Y.: McBride, Nast	1917
Brood of the Witch Queen	London: C. Arthur Pearson	1918
	N.Y.: Doubleday, Page	1924
Tales of Secret Egypt	London: Methuen	1918
	N.Y.: McBride	1919

[Tales of Abû Tabâh: The Yashmak of Pearls, The Death-Ring
        of Sneferu, The Lady of the Lattice, Omar of Ispahân,
        Breath of Allah, The Whispering Mummy;
  Other Tales: Lord of the Jackals, Lure of Souls, The Secret of Ismail,
        Hurûn Pasha, In the Valley of the Sorceress, Pomegranate
        Flower]

The Orchard of Tears	London: Methuen	1918
The Quest of the Sacred Slipper	London: C. Arthur Pearson	1919
	N.Y.:Doubleday, Page	1919
Dope	London: Cassell	1919
	N.Y.: McBride	1919
The Golden Scorpion	London: Methuen	1919
	N.Y.: McBride	1920
The Green Eyes of Bâst	London: Cassell	1920
	N. Y. : McBride	1920
The Haunting of Low Fennel	London: C. Arthur Pearson	1920

[The Haunting of Low Fennel, The Valley of the Just,
        The Blue Monkey, The Riddle of Ragstaff, The Master of
        Hollow Grange, The Curse of a Thousand Kisses, The
        Turquoise Nacklace]

The Dream Detective	London: Jarrolds	1920
	N.Y.: Doubleday, Page	1925

[The Tragedies in the Greek Room, The Potsherd of Anubis,
    The Crusader's Ax, The Ivory Statue, The Blue Rajah,
    The Whispering Poplars, The Headless Mummies,
    The Haunting of Grange, The Veil of Isis;

U.S. edition contains an additional episode: The Chord in G]

Bat Wing	London: Cassell	1921
	N.Y.: Doubleday, Page	1921
Fire-Tongue	London: Cassell	1921
	N.Y.: Doubleday, Page	1922
Tales of Chinatown	London: Cassell	1922
	N.Y.: Doubleday, Page	1922

[The Daughter of Huang Chow, Kerry's Kid, The Pigtail of
    Hi Wing Ho, The House of Golden Joss, The Man with
    the Shaven Skull, The White Hat, Tchériapin, The Dance
    of the Veils, The Hand of the Mandarin Quong, The Key
    of the Temple of Heaven]

Grey Face	London: Cassell	1924
	N.Y.: Doubleday, Page	1924
Yellow Shadows	London: Cassell	1925
	N. Y. : Doubleday, Page	1926
Moon of Madness	N.Y.: Doubleday, Page	1927
	London: Cassell	1927
She Who Sleeps	N.Y.:Doubleday, Doran	1928
	London: Cassell	1928
The Emperor of America	N.Y.:The Crime Club	1929
	London: Cassell	1929
The Book of Fu-Manchu	London: Hurst & Blackett	1929

[The Mystery of Dr. Fu-Manchu, The Devil Doctor,
    The Si-Fan Mysteries]

The Book of Fu-Manchu	N.Y.:McBride	1929

[The Insidious Dr. Fu-Manchu, The Return of Dr. Fu-Manchu,
    The Hand of Fu-Manchu, The Golden Scorpion]

The Day The World Ended	N.Y.: The Crime Club	1930
	London: Cassell	1930
Daughter of Fu Manchu	N.Y.:The Crime Club	1931
	London: Cassell	1931

Yu'an Hee See Laughs	N.Y.: The Crime Club	1932
	London: Cassell	1932
Tales of East and West	London: Cassell	1932

[Tales of the East: The Black Mandarin, Father of Thieves,
     The Turkish Yataghan, Spirit of the Black Hawk, Fires of Baal;
   Tales of the West: Mark of the Monkey, The Squirrel Man,
     The Cardinal's Stair, Torture, The M'Villin]

The Mask of Fu Manchu	N.Y.: The Crime Club	1932
	London: Cassell	1933
Tales of East and West	N.Y.: The Crime Club	1933

[Tales of the East: The Black Mandarin, The Valley of the Just,
     The Turquoise Necklace, The Curse of a Thousand Kisses,
     Spirit of the Black Hawk, The Turkish Yataghan, Light of Atlantis;
   Tales of the West: The Haunting of Low Fennel, At the Palace da Nostra,
     The Master of Hollow Grange, The Cardinal's Stair,
     The Riddle of Ragstaff, Torture]

Fu Manchu's Bride	N.Y.:The Crime Club	1933
as *The Bride of Fu Manchu*	London: Cassell	1933
The Trail of Fu Manchu	N.Y.: The Crime Club	1934
	London: Cassell	1934
The Bat Flies Low	N.Y.: The Crime Club	1935
	London: Cassell	1936
President Fu Manchu	N.Y.: The Crime Club	1936
	London: Cassell	1936
White Velvet	N.Y.:Doubleday, Doran	1936
	London: Cassell	1936
The Golden Scorpion Omnibus	N.Y.: Grosset & Dunlap	1938

    [The Golden Scorpion, Dope]

The Sax Rohmer Omnibus	N.Y.: Grosset & Dunlap	1938

   [The Yellow Claw, Tales of Secret Egypt]

Salute to Bazarada and Other Stories	London: Cassell	1939

[Salute to Bazarada (a novel), The Treasure Chest Murders,
     Death of Boris Korsakov, Skull Face, Sheba's Love-Pearls,
     Limehouse Rhapsody]

The Drums of Fu Manchu	N.Y.: The Crime Club	1939
	London: Cassell	1939
The Island of Fu Manchu	N.Y.:The Crime Club	1941
	London: Cassell	1941
Seven Sins	N.Y.: McBride	1943
	London: Cassell	1944
Egyptian Nights	London: Robert Hale	1944
as Bimbâshi Barûk of Egypt	N.Y.: McBride	1944

[Mystery Strikes at Ragstaff Hall, The Bimbâshi Meets Up with
A 14, Murder Strikes at Lychgate, The Laughing Buddha
Finds a Purchaser, Warning from Rose of the Desert,
Lotus Yuan Loses her Vanity Case, The Scarab of Lapis Lazuli,
Vengeance at the Lily Pool, Adventure in the Libyan Desert,
Pool-o'-the-Moon Sees Bimbâshi Barûk]

Note: *Egyptian Nights and Bimbâshi Barûk of Egypt* are the same, except
that the former is presented as a novel and the latter as a collection of
ten separate short stories.

Shadow of Fu Manchu	N.Y.: The Crime Club	1948
	London: Herbert Jenkins	1949
Hangover House	N.Y.: Random House	1949
	London: Herbert Jenkins	1950
Nude in Mink	N.Y.: Fawcett (pb)	1950
as Sins of Sumuru	London: Herbert Jenkins	1950
Sumuru	N.Y.: Fawcett (pb)	1951
as Slaves of Sumuru	London: Herbert Jenkins	1952
The Fire Goddess	N.Y.: Fawcett (pb)	1952
as Virgin in Flames	London: Herbert Jenkins	1953
The Moon is Red	London: Herbert Jenkins	1954
The Return of Sumuru	N.Y.: Fawcett (pb)	1954
as Sand and Satin	London: Herbert Jenkins	1955
Sinister Madonna	London: Herbert Jenkins	1956
	N.Y.: Fawcett (pb)	1956
Re-Enter Fu Manchu	N.Y.: Fawcett (pb)	1957
as Re-enter Dr. Fu Manchu	London: Herbert Jenkins	1957

Emperor Fu Manchu	London: Herbert Jenkins	1959
	N.Y.: Fawcett (pb)	1959
The Secret of Holm Peel and *Other Strange Stories*	N.Y.: Ace Books (pb)	1970

[The Secret of Holm Peel, The Owl Hoots Twice, A House
Possessed, The Eyes of Fu Manchu, The Mystery of
the Marsh Hole, Bazarada, For Love of Mistress Mary,
Brother Wing Commanders]

ANONYMOUS AND PSEUDONYMOUS BOOKS

Pause (as by Anonymous)   London: Arthur Greening & Co. 1910
    A collection of short stories by Rohmer, based on ideas supplied by
    George Robey, although neither man's name appears on the book.

Little Tich: A Book of Travels and Wanderings (as by Little Tich)
                    London: Arthur Greening & Co. 1911
    An "autobiography" ghost-written by Rohmer.

Wulfheim (as by Michael Furey)   London: Jarrolds   1950
    An occult novel; Furey was Rohmer's mother's maiden name.

MORE ON AUTHOR AND SUBJECT

*Robert E. Briney was born in Michigan in 1933, was raised in
a house filled with books, and began collecting fantasy and science
fiction in his teens. In 1955 he became a co-founder of Advent:
Publishers, the only publishing house devoted exclusively to
critical and bibliographical works on science fiction. (It is still in
business.) While in graduate school he developed an interest in
mystery and detective fiction which, as the above essay shows, has
not lessened over the years. He received his Ph.D. from M.I.T.
and is presently an Associate Professor of Mathematics at the
State College in Salem, Massachusetts. Among his other recent
publications is an awesome bibliography of John Creasey which
appeared in* The Armchair Detective *for October 1968.*

*Those who are further interested in Sax Rohmer would do
well to look into a little magazine called* The Rohmer Review,
*edited originally by Douglas Rossman and presently by Mr. Briney
himself, which appears twice yearly. They might also keep an eye*

out for a study of Rohmer's life and writing entitled Master of Villainy, *by Elisabeth Sax Rohmer and Cay Van Ash, which will at a later date be published by this Press.*

†As day follows night, scientific rationality succeeds Oriental fantasy. R[ichard] Austin Freeman, a medical man by profession, performed two services that earned him a place in every history of crime fiction since his own time. He brought the concept of scientific detection to full maturity when he created Dr. John Thorndyke, and he gave birth to a new and brilliant approach to the telling of detective stories when he created the inverted tale. Mr. Donaldson now gives us full details as to the latter achievement.

R. Austin Freeman: The Invention of Inversion
by Norman Donaldson

Between the first group of Dr. Thorndyke short stories (1908-09) and the second, seventeen months elapsed. We know very little about Freeman's life at that time. He was engaged in writing another Thorndyke novel—his third—which was to be titled *The Eye of Osiris*, while his first still lay around the house, unpublished.

During this period he had an inspiration, a happy thought which was to bring him fame in histories of detection. He had already made his mark—although the fact was evident only to a limited number of readers—by introducing the first real scientific investigator into the pages of detective fiction. Now he was to

devise an entirely new form of story, in which he would give away
the secret from the start and rely entirely on the ingenuity of his
detective, or the sheer excitement of the deductive process in
action, to draw the reader along to the end of the story.

It was a bold stroke for a writer with so little success behind
him and such a tiny amount of money in the bank. "Would there
be any story left to tell when the reader had all the facts?"
wondered Freeman. "I believed that there would; and, as an
experiment to test the justice of my belief, I wrote 'The Case of
Oscar Brodski'. Here, the usual conditions are reversed; the reader
knows everything, the detective knows nothing, and the interest
focuses on the unexpected significance of trivial circumstances."[1]

In the first part of this story (and of all the other stories of
the same type which Freeman was to write) the third-person
narrative style is employed. We are able to view the murder scene
as detached observers and, in addition, have the advantage of
entering into the thoughts of one of the principals, usually the
murderer.

The second part of each story is related by Jervis, and
describes how Thorndyke is brought into each case and, with
remarkable dispatch, soon knows more about the crime than we
do.

The first and best of the stories recounts the murder of Oscar
Brodski, dealer in precious stones, in the home of a small-time
burglar, Silas Hickler, near a country railway station. Hickler's
motive is possession of the packet of diamonds he knows his victim to be carrying, and his method of disposing of the body is to
lay it across the railway track shortly before a freight train is
expected, thus simulating suicide or accidental death. His greatest
mistake is to forget Brodski's felt hat, which he leaves behind at
his home when he carries the body away; however, he remembers
it when he returns to the house and is able to burn it in the fire-
place.

There are many explanations for the fascination the story
holds for connoisseurs of the detective story. If detection is what
the customers like, here is detection in its purest form, with more

inferences per page than in any other story up to that time or probably since. The dramatic impact is enhanced by Freeman's skillful construction. The two halves of the tale overlap, and we see Thorndyke first through the murderer's eyes, as a stranger in the excited throng on the railway platform, and later as Jervis describes him, his antecedents nicely in place. Some of the dialogue of this scene is heard twice. It is all remarkably effective. There is a striking unity of time and place. Thorndyke is on the spot when the body is brought into the station; and he has the murder solved, thanks to his invaluable green research case, without ever leaving the scene.

Finally there is that useful foil, the hostile local official—in this case a police inspector—eager to interfere with Thorndyke's activities at every turn, by means of sarcasm when all else fails. And against Thorndyke's imperturbable bonhomie, sarcasm invariably fails too.

Altogether the story deserves its honored place in the history of detection, though few of its admirers are aware that it is based on an actual case. Here is Freeman's brief account of it, written many years later.

> The methods of even famous murderers are commonly crude and even foolish, and the gross and palpable traces that they leave can be followed by the most obvious and commonplace means. Indeed in the whole of my reading—with some experience as a prison medical officer—I have met with but a single case which seemed to be worth using for fiction: the one on which I founded my story of 'The Case of Oscar Brodski.' And even this case was selected less for its ingenuity of plan than for the excellent opening that it offered for medico-legal investigation.[2]

The case was that of R. v. Watson and wife (Nottingham Assizes, March 15, 1867). John and Mary Watson were accused of the murder of Henry Raynor on the evening of 17th November, 1866. Raynor was a rent collector who lived with his wife and large family in Nottingham. He had formerly lived in half a cottage in Carlton, a village two or three miles to the east of the city, the other half of the modest dwelling being occupied by the Watsons and their only child. The two families had lived, by all accounts, in an atmosphere made acrimonious by constant dispute over such matters, for example, as who should have the use of the vegetable produce from the garden. When Raynor left the village he kept ownership of the Carlton property, and visited the village frequently. He had reason to suspect the Watsons of using a copper in one of his outhouses to boil potatoes for their pigs, and was determined to put a stop to the practice.

On the fatal day, a Saturday, he travelled to Carlton with a padlock in his pocket, and was seen fit and well at six in the evening. At 7:40 P.M. a railway worker observed his dead body on the line with the neck across one of the rails, in such a position that it would surely have been decapitated by the 8:10 train. There were blows about the head such as a poker might have caused, and some bleeding, but no great vessels had been damaged. His watch and money had disappeared and his hat was nowhere to be seen. Medical examination showed that death had been caused by manual strangulation.

Professor Alfred Swaine Taylor was called in, and he later described the medico-legal aspects in his textbook, where Freeman picked them up. "There were marks of dragging between the cottage and the railway, and marks corresponding with Watson's boots."

> On searching the house [wrote Taylor] an iron rake was found concealed on a shelf. This was delivered to me for examination. A cindery substance adhered to one end of it, looking as if it had undergone fusion. On heating a portion of it the smell of burnt shellac was emitted, and on acting on it with alcohol a resinous solution like that of shellac was obtained. The alcohol caused the separation of some fibres which under the microscope proved to be the hair of some animal of the

order rodentia. . . . On being questioned respecting the rake the male prisoner said he himself had used it. . . . . . for cleaning out a cesspool.

A hat similar to that worn by the deceased, and purchased at the same shop, was burnt. The cindery ash was collected, and submitted to examination with precisely similar results. These hats are made of felt chiefly from rabbit's and hare's fur, and this is combined with a quantity of shellac.

. . . . . . Where was the hat of the deceased? . . . . . It was suggested for the prosecution that, in dragging the body to the railway track to conceal the murder, the hat was accidentally left in the cottage. To have returned with it to the railway might have led to detection [so they burned it in the grate].[3]

The prisoners had no effective defense to offer. To explain blood-stained clothes found in their home, they called witnesses to testify to the killing of a pig three days before the murder. Taylor, in the witness box, expressed disbelief in this explanation, but could not swear that the bloodstains were human. In spite of the grave suspicions attaching to the Watsons, the jury found them "not guilty," and they were forthwith acquitted. (Taylor does not make this fact clear in his account, and Freeman appears to have believed that a guilty verdict was returned.)

It will not be possible to examine in such detail Freeman's other inverted stories. All are fine examples of detection, and most have convincing dramatic and human qualities. One of them, however, did not satisfy *Pearson's*, and was published instead in *The Novel Magazine,* another A.C. Pearson publication, ahead of the others. This story, "The Willowdale Mystery," better known by its *Singing Bone* title, "A Wastrel's Romance," is the only one of the series which does not involve a capital crime; moreover, it is excessively sentimental. Nevertheless, the central feature of the detectival process has a fascination all its own. Is it possible to determine a thief's approximate place of residence solely from the dust found on a coat left behind at the scene of an attempted robbery? If he chooses his residence carefully, with a rice mill on one side, a flour mill on the other, and cocoa and black-lead factories within sniffing distance, why not? Thorndyke with his microscope and Post Office directory can work wonders with such clues as that.

Incidentally, John Freeman remembers his father's researches for this story. He left microscope slides, no doubt moistened with glycerine, on the wall of one of the factories concerned, in the Dockhead area of East London, south of the Thames, to satisfy himself of the nature and quantity of dust likely to be deposited in the locality.

For another of the excellent inverted stories, "The Echo of a Mutiny," published in *Pearson's* as "Death on the Girdler," Freeman used his memories of his stay in Ramsgate, his journeys down the Thames estuary, and the investigation he had made for his articles in *Cassell's Magazine* on lighthouses. While Freeman lived in Ramsgate, reports his son, two collier brigs were still using the harbor there, and the Trinity House tender *Lord Warden* was stationed in the other harbor; this accounts for all the craft mentioned in the story.

The remaining story of the "inverted" type to be published in *The Singing Bone* was "A Case of Premeditation," in which Freeman illustrated a point he felt was misunderstood: that bloodhounds, like fingerprints, are no use without corroboration for fixing a crime on an individual. As Thorndyke put it: "The hound possesses a special sense—the olfactory—which in man is quite rudimentary. He thinks, so to speak, in terms of smell, and his thoughts are untranslatable to beings in whom the sense of smell is undeveloped. We have presented to the hound a knife, and he discovers in it certain odorous properties; he discovers similar or related odorous properties in a tract of land and a human individual—Ellis. We cannot verify his discoveries or ascertain their nature. What remains? All that we can say is that there appears to exist some odorous relation between the knife and the man Ellis. But until we can ascertain the nature of that relation, we cannot estimate its evidential value or bearing."

Pearson's published one more inverted story, "The Dead Hand," in October and November 1912; but by that time *The Singing Bone* had been issued as a collection of five stories, comprising the first four inverted stories from *Pearson's* together with an as yet uncollected tale from the earlier series, "The Scarred Finger," which was retitled "The Old Lag" and rather awkwardly divided into two parts so that it took on the semblance, though not the substance, of the inverted stories which appeared with it.

"The Dead Hand" was much longer than the previous inverted stories published in *Pearson's,* but it was accepted by the magazine eagerly enough, for they recognized its high quality; and it appeared in the two parts into which it so naturally falls. Freeman thought highly of the story, and when his next volume of short tales, *The Great Portrait Mystery,* was brought out in 1918, he included therein two other inverted short stories he had written during 1913 and 1914—"Percival Bland's Proxy" and "The Missing Mortgagee"—but deferred book publication of "The Dead Hand." This story he put to one side for a few more years, and it finally appeared, greatly increased in length, as a full-scale Thorndyke novel, *The Shadow of the Wolf* (1925).

Critical interest at the time *The Singing Bone* was published was only moderate. It has taken many years for critics to appreciate Freeman's masterstroke, and he has continued to appeal only to a small minority of readers, but an important minority. As John Adams said in an important contemporary article on Freeman:

> The objection to this duplicate method, which Mr. Freeman claims to have been justified by its success, is that it emphasises the purely logical aspects of the different cases. It is not so much a series of stories as a set of exercises. A teacher might be tempted to use them as problems in applied logic. This logical interest is no doubt prominent in other books, notably in the summing up at the symposium at the end of "The Eye of Osiris," but in the short stories it is deliberately brought

forward as the chief matter. Nothing but the author's remarkable skill in character delineation and graphic narrative could save the stories from being regarded as technical studies, such as find a suitable place in a course on forensic medicine.

Indeed, the whole position of Mr. Freeman depends upon the class of readers to whom he appeals. His work is certainly beyond the range of the ordinary devourer of "sleuth" novels. He makes very great demands on the attention of his readers. To read these books intelligently implies a definite exercise in the use of Mill's Canons of Inductive Logic and the books might form a very practical means of testing the student's mastery of these canons. A very obvious and natural criticism of the stories is that they are too clever: they ask too much of the reader. But unlike some clever writers, Mr. Freeman is clever enough to carry off his cleverness. His exposition is so clear, his arrangement of events so methodical, that the reader is led along with the minimum amount of effort consistent with a very definite exercise of the reason. Stupid and lazy readers may be warned off, but the ordinary intelligent reader may rely upon having from Mr. Freeman a course in mental gymnastics conducted under the pleasantest conditions.[4]

It may be added that the class of readers to whom Freeman's books appeal has steadily increased in proportion since these words were written, so that in recent years, with a new emphasis on the scientific method as opposed to the romantic or intuitive—in detection as in most other matters—Freeman can be said to be well suited to those modern readers who stumble upon his books. At least one reader can testify to Freeman's capacity for teaching a young mind, in a most fascinating way, the validity of the scientific approach, not only to criminal problems but, by extension, to the affairs of life.

NOTES

[1]R. Austin Freeman, *The Singing Bone* (1912), preface.

[2]R. Austin Freeman, in *Strand Magazine*, Vol. 73 (January, 1927), pp. 90-91. Freeman forgot his use of R. v. Castleton in *Danby Croker* (1916). After writing this account in *The Strand* he was to make use of another real-life case in *Dr. Thorndyke Intervenes* (1933).

[3]Alfred Swaine Taylor, *Principles and Practice of Medical Jurisprudence* (London: J. & A. Churchill, 1883), I, 541-43; see also *Times* (London), 19-20 November 1866 and 16-18 March 1867.

[4]John Adams, in *The Bookman* (London), April, 1913, pp. 6-7. The author, who was later knighted, was Professor of Education at the University of London.

MORE ON AUTHOR AND SUBJECT

Norman Donaldson was born in Carlisle, England in 1922. In his teens he discovered the Dr. Thorndyke stories, which afforded him an early insight into the meaning of scientific method and influenced his choice of a scientific career. After four years in the Royal Army Medical Corps, he attended St. Andrews University in Scotland, graduating in 1950 with a degree in chemistry. He came to the United States in 1957, and presently makes his home with his wife and four children in Columbus, Ohio, where he works as an organic indexer for the Chemical Abstracts Service. For relaxation he plays the violin and (of course) collects R. Austin Freeman books.

Mr. Donaldson's In Search of Dr. Thorndyke, *the first book-length study of Freeman's life and work, has recently been issued by this press.*

†The Golden Age of the formal detective story may be dated from Agatha Christie's first novel (1920), or from S.S. Van Dine's (1926), or from any of several other landmark events. But all are agreed that the great names of that age are Carr, Christie, Queen, Sayers, Allingham, Blake, Innes, Marsh, and a dozen or so others. One of the least known of the masters of formal detection in its finest flower is the subject of the following essay. If Mr. Shibuk's descriptions tempt you to rummage through all accessible second-hand bookstores for old Henry Wade novels, by all means don't resist.

Henry Wade
by Charles Shibuk

*One of our best and soundest writers—*Dorothy L. Sayers.
*One of the greatest English writers of detective stories—*London Times.
Today Wade seems a curiously neglected master— C.S.

Henry Wade has written twenty detective novels since 1926. At least half a dozen of them are worthy of the most serious attention. But only thirteen of these novels have been published here. His two historically important books of short stories have never seen American publication either. Only two of his most recent novels have ever been issued in paperback by an American publisher, and they, like Wade's other work, are now completely out of print in this country.

Wade was a practitioner of the school of modern British realism and a master of the police novel. A staunch advocate of the classical detective novel in its purest form, he also wrote "inverted" stories—tales related wholly or partly from the viewpoint of the criminal—that are among the best in the genre.

He can most aptly be compared to Freeman Wills Crofts, in whose demanding tradition Wade was second to none. Wade's police novels and inverted tales never quite reached the pinnacle of Crofts' *The Cask* or *The 12.30 from Croydon*, but his characterizations were deeper, especially in his inverted stories. His personal experiences brought skill to his depiction of the rural police, and his strongly developed sense of irony, in particular his "ironical criticism of legal procedure" (Dorothy L. Sayers), anticipated the work of Richard Hull, Cyril Hare, Raymond Postgate, Henry Cecil, Michael Underwood and Roderic Jeffries. He accurately limned the changing values of postwar England in his later novels, and throughout his entire career he has done more to explicate the psychology and mores of the English people than any other writer in the field.

Major Sir Henry Lancelot Aubrey-Fletcher was born in Surrey on September 10, 1887. He was educated at Eton College and New College, Oxford. His marriage to Mary Augusta Chilton in 1911 produced four sons and a daughter before it was terminated by the first Mrs. Wade's death in 1963. He served with distinction in the Grenadier Guards in World War One, being wounded twice and receiving both the Distinguished Service Cross and the Croix de Guerre. He retired in 1920 and has since served in various capacities such as Justice of the Peace, Alderman, High Sheriff, and Lord Lieutenant of Buckinghamshire (the Queen's representative in the county) from 1954 to 1961. He now resides in Oxfordshire, having remarried in 1965. He is the author of the definitive *A History of the Foot Guards to 1856* (1927) in addition to the long series of detective stories under the pseudonym of Henry

Wade, which was taken from his mother's maiden name.

1. *The Verdict of You All* (London: Constable, 1926. Reprinted in paperback by Penguin. New York: Payson & Clarke, 1927.) Inspector Dobson.

An elderly and wealthy man is murdered in his study. The police investigate but there are no clues.

Wade's first police novel contains a trial scene culminating in a verdict that questions the entire legal system. Reviewers drew the inevitable comparisons with Crofts. Dorothy L. Sayers called it "A first rate story."

2. *The Missing Partners* (London: Constable, 1928. New York: Payson & Clarke, 1928.) Superintendent Dodd.

Two partners fade into thin air. One is found murdered and the other is presumed to be guilty. He returns and is sent to jail, but manages to prove his innocence. It is now up to the police to find the guilty party.

This is perhaps Wade's closest emulation of Crofts' methods, but his scrutiny of the legal system wherein there is a near miscarriage of justice is all his own. At the time of publication of this novel Wade's real identity was made known.

3. *The Duke of York's Steps* (London: Constable, 1929. New York: Payson & Clarke, 1929.) Inspector Poole.

A financier with a well-known heart condition collapses and dies at the foot of the Duke of York's Steps. Who was the unknown man who jostled him just before he fell?

This was the most favorably received of all Wade's novels, and is usually cited by the historians as his best work. It is also the last of Wade's novels to receive any mention in the standard historical surveys. Debuting herein is John Poole, Wade's most frequently used detective. Poole was representative of the new breed of policeman: college educated and police school trained, he rose from the ranks to become the youngest Inspector in the C.I.D. at New Scotland Yard. "There is a quiet persuasive charm about Henry Wade's Inspector Poole," wrote Dorothy L. Sayers.

4. *The Dying Alderman* (London: Constable, 1930. Reprinted in paperback by Penguin. New York: Brewer & Warren, 1930.) Inspector Lott. Alderman Trant manages to leave a dying message as a clue to his murderer.

The Verdict of You All and *The Duke of York's Steps* are acknowledged classics of their type and have received sufficient critical fanfare. From this early period I personally prefer *The Dying Alderman,* which is written and plotted with great clarity and precision, and remains surprisingly fresh today.

5. *No Friendly Drop* (London: Constable, 1931. New York: Harcourt Brace, 1932. Later revised (late 1930's?). Revived in the U.S. as #17 in the *Murder Revisited* series. New York: Macmillan, 1957.) Inspector Poole.

The two drugs were harmless in themselves, but not when mixed in the human stomach. An intriguing subplot concerns illicit traffic in antique furniture.

The novel was originally criticized for having too much love interest, but on its revival reviewers thought it better than competent.

6. *The Hanging Captain* (London: Constable, 1932. New York: Harcourt Brace, 1933. English paperback reprint by Chariot Books, 1952.) Superintendent Dawle.

A body is found. Was it suicide or was it murder?

This novel marks the end of Wade's apprentice period.

7. *Policeman's Lot: Stories of Detection* (London: Constable, 1933. Reprinted in paperback by Penguin, 1946. Never published in the U.S.)

This collection contains seven cases for Inspector Poole ("Duello," "The Missing Undergraduate," "Wind in the East," "The Sub-Branch," "The Real Thing," "The Baronet's Finger," "The Three Keys"), and six other stories ("A Matter of Luck," "Four to One—Bar One," "Payment in Full," "Jealous Gun," "The Amateurs," "The Tenth Round").

The book was praised by Ellery Queen and selected as #85 in

Queen's Quorum. "The Sub-Branch" and "Four to One—Bar One" were included in the anthology *Detection Medley,* edited by John Rhode (London: Hutchinson, 1939. Partial contents published in the U.S. as *Line-Up,* New York: Dodd Mead, 1940). Dorothy L. Sayers reprinted "Duello" in her *Second Omnibus of Crime.*

This excellent collection proves that Wade, like Crofts, could write masterly and incisive short stories. "The Tenth Round" in particular deserves classic status, and contains hints of thematic material later to appear in *Heir Presumptive, The High Sheriff, Too Soon to Die* and *A Dying Fall.*

8. *Mist on the Saltings* (London: Constable, 1933. Never published in the U.S.) Superintendent Jett and Inspector Lamming.

This fusion of the inverted tale and the police novel anticipates Crofts' *The 12.30 from Croydon* (1934), but by Crofts', Wade's own or anybody else's standards it is an unexpected and unprecedented masterpiece. It boasts penetrating characterizations, superb East Anglian marshland atmosphere, and a powerful climax. It is easily one of the thirty best detective novels ever written, and ·probably the greatest detective novel that has not been published in America.

9. *Constable, Guard Thyself!* (London: Constable, 1934. New York: Houghton Mifflin, 1935.) Inspector Poole.

Isn't Police Headquarters a perfect setting for a murder?

The reviews were generally good, with Will Cuppy dissenting by finding it slow and lacking in character interest. On the other hand, Dorothy L. Sayers thought it a model of the classical detective story. No subsequent Wade novel was to be published in the U.S. for the next 17 years.

10. *Heir Presumptive* (London: Constable, 1935. New York: Macmillan, 1953, as #2 in the *Murder Revisited* series.) Chief Inspector Darnell.

Eustace Hendel must kill several of his relatives in order to inherit a huge fortune.

This fully inverted tale is ingenious and highly devious, and has a fine ironic ending. It is Wade's second-best novel, and marks the end of his best and most creative period, and took almost twenty years to cross the Atlantic. When it did, the reviews were excellent. "Puts most of its present day rivals and many of its own contemporaries to shame," James Sandoe wrote. Anthony Boucher commented: "Chalk up a black mark against all of New York's mystery editors who, in 1935, shipped this one back to London, unbought."

11. *Bury Him Darkly* (London: Constable, 1936. Never published in the U.S.) Inspector Poole.

A night watchman is found murdered in a shop. The usual blunt instrument is the murder weapon. A group of valuable diamonds is missing.

A straight police novel, but only average for Wade.

12. *The High Sheriff* (London: Constable, 1937. Never published in the U.S.) Superintendent Clewth.

A blackmailer dies while out hunting. Was it suicide, accident, or murder? The blackmail victim had means, motive and opportunity, but is he really guilty?

Set in the same environment as *No Friendly Drop* (but without the services of Inspector Poole), this is Wade's fifth-best novel, and is distinguished by a truly horrifying climax. Its sincere depth of characterization and dazzling narrative technique are unexpected surprises, representing in many ways an advance over Wade's previous work and looking forward to his major novels of the 1950's, especially *A Dying Fall*.

13. *Here Comes the Copper* (London: Constable, 1938. Reprinted in paperback by Penguin. Never published in the U.S.) John Bragg.

This collection contains thirteen short stories: "These Artists!," "The Seagull," "The Ham Sandwich," "Summer Meeting," "Anti-Tank," "A Puff of Smoke," "Steam Coal," "Toll of the Road," "November Night," "The Little Sportsman," "Lodgers,"

"One Good Turn," and "Smash and Grab." The series traces the career of rural police constable John Bragg, whose motto is "Notice and Remember," and who eventually rises to become a member in good standing of London's famed C.I.D. "Smash and Grab," detailing Bragg's first case as a member of the C.I.D., was reprinted in *Ellery Queen's Mystery Magazine* for July 1945.

The book is an excellent collection of shorts, with the emphasis on crime and deduction.

14. *Released for Death* (London: Constable, 1938. Never published in the U.S.) Detective-Constable John Bragg.

An ex-convict finds that it isn't always easy to follow the straight and narrow path.

John Bragg makes his only novelistic appearance in this book, wherein he is obliged to disprove the Yard's own iron-clad case against an innocent man accused of murder. It's a well above average novel, sympathetic and perceptive in its view of the criminal protagonist.

15. *Lonely Magdalen* (London: Constable, 1940. Revised edition, London: Constable, 1946. Never published in the U.S.) Inspector Poole.

The abandoned body of a woman who was no better than she should be is found on a lonely road. This highly complicated police novel features a long flashback sequence.

For the six long years between the first and the revised editions of *Lonely Magdalen,* war service halted Wade's pen. His subsequent work indicates that this period and its aftermath had a profound effect on his outlook.

16. *New Graves at Great Norne* (London: Constable, 1947. Never published in the U.S.) Chief Inspector Myrtle and Inspector Joss.

The investigators are confronted with three murders, including the strangulation of two old ladies. This is a straight police novel, marked by more bloodshed than usual.

17. *Diplomat's Folly* (London: Constable, 1951. New York: Macmillan, 1952.) Chief Constable Cannon and Superintendent Peck.

Add one unsavory diplomat to a blackmail scheme and the result is murder.

Wade, who had in his earlier inverted tales been heavily influenced by Francis Iles, here pays tribute to Iles by writing his third partially inverted novel from the viewpoint of the murderee. This was the first Wade novel to be published here since 1935. The reviews were mixed but Anthony Boucher called it "reminiscent of the best Crofts."

18. *Be Kind to the Killer* (London: Constable, 1952. Never published in the U.S.) Chief Inspector Vine.

The murder of a policeman turns into another criticism of the legal system. The book was cited by W.B. Stevenson in his *Detective Fiction* (1958 edition), more for its availability, I presume, than for any superior merit.

19. *Too Soon to Die* (London: Constable, 1953. New York: Macmillan, 1954. Reprinted in paperback by Collier Books.) Chief Inspector Poole. A family's attempt to evade paying exorbitant inheritance taxes that will mean financial ruin soon turns into a murder problem for newly promoted Chief Inspector Poole. This partially inverted story is Wade's third-best novel and the start of a brief renaissance in his writing career.

20. *Gold Was Our Grave* (London: Constable, 1954. New York: Macmillan, 1954.) Chief Inspector Poole.

An almost fatal car accident occurs. Was it an attempt at murder? Among the elements Poole encounters in trying to find out are blackmail and Bolivian gold mine stock certificates.

The reviewers agreed that this was a comedown after such masterpieces as *Too Soon to Die*.

21. *A Dying Fall* (London: Constable, 1955. New York: Macmillan, 1955. Reprinted in paperback by Collier Books.) Chief Constable Colonel John Netterly and Detective Hant.

An unwanted wife falls to her death from a high balcony. Suicide or murder?

Excellent characterization, a perceptive view of changing postwar values in England and an ironic ending combine to make this Wade's fourth-best novel. It was also his last major work, a highly personal novel to which he gave the best of his capabilities.

22. *The Litmore Snatch* (London: Constable, 1957. New York: Macmillan, 1957.) Chief Inspector Vine.

This is one of the few stories of child-kidnapping that is given the form of the classical detective novel, thus enabling Wade to treat sensational subject-matter in his own inimitable style. Wade's last novel to date is a successful attempt to come to terms with postwar values, and was well received, though not on his highest level of achievement.

Henry Wade was not only a pioneer of historical significance but also a writer of extreme merit. Unfortunately not many people read him now, largely because no publisher is printing his work today. Hopefully, however, these notes may serve to revive some interest in an unsung master.

(The author wishes to extend a note of thanks to Edward Gorey for his cooperation in the preparation of this tribute to Henry Wade.)

MORE ON AUTHOR AND SUBJECT

Charles Shibuk is a native and inhabitant of the Bronx, and his two greatest interests are mystery fiction and the cinema (silent films in particular). He has published material on the films of Alexander Dovzhenko and Lewis Milestone among others, has contributed articles and letters to Films in Review, *and is vice president of the Theodore Huff Memorial Film Society (whose president, William K. Everson, is represented later in this book). In the field of crime fiction criticism, he is the author of "A Preliminary Checklist of the Detective Novel and its Variants" (with two supplements), of articles on Anthony Berkeley and Cyril Hare among others, and of the excellent column "The Paperback Revolution" in* The Armchair Detective.

Aside from reviews, and a few sentences in each of the standard reference books on mystery fiction, the present essay is the only material on Henry Wade published to date.

†Dashiell Hammett is world-renowned as the first "ace performer" of the hard-boiled or realistic school of crime fiction. It is not so well known, but should be, that he was also a brilliant craftsman of intricate formal plot-puzzles; even Red Harvest, *for all its dozens of bloody deaths, is a masterpiece of tight construction, with quite a bit of creditable deductive reasoning (including a dying-message situation that ranks with the best of Queen). Prof. Edenbaum, however, approaches Hammett more from the literary critic's viewpoint, and his analysis of Hammett's novels and why they deserve serious attention is one of the best pieces on a mystery writer ever written by an academic.*

The Poetics of the Private Eye:
The Novels of Dashiell Hammett
by Robert I. Edenbaum

[The daemonic agent] will act as if possessed. . . .
He will act part way between the human and divine
spheres, touching on both, which suggests that he can
be used for the model romantic hero, since romance
allows its heroes both human interest and divine
power. His essentially energic character will delight
the reader with an appearance of unadulterated
power. Like a machiavellian prince, the allegorical
hero can act free of the usual moral restraints, even
when he is acting morally, since he is moral only in
the interests of his power over other men. This sort

98

of action has a crude fascination for us all; it impels
us to read the detective story, the western, the saga of
space exploration and interplanetary travel.
—Angus Fletcher, *Allegory*

Raymond Chandler, Dashiell Hammett's major successor in
the tradition of the tough detective novel, Howard Haycraft, a
historian of the form, and David T. Bazelon, a far from sympathetic critic, all agree that Hammett shaped the archetype and
stereotype of the private-eye. Hammett's third novel, *The Maltese
Falcon*, heads any list of tough guy novels of the thirties. The pre-
eminence and popularity of that novel is not only due to its date
of publication at the very start of the new decade, nor to the fact
that eleven years later John Huston turned it into "the best
private-eye melodrama ever made," according to James Agee (*Agee
on Film*). And it is not only the vagaries of camp taste that have
made Humphrey Bogart's Sam Spade a folk-hero a third of a century later. Sam Spade of *The Maltese Falcon* (1930), together
with the nameless Continental Op of the earlier novels, *Red Harvest* and *The Dain Curse* (both 1929), and to a lesser extent Ned
Beaumont of *The Glass Key* (1931) and Nick Charles of *The Thin
Man* (1934) constitute a poetics of the tough guy hero of novel,
film, and television script from 1929 to the present.

The characteristics of Hammett's "daemonic" tough guy,
with significant variations in the last two novels, can be schema-
tized as follows: he is free of sentiment, of the fear of death, of
the temptations of money and sex. He is what Albert Camus calls
"a man without memory," free of the burden of the past. He is
capable of any action, without regard to conventional morality,
and thus is apparently as amoral—or immoral—as his antagonists.
His refusal to submit to the trammels which limit ordinary mortals
results in a godlike immunity and independence, beyond the
power of his enemies. He himself has under his control the pure
power that is needed to reach goals, to answer questions and solve
mysteries, to reconstruct the (possible) motivations of the guilty
and innocent alike. Hammett's novels—particularly the first three,
with which this essay will be primarily concerned—present a "cri-

tique" of the tough guy's freedom as well: the price he pays for his power is to be cut off behind his own self-imposed masks, in an isolation that no criminal, in a community of crime, has to face.

The Maltese Falcon is the most important of the novels in the development of the poetics of the private-eye because in it Hammett is less concerned with the intricacies of the detective story plot than with the combat between a villain (ess) who is a woman of sentiment, and who thrives on the sentiment of others, and a hero who has none and survives because he has none. As a result of that combat itself, the novel is concerned with the definition of the private-eye's "daemonic" virtue—with his invulnerability and his power—and with a critique of that definition.

The word "combat" has to be qualified immediately, for there can only be unequal combat when one antagonist holds all the cards and the other is always victim; when the one manipulates and the other is deceived; when the actions of the one are unpredictable and the responses of the other stock. These terms would seem to describe the villain and his victim in Gothic fiction from The Mysteries of Udolpho to The Lime Twig. But Hammett, in Maltese Falcon, reverses the roles. Brigid O'Shaughnessy, the murderer of Sam Spade's partner Miles Archer, is the manipulated, the deceived, the predictable, finally, in a very real sense, the victim. Customarily in the detective story, the solution to the mystery—for example, the identity of the murderer—is known only to the murderer himself; terror makes everyone victim but the murderer, for only the murderer, the unpredictable element, can know what will happen next. In the first few pages of The Maltese Falcon Miles Archer is murdered, apparently by Floyd Thursby. Thursby is killed; that is apparently a mystery (though it takes no great imagination to settle on the young hood Wilmer as the likely culprit). The ostensible mystery, then, is why Thursby killed Archer, and why he in turn was killed. In the last pages of the novel, however, the reader (and Brigid O'Shaughnessy) discovers that he (and she) has been duped all along, for Spade has known from the moment he saw Archer's body that

Brigid is the murderer. Spade himself, then, is the one person who holds the central piece of information; he is the one person who knows everything, for Brigid does not know that he knows. And though Spade is no murderer, Brigid O'Shaughnessy is his victim.

Once the reader knows, finally, that Spade has known all along that Miles Archer, with his pistol tucked inaccessibly under his arm, would not have gone up a dark alley with anyone but a girl as beautiful as Brigid, and therefore must have gone with *her*, he can make sense out of an apparently irrelevant anecdote that Spade tells Brigid early in the novel. The story, about a case Spade once worked on, concerns a man named Charles Flitcraft who had disappeared without apparent motive. The likely possibilities—as nearly always in Gothic fiction, sex and money—are eliminated beyond doubt. The mystery is cleared up when Spade finds the missing man. Flitcraft's life before his disappearance had been "a clean orderly sane responsible affair," Flitcraft himself "a man who was most comfortable in step with his surroundings." The day of his disappearance, on his way down a street, a beam had fallen from a building under construction and missed killing him by an inch. At that moment Flitcraft "felt like somebody had taken the lid off life and let him look at the works." He left his old life on the spot, for "he knew then that men died at haphazard like that, and lived only while blind chance spared them." Flitcraft spends several years living under that Dreiserian philosophy, working at a variety of jobs, until he meets another woman identical to his first wife except in face, marries her, has children identical to those by his first wife, leads a life identical to the one he had led before his black epiphany. Spade had returned to the first Mrs. Flitcraft to tell her what he had learned. Mrs. Flitcraft had not understood; Spade had no trouble understanding. Brigid O'Shaughnessy, despite her fascination with Spade's story almost against her will (she is trying to find out what he intends to do in her case) understands no more than Mrs. Flitcraft did.

Flitcraft moves from a life—and a commensurate philosophy—in which beams do not fall, to one in which beams do, back to one in which they don't. There can be no doubt which of the two Spade subscribes to: "Flitcraft *knew* then that men died at haphazard" (my emphasis). That commonplace enough naturalistic conception of the randomness of the universe is Spade's vision throughout. The contrast is of Spade's life (that of the private-eye) in which beams are expected to fall, and do fall, and that of the suburban businessman, in which they do not—or, at least, do not until they do. Since they did stop in the years between, Flitcraft merely adjusted himself back to a world where they did not. In Spade's world, of course, they never stop falling. If Brigid were acute enough—or less trammelled by conventional sentiment—she would see in the long, apparently pointless story that her appeals to Spade's sense of honor, his nobility, his integrity, and finally, his love, will not and cannot work. That essentially is what Spade is telling her through his parable. Brigid—totally unscrupulous, a murderess—should understand rather better than Mrs. Flitcraft, the bourgeois housewife. But she doesn't. She falls back on a set of conventions that she has discarded in her own life, but which she naively assumes still hold for others'. At the end of the novel, Brigid is not merely acting her shock at Spade's refusal to shield her; that shock is as genuine as Effie Perine's at Spade for that same refusal—and as sentimental. Paradoxically, in *The Maltese Falcon* the good guy is a "blonde satan" and the villain is as innocent as she pretends to be. For that matter Gutman, Cairo, even Wilmer, are appalled by Spade, and in their inability to cope with him are as innocent as Brigid.

This reading of the Flitcraft story accounts for Spade's overriding tone of mockery with Brigid whenever she appeals to his gallantry and loyalty based on her trust and confidence in him. His response to her talk of trust is, "You don't have to trust me. . as long as you can persuade me to trust you." But, as we have seen, that is impossible from the very start, and Spade's saying so is a cruel joke on an unsuspecting murderer. To Brigid, Spade is "the wildest person I've ever known," "altogether unpredictable." Had she understood the Flitcraft story, she would have known that he is not unpredictable at all, but simply living by Flitcraft's vision of meaninglessness and the hard knowingness that follows from that vision. Spade is in step with his surroundings as much as Flitcraft is in step with his. Except for a brief (but important) moment at the end when he is nonplussed by Effie, Spade is never surprised by anyone's actions as Brigid is continually surprised by his. Spade several times picks up mockingly on Brigid's words "wild and unpredictable." She asks at another point what he would do if she were to tell him nothing about the history of the falcon and the quest for it; he answers that he would have no trouble knowing "what to do next." Sam Spade (cf. Humphrey Bogart) never has to hesitate about what to do next. Brigid, of course, has no idea what he will do. When a thousand dollar bill disappears from the envelope holding Gutman's "payment" to Spade, the detective takes Brigid into the bathroom and forces her to undress so that he can make sure she does not have it hidden on her person. Brigid, incredulous, responds with the appropriate clichés: "You'll be killing something." "You shouldn't have done that to me, Sam. . ." But Spade will not be stopped by "maidenly modesty," for he knows that Gutman is testing him to see what he will do. The fat man finds out; Brigid still does not, and learns only when it is too late.

The rejection of the fear of death, perhaps the most obvious characteristic of the tough guy in general, is but another aspect of the rejection of sentiment. Spade fully expects those falling beams, and thus detective work is as much a metaphor for existence as war is in *The Red Badge of Courage* or *A Farewell to Arms*. In an exchange with the driver of a rented car on its way to one unknown destination in the unending series that is the fictional detective's life, the driver comments on Miles Archer's death and on the detective business.

> "She's a tough racket. You can have it for mine."
> "Well [Spade answers], hack-drivers don't live forever."
> "Maybe that's right. . . but just the same, it'll always be a surprise to me if I don't."

The driver is a working-class Flitcraft; Spade, on the other hand, is heading towards another potential falling beam—though, in fact, the trip turns out to be a wild-goose chase planned by Gutman. And the final sentence of the dialogue—"Spade stared ahead at nothing. . ."—bears a double force.

Hammett's reversal of the trap of naturalism gives his heroes a kind of absolute power over their own destiny, a daemonic power, in Angus Fletcher's useful phrase. To stare into nothing and know it; to be as dispassionate about death as about using others—Wilmer, Cairo, or Brigid—as fall-guy: all this means that Spade can rob a Gutman of his ultimate weapon, the threat of death. When Gutman threatens Spade, the detective can argue that the fat man needs him alive; Gutman returns that there are other ways to get information; Spade, in his turn, insists that there is no terror without the threat of death, that he can play Gutman so that the fat man will not kill him, but that if need be he can *force* Gutman to kill him. Who but the tough guy can *make* the beam fall? In that lies the tough guy's power to set his own terms in life and death, a power that is the basis of his popularity in detective and other fiction.

To a generation of readers suckled on the violence of Mickey Spillane and Ian Fleming, it will hardly come as a shock to learn that detectives are as unscrupulous and amoral as "the enemy," as Spade calls them. In this book, though, Hammett seems to be consciously defining the nature of that unscrupulousness through Spade's relationship with Brigid, a relationship which itself becomes the major subject of *The Maltese Falcon* and itself exemplifies the terms of the detective's existence in the novel and in the fiction that ultimately derives from it. The dialogue between Sam Spade and Brigid does much of the work of developing that definition. For example, at one point Brigid says that she is afraid of two men: Joel Cairo and Spade himself. Spade answers, with his total awareness of what she means and what she is, "I can understand your being afraid of Cairo. . .He's out of your reach" (that is, because he is homosexual). And she: "And you aren't?" And he: "Not that way." Under the terms I am suggesting, this exchange must be read as follows: she says she is afraid of him; he says that that's not true because he's not out of her reach; he's right, she's not afraid of him; she should be because he *is* out of her reach. If she thinks him unscrupulous it is because she thinks he is after her and/or her money. She "seduces" him, thinking it will make a difference, but it doesn't. As soon as he climbs out of bed in the morning he steals her key to ransack her apartment, to find further evidence of her lies, though once again the reader doesn't know what he finds until the very end. The fact that Spade does not "cash many checks for strangers," as his lawyer puts it, is the key to his survival, and it leaves him outside the pale of tenderness.

One further key to Hammett's demolition of sentiment is the all but passionless figure of Sam Spade and one further indication of the price immunity exacts is Effie Perine, the archetypal tough guy's archetypal secretary. Spade pays Effie the highest compliment of all in the classic line, "You're a damned good man, sister," but unlike many of her later peers Effie is not tough. In the course of the novel Spade baits Effie again and again by asking what her "woman's intuition" tells her about Brigid O'Shaughnessy; Effie is "for her"; "that girl is all right." The point is not simply that Effie is wrong. Even at the end, knowing that she has been wrong all along, that Brigid has murdered one of her bosses, she responds as a woman, with a woman's (from Hammett's point of view?) sentimental notions, with appalled distaste for Spade. The last word in the novel is Effie's. She has learned of Brigid's arrest through the newspapers; Spade returns to his office.

> Spade raised his head, grinned, and said mockingly: "So much for your woman's intuition."
> Her voice was queer as the expression on her face. "You did that, Sam, to her?"
> He nodded. "Your Sam's a detective." He looked sharply at her. He put his arm around her waist, his hand on her hip. "She did kill Miles, angel," he said gently, "offhand, like that." He snapped the fingers of his other hand.

She escaped from his arm, as if it had hurt her. "Don't, please, don't touch me," she said brokenly. "I know—I know you're right. You're right. But don't touch me now—not now."

Effie's response amounts to a definition of sentiment: the impulse that tells you to pretend that what you know to be true is not true, to wish that what you know has to be, did not have to be. In the vein of the romanticism of action that becomes doing what everything sensible tells you you cannot do. You're right, you're right, but couldn't you better have been wrong? As Hammett has made sufficiently clear in the course of the book, and particularly in the final confrontation with Brigid, exactly the point about Spade—and about the tough guy in general—is that he could not have.

The confrontation of Spade and Brigid rather than the doings of Gutman, Cairo, and Wilmer, who are disposed of perfunctorily offstage, is the climax of the novel. Spade makes Brigid confess to him what, as we have seen, he has known all along— that she is Miles Archer's murderer; then he tells her, to her horror, that he is going to "send her over." His theme throughout this sequence is, "I won't play the sap for you." Though he says, "You'll never understand me" (anymore than Mrs. Flitcraft understood her husband), he goes on, in an astonishing catalogue, to tote up the balance sheet on the alternatives available to him. He ticks off the items on one side: "when a man's partner is killed he's supposed to do something about it"; "when one of your organization gets killed it's bad business to let the killer get away with it"; a detective cannot let a criminal go any more than a dog can let a rabbit go; if he lets her go, he goes to the gallows with Gutman, Cairo, and Wilmer; she would have something on him and would eventually use it; he would have something on her and eventually she couldn't stand it; she might be playing him for a sucker; he could go on "but that's enough." On the other side of the ledger is merely "the fact that maybe you love me and maybe I love you."

The tabulation of pros and cons suggests that Spade is a book-keeper calculating the odds for getting away with breaking the law. But that is inaccurate, for his final statement demolishes his own statistics and suggests that something else is at stake: " 'If that [all he has been saying] doesn't mean anything to you forget it and we'll make it this: I won't because all of me wants to—wants to say to hell with the consequences and do it—and because—God damn you—you've counted on that with me the same as you counted on that with the others.' " The rejection of sentiment as motivating force, i.e., of sentimentality, is at the heart of the characterization of Sam Spade and of the tough guy in general. It is not that Spade is incapable of human emotions—love, for example—but that apparently those emotions require the denial of what Spade knows to be true about women and about life. The sentiment Spade rejects is embodied in all three women in *The Maltese Falcon*—Brigid, Iva Archer, and Effie: murderer, bitch, and nice girl, respectively. It is in this theme itself, paradoxically, that *The Maltese Falcon* has been weakened by the passage of time. As one reads the novel now, Spade himself still retains his force; he is still a believable, even an attractive (if frightening) character. Brigid, on the contrary, is not. (Just so, Hemingway's assertion of Jake Barnes' stoical mask in *The Sun Also Rises* still works, but the attack on Robert Cohn's romanticism seems to be beating a dead horse.) And yet it is the pitting of Brigid's sentimental platitudes against Spade's mocking wisecracks that may make this book the classic it is. This theme, too, signals a reversal in the naturalistic novel, for the tough guy in the tradition of Sam Spade can no longer be the victim of sentiment (cf., for example, Dreiser's Hurstwood or Clyde Griffith, or a Hemingway character defeated by the death of the woman he loves). On the contrary, he hedges himself so thoroughly against betrayal that he lives in total isolation and loneliness. Spade is last seen shivering (temporarily) in revulsion as Effie Perine sends the moral slug Iva in to him. The attractions of Brigid given up to the law, the possibilities of Effie lost, Spade is left with only Iva—or an unending string of Iva's successors.

The Hammett detective most pure, most daemonic, is the Continental Op of the first two novels, his purity indicated even in his namelessness. The Op, perhaps more than Spade, is free of sentiment, of the fear of death, of a past, of the temptations of sex and money. Like Spade he is capable of anything that his opponents are in the pursuit of his goals; in *Red Harvest* he goes further than Spade ever does in his responsibility for setting criminals against one another murderously. The Op in *Red Harvest* is much like Mark Twain's mysterious stranger that corrupts Hadleyburg: the stranger drops the bag of "gold" in the laps of the townsmen and watches them scramble; and so the Op in Personville (pronounced Poisonville). Both manipulate matters with absolute assurance and absolute impunity (*cf.* Spade as well). In *Red Harvest* twenty-five people are killed, not counting an additional unspecified number of slaughtered hoodlums, yet the only mishaps to befall the Op are to have a hand creased by a bullet and an arm stunned by the blow of a chair-leg. His powers come to seem almost supernatural, his knowledge of the forces that move men (sex and money) clairvoyance. His single-minded mission is to clean up the corruption no matter what the cost in other men's lives. The Op's own explanation of his motives—like those voiced to Gutman by Spade, a kind of personal grudge against those who have tried to get him—is not particularly convincing. It is tempting to say that the Op's apparently personal response to being picked on is the equivalent of the response of Hemingway's characters when they are picked off, but Hemingway's characters do have identifiable human emotions, whether disgust, or relief from disgust, or love; Hammett's, because of the purely external mechanistic method, do not. The superhuman is so by virtue of being all but nonhuman.

Red Harvest offers a perfect role for the Hammett private-eye. Elihu Willsson, aristocratic banker-boss of Poisonville, gives the Continental Detective Agency in the person of the Op ten thousand dollars to clean up the town because Willsson thinks the local gangsters responsible for the murder of his son. After the Op discovers that the crime was one of passion (if passion bought and sold) unrelated to the bootlegging-gambling-political corruption of the town, Willsson tries to dismiss the Op, who refuses to be dismissed, " 'Your fat chief of police tried to assassinate me last night. I don't like that. I'm just mean enough to want to ruin him for it. Now I'm going to have my fun. I've got ten thousand dollars of your money to play with. I'm going to use it opening Poisonville up from Adam's apple to ankles.' " Ten thousand dollars of *your* money to play with—there is the role of invulnerable power with the most possibilities open. The Op almost seems to forget he has the money; aside from his day-to-day expenses, all he uses of it is $200.10 that he reluctantly pays Dinah Brand for information. Hammett seems to want to establish the financial freedom of his character: with ten thousand dollars in hand how can the Op be suborned? Once that immunity is established it does not matter how (or whether) the money is spent.

The Op's immunity from temptation indicates something of the allegorical nature of these novels. Rather than being amoral, they establish moral oppositions of the simplest kind: if the proletarian novel is a version of pastoral, in William Empson's witty formulation, the tough detective novel is a version of morality, with allegorical combat between the forces of good and evil, and the most obvious of object lessons. Don't be a sucker for sex (read "love"): better Spade with Iva than Spade with Brigid. Don't be a sucker for money: it leaves you wide open for the crooks *and* the cops. Myrtle Jennison (a minor character in *Red Harvest*) was once as beautiful as Dinah Brand: now she's bloated with Bright's Disease (and Dinah herself dies of an ice-pick wound). Twenty-five men, slaughtered, were once alive (*Red Harvest*). And so on.

The morality of Hammett's detectives is basically defensive, as it must be in the Gothic world posited. As I indicated earlier, in the traditional Gothic novel (and as well in the naturalistic novel in this century) corruption and evil stem from two sources of power, two kinds of end—money and sex. Innocence (virginity in the older Gothic) is eternally threatened, usually for money;

sex is used to gain money, and is in turn corrupted by money. Sexual and financial power are at most equatable, at least inextricable, for it is money which makes sex purchasable and sex which makes money attainable. The Op functions as a monk-ish ascetic who in order to survive must stay clear of money and sex, the only real temptations. Presumably he could walk off with Elihu Willsson's ten thousand, but of course he is no more tempted to abscond than he is to seduce Dinah Brand (he is just about the only male in the novel who doesn't). He unfixes a prizefight, lets Dinah win a pile of money, but does not himself bet. When Dinah, puzzled, questions him, he claims he was not sure his plan would work; but there is no evidence that that is anything but bluff. Dinah no more understands the Op's im-munity to cash than Brigid understands Spade's to love. For Dinah, trying to get money out of the Op in exchange for the information she has on the inner workings of Poisonville, "It's not so much the money. It's the principle of the thing." The Op, refusing, parodies her with her own words: "It's not the money . . . It's the principle of the thing." Everything about Dinah, particularly her body, can be bought; nothing about the Op can be, by money or sex or sentiment. In self-defense he must be untouchable; otherwise his invulnerability would be seriously compromised.

Like Spade, the Op in his immunity from temptation be-comes god-like, perhaps inseparable from a devil, his concern not a divine plan but a satanic disorder. "Plans are all right sometimes . . . And sometimes just stirring things up is all right—if you're tough enough to survive, and keep your eyes open so you'll see what you want when it comes to the top." The Op's way of un-ravelling the mess in Poisonville is to "experiment," in his word, to see if he can pit one set of crooks against another, when he un-fixes the prizefight, for example. The result, in that case and always, is more murder and further chaos impending. Dinah Brand's irony—"So that's the way you scientific detectives work"—is Hammett's as well. The Op's metaphor makes him the same kind of godlike manipulator the naturalist novelist himself becomes in *his* experiments with the forces that move human beings to destruction. The stranger in "The Man That Corrupted Hadleyburg" may drop the bag of money in the town, but it is Mark Twain who drops the stranger there; and Hammett the Op in Poisonville. The bitter enjoyment may be Hammett's and Mark Twain's as well as their characters'.

Ultimately the Op does discover that he is paying the price for his power—his fear that he is going "blood simple like the natives." "Play with murder enough and it gets you one of two ways. It makes you sick or you get to like it," he says as he tabulates the sixteen murders to that moment. The blood gets to the Op in both ways. He finds that he cannot keep his imagination from running along murderous lines on the most common of objects; he carries an ice-pick into Dinah's living room, and Dinah asks why.

> "To show you how my mind's running. A couple of days ago, if I thought about it at all, it was as a good tool to pry off chunks of ice." I ran a finger down its half-foot of round steel blade to the needle point. "Not a bad thing to pin a man to his clothes with. That's the way I'm getting, on the level. I can't even see a mechanical cigar lighter without thinking of filling one with nitroglycerine for somebody you don't like. There's a piece of copper wire lying in the gutter in front of your house—thin, soft, and just enough to go around a neck with two ends to hold on. I had one hell of a time to keep from picking it up and stuffing it in my pocket, just in case—"
>
> "You're crazy," [Dinah says].
>
> "I know it. That's what I've been telling you. I'm going blood-simple."

Out of his head on the gin and laudanum which he takes to relieve his own morbidity, the Op wakes the next morning to find his hand around the ice-pick, buried in Dinah's breast. It is not surprising that not only the authorities but one of the other operatives sent down from San Francisco and the Op himself think he may be Dinah's murderer. If the Op, like all men, is capable of all things, then he is capable of unmotivated murder. If the calculatedly nonhuman yields to human emotion and human weakness, defenses are down; loss of control and near-destruction follow. The point would seem to be, don't let your defenses down. No one, including the detective, is exempt from the possibility of crime. Thus, in *The Dain Curse* and *The Thin Man* the murderer turns out to be an old friend of the detective; in *The Maltese Falcon* it is the girl the detective loves (or may love); in *The Glass Key* a father (and U.S. Senator) murders his own son; and in *Red Harvest* there is no one who might not be a killer—and most of them are, given those twenty-five some odd murders.

In *The Rebel* (Vintage Books) Albert Camus offers a brilliant analysis of the implications of the fear of emotion in the tough guy novel. The concomitant of the rejection of sentiment is the rejection of psychology, of everything that comprises the inner life, in favor of the defenses themselves.

> The American novel [the tough novel of the thirties and forties, Camus explains in a note] claims to find its unity in reducing man either to elementals or to his external reactions and to his behavior. It does not choose feelings or passions to give a detailed description of. . . It rejects analysis and the search for a fundamental psychological motive that could explain and recapitulate the behavior of a character. . . Its technique consists in describing men by their outside appearances, in their most casual actions, of reproducing, without comment, everything they say down to their repetitions, and finally by acting as if men were entirely defined by their daily automatisms. On this mechanical level men, in fact, seem exactly alike, which explains this peculiar universe in which all the characters appear interchangeable, even down to their physical peculiarities. This technique is called realistic only owing to a misapprehension. . . it is perfectly obvious that this fictitious world is not attempting a reproduction, pure and simple, of reality, but the most arbitrary form of stylization. It is born of a mutilation, and of a voluntary mutilation, performed on reality. The unity thus obtained is a degraded unity, a leveling off of human beings and of the world. It would seem that for these writers it is the inner life that deprives human actions of unity and that tears people away from one another. This is a partially legitimate suspicion. . . [but] the life of the

body, reduced to its essentials, paradoxically produces an abstract and gratuitous universe, continuously denied, in its turn, by reality. This type of novel, purged of interior life, in which men seem to be observed behind a pane of glass, logically ends, with its emphasis on the pathological, by giving itself as its unique subject the supposedly average man. In this way it is possible to explain the extraordinary number of "innocents" who appear in this universe. The simpleton is the ideal subject for such an enterprise since he can only be defined—and completely defined—by his behavior. He is the symbol of the despairing world in which wretched automatons live in a machine-ridden universe, which American novelists have presented as a heart-rending but sterile protest (pp. 265-66).

Camus' analysis isolates both the success and the sadness of the tough novel. The success is that of the serious novel in general in that the correlation between the "voluntary mutilation" performed on reality by the author and that of the characters is complete; technique is subject matter in Hammett as much as in Joyce (though the analogy ends there). The excision of mind and emotion in tough dialogue, the understatement, the wise-guy joke-cracking cynicism—all the characteristics of Hammett's particular stylization—are matter as much as method. The sadness lies in the thinness of the world that remains and in the terror that is the common denominator of all men, who must fear all other men *and* themselves, and whose primary occupation would seem to be the development and maintenance of a reflexive self-defense. Finally, the detective's motives are as hidden as the murderer's and as indeterminable. The inner world is so thoroughly left to shift for itself (if it exists at all) that there is some question as to whether Hammett's characters *are* more than Camus' "wretched automatons"—with credits to Hollywood for the terrorless charms of Bogart, Greenstreet, *et al.*

The Dain Curse is one of the more interesting of Hammett's novels, in part because it is concerned with the implications and consequences of the mechanistic method and the mechanical world, with the difficulty of discovering, not only the motives of the actors, but the actual events that took place. As a result *The*

Dain Curse is by far the most complicated of the novels. It consists of three separate plots concerning the events surrounding the
drug-addict Gabrielle Leggett, events which eventually include the
deaths of her father, mother, step-mother, husband, doctor, and
religious "counselor," among others. In the first sequence, an
apparently trivial theft of a batch of inexpensive diamonds leads
to several murders and to incredible disclosures about the history
of Edgar Leggett and his two wives, the Dain sisters Alice and Lily,
a history that includes, for example, Alice's training of the three-
year-old Gabrielle to kill Lily. In the second sequence, her father
and aunt/step-mother dead, Gabrielle, a virtual prisoner in the
quack Temple of the Holy Grail, is involved in another round of
deaths, and the Op does battle with a man who thinks he is God
and with a spirit that has weight but no solidity. In the third,
after still more murders and maimings—a total of nine, plus three
before the time of the novel—the Op discovers that there was, as
he had suspected, a single mind behind the many criminal hands
at work in all three apparently unrelated sequences of events. The
man the Op has known for several years as Owen Fitzstephan is
actually a Dain, a mastermind whose prime motive is love for
Gabrielle.

After the second part, the Op gives the still-unsuspected
Fitzstephan his reconstruction of the events at the Temple of the
Holy Grail, then adds,

> "I hope you're not trying to keep this nonsense straight in
> your mind. You know damned well all this didn't happen."
> "Then what did happen?" [Fitzstephan asks]
> "I don't know. I don't think anybody knows. I'm telling
> what I saw plus the part of what Aaronia Haldorn [the woman
> who runs the Temple, and, it is later disclosed, Fitzstephan's
> mistress and tool] told me which fits in with what I saw. To fit
> in with what I saw, most of it must have happened very nearly
> as I've told you. If you want to believe that it did, all right. I
> don't. I'd rather believe I saw things that weren't there."

And again the Op asks, "You actually believe what I've told you so far?" Fitzstephan says that he does, and the Op answers, "What a childish mind you've got," and starts to tell the story of Little Red Riding-Hood. In these novels there is no question of the complexity of, say, the relativity of guilt, for there is no ambiguity in human actions. As I have suggested, the allegory is fairly simple. The complexity is in the mystery of motive which results in the thorough-going ignorance that even the detective must admit to. What, finally, does move any human being—here, a criminal—to act? Put together a gaggle of the criminal and semi-criminal, the tempted and the merely self-interested, and it may be nearly as difficult to find out what happened as why. Similarly in *The Thin Man* Nora Charles is thoroughly dissatisfied with Nick's "theories" and "probablys" and "maybes" in his reconstruction of the events surrounding the death of Clyde Wynant. To the Op "details don't make much difference," details, that is, such as whether Joseph Haldorn really came to think himself God or merely thought he could fool everyone into thinking he was God. All that matters is that Joseph "saw no limit to his power." The same impossibility of determining truth recurs at the end of the novel: is Fitzstephan a sane man pretending to be a lunatic or a lunatic pretending to be sane? It's not clear whether the Op himself thinks Fitzstephan sane. That again is a detail that doesn't make much difference, especially since people are capable of anything. Fitzstephan, like Haldorn, saw no limit to his power. The exact terms of the curse are irrelevant; he is lost in any case.

In *The Dain Curse* Hammett once again explores the detective's mask by means of a woman's probing, but the Op's motives are no more susceptible to analysis than the criminals'. Gabrielle wants to know why the Op goes to the trouble of convincing her that she is not degenerate or insane, cursed by the blood of the Dains in her veins. She asks the questions the reader might ask: "Do I believe in you because you're sincere? Or because you've learned how—as a trick of your business—to make people believe in you?" The Op's response—"She might have been crazy, but she wasn't so stupid. I gave her the answer that seemed best at the time. . ."—doesn't answer the question for the reader any more

than it does for the girl. Is it only a trick of his business or does
he have a heart of gold beneath his tough exterior? Gabrielle is
asking unanswerable questions, finally, because the removal of one
mask only reveals another beneath. That may amount to saying
that the toughness is not a mask at all, but the reality.

In their next encounter Gabrielle asks specifically why the
Op went through the ugliness of supervising her withdrawal from
drugs. He answers, with exaggerated tough guy surliness, "I'm
twice your age, sister; an old man. I'm damned if I'll make a
chump of myself by telling you why I did it, why it was neither
revolting nor disgusting, why I'd do it again and be glad of the
chance." By refusing to expose himself he is suggesting that he is
exposing himself. Certainly his words suggest love for the girl, but
he's hardly to be believed. He pretends to be hiding his senti-
ments under his tough manner, but it is more likely that he is pretending to pretend. Gabrielle has been the object of the "love" of
a whole series of men: of the insane passion of Owen Fitzstephan
and the only less insane of Joseph Haldorn, the High Priest and
God of the Cult of the Holy Grail; of the petty lechery of her
lawyer, Madison Andrews; and of the fumbling, well-meant love of
Eric Collinson, who gets himself (and nearly Gabrielle) killed as a
result. This view of love as destructive force, as we have seen, is
an essential part of the occasion for the tough role. The Op, like
Spade, has to think himself well out of it, though the reader does
not have to agree.

In the last of this series of interviews in which Gabrielle, acting as the reader's friend, tries to comprehend the Op's tough guy
role, the girl accuses the detective of pretending to be in love with
her during their previous talk.

> "I honestly believed in you all afternoon—and it did help me.
> I believed you until you came in just now, and then I saw—" She
> stopped.
> "Saw what?"
> "A monster. A nice one, an especially nice one to have a-
> round when you're in trouble, but a monster just the same, with-
> out any human foolishness like love in him, and—What's the

matter? Have I said something I shouldn't?"

"I don't think you should have," I said. "I'm not sure I wouldn't trade places with Fitzstephan now—if that big-eyed woman with the voice [Aaronia Haldorn] was part of the bargain."

"Oh , dear!" she said.

It's tempting to take the Op at his word here, at least, and believe that he has been hurt by Gabrielle's unwittingly cruel words. But the pattern I have been developing makes it difficult to accept the Op's sensitivity about his toughness. It is more reasonable to assume that he is telling her, once again, what she wants to hear, suggesting that she is in some way unique in his life. If no sentiment whatever is involved in his actions, he *is* the monster she calls him. And, in fact, that is the case with the Op as with Sam Spade. Seen as figures in stylized romance, both men may be seen as daemons; as characters in realistic fiction they are monsters both.

The Glass Key is Hammett's least satisfactory novel, perhaps precisely because it is not allegorical Gothic romance, lacking as it does a godlike Spade or Op. It may be the case, as David T. Bazelon writing in *Commentary* suggests, that Hammett was trying to write a book closer to a conventional novel, one in which characters are moved to action for human reasons such as loyalty and love. But Hammett's mechanistic method is unchanged and, as a result, it is still impossible to tell what is under Ned Beaumont's mask. Does Ned take the punishment he does out of loyalty to the political boss Paul Madvig, because Madvig picked him out of the gutter fifteen months earlier? Perhaps the reader's sense of propriety or decency fills in that answer, but there is no evidence that it is accurate. It can be argued, on the contrary, that Ned takes the vicious beatings, not out of loyalty but out of indifference to death (to falling beams, if you will). He "can stand anything [he's] got to stand," a gangster's sadism no more and no less than his (apparent) tuberculosis or a purely fortuitous traffic accident in a New York taxi. But "standing" punishment stoically (or suicidally) is not loyalty, not a basis for positive action; and without some clarification of motive, the sense of Ned's activities is merely muddy.

In a sequence that goes on for four brutal pages Ned tries repeatedly to escape his enemies despite being beaten after each attempt. But nothing stops him; as soon as he regains consciousness, he goes to work on the door again. It is tempting, once again, to take this behavior (which includes setting fire to the room) as motivated by loyalty, by Ned's overwhelming desire to warn Paul. But nothing of the sort is possible, for Hammett's descriptions of Ned's actions make it clear that most of his behavior—both his attempts to escape and to kill himself—are instinctual. He remembers nothing beyond his first beating, we are told. Action is determined mechanistically—or animalistically.

Ned's motives are essential to make sense of the climax of the novel when Ned allows Janet Henry, Paul's ostensible fiancee, to go off with him. His response to her "Take me with you" is hardly romantic: "Do you really want to go or are you just being hysterical?. . . It doesn't make any difference. I'll take you if you want to go." Yet there are indications earlier that Hammett wants to suggest the development of some kind of love between the two, growing out of their original mutual dislike, a love about which Paul Madvig has no doubt. The men have a falling out when Paul accuses Ned of lying to him because of Ned's own interest in Janet; at the end of the novel, Paul is confronted with the couple going off together. The question remains whether Paul was right in the first place, whether Ned acted out of desire for the girl rather than loyalty to Paul, or for neither reason. But there is no basis for judgment, by Janet or the reader. Motives are once again indeterminable, but in this book it is necessary that they be determined. The result is not the richness of fruitful ambiguity but the fuzziness of inner contradiction.

The title of this novel, from a dream recounted to Ned Beaumont by Janet Henry, suggests once again the fear of unhedged emotion and thus of all human relationships despite the matching of Ned and Janet with which it ends. In the dream Janet and Ned are starving and come upon a locked house within which they can see food—and a tangle of snakes. To open the door there is a glass key; to get access to the food is to release the snakes. The fragile key breaks as the door opens, and the snakes attack: apparently to get at the heart's need is to open a Pandora's box. Given the tawdriness of the "love" relations in *The Glass Key*— Taylor Henry's unscrupulous use of Opal Madvig's love, Janet Henry's of Paul's—there is not much chance that Ned and Janet will escape the snakes ("I'll take you if you want to go"). Once again in these novels, it would seem that the only safety is in not letting down your guard in the first place: do without the food and you escape the snakes.

It is perhaps significant that Ned Beaumont is not actually a detective, though he functions as one in trying to clear up the mystery of the murder of Taylor Henry. However, there is a professional detective in the novel, Jack Rumsen, who is interesting for his unHammett-like behavior; it is not Sam Spade or the Op who would say to a man trying to solve a crime, "Fred and I are building up a nice little private-detective business here. . . A couple of years more and we'll be sitting pretty. I like you, Beaumont, but not enough to monkey with the man who runs the city."   That modification of the private-eye character in the direction of the cynicism and timidity of self-interest prepares the way for Hammett's last novel, *The Thin Man,* published three years later.   Nick Charles is the least daemonic of Hammett's heroes, but then he's only an ex-detective. However indifferent he may have been to death in the past, now he wants to be left out of danger, to be able to enjoy his wife, her wealth, and his whiskey. Nick Charles and his boozing is what happens to the Op/Spade when he gives up his role as ascetic demi-god to become husband, man of leisure, investor in futures on the stock market.

The Thin Man is perhaps less concerned with murder and the private-eye than with the people around the murder—with a wide range of social types spiritually sibling to the Alfred G. Packer of the long entry Gilbert Wynant reads in *Celebrated Criminal Cases of America.* The man-eaters Mimi, Dorothy, and Gilbert Wynant; Christian Jorgensen, Herbert Macauley, the Quinns, the

Edges; as well as underworld characters like Shep Morelli and Julia Wolfe are little less cannibalistic than Packer. Nick Charles has no interest in their problems; it is his wife who drags him into the search for the missing Wynant against his will. The martini-for-breakfast cracking wise of William Powell and Myrna Loy more than anything else accounts for the popularity of *The Thin Man*. Despite Nick Charles' tough manner, Hammett's tough guy had been retired for good before this book appeared.

In Hemingway's story "In Another Country" the Italian major whose wife has just died fortuitously of a cold says, "[A man] must not marry. He cannot marry. . . If he is to lose everything, he should not place himself in a position to lose that. He should not place himself in a position to lose. He should find things he cannot lose." Knowing that, and despite that knowledge, Hemingway's characters of course always put themselves in a position to lose. They continually fall in love, knowing just how vulnerable that makes them, and they continually lose. Their hard exterior is merely a mask for the fine sensibility on a perpetual quest for good emotion. Hammett, in his best novels, literalizes the Hemingway mask and produces "monsters" who take the major's advice. The Hemingway mask is lifted every time the character is alone; he admits his own misery to himself—and to the reader—and exposes his inner life. The Hammett mask is never lifted; the Hammett character never lets you inside. Instead of the potential despair of Hemingway, Hammett gives you unimpaired control and machinelike efficiency: the tough guy refuses "to place himself in a position to lose." For all (or most) intents and purposes the inner world does not exist: the mask is the self. It is that "voluntary mutilation" of life that is the subject matter of these novels as much as Hemingway's stoical mask is of his. Hammett uses the relationships of Sam Spade with Brigid O'Shaughnessy, of the Continental Op with Dinah Brand and then with Gabrielle Leggett as proving grounds to indicate just how invulnerable his tough guys are. In each case the woman tries to find out what the man is; in each case the toughness is tested—and found not wanting. In the fantasy of detective novel readers and movie-goers who are themselves victims of a machine-ridden universe, loneliness is not too high a price to pay for invulnerability.

MORE ON AUTHOR AND SUBJECT

Robert I. Edenbaum is an Associate Professor of English at Temple University, where he has been teaching since 1961. Among the subjects of his other articles are Nathanael West, F. Scott Fitzgerald, Henry Adams, dadaism and surrealism, and the draft.

Since the original publication of Prof. Edenbaum's essay on Hammett, the first book-length study of the author has appeared, William F. Nolan's Dashiell Hammett: A Casebook (Santa Barbara: McNally & Loftin, 1969). Nolan's book is well worth the serious mystery reader's attention, not only on its own merits but for its exhaustive bibliography of commentary on American crime fiction. An intimate personal memoir of Hammett is provided by the playwright Lillian Hellman in An Unfinished Woman (Little, Brown, 1969).

†Frederic Dannay and Manfred B. Lee are Ellery Queen, but Ellery Queen is also Barnaby Ross—the "alter-pseudonym" under which Queen wrote a remarkable tetralogy (1932-33) about a retired Shakespearean actor named Drury Lane. If the following piece helps dispel the myth that Queen's early novels are nothing but brilliant artificial puzzles, the author will be content.

The Drury Lane Quartet
by Francis M. Nevins, Jr.

Having published three near-perfect novels dealing with Ellery and Richard Queen, the cousins proceeded in 1932 to adopt a second pseudonym—that of Barnaby Ross—and to create a second world. This world existed only for the length of four novels; then its creators terminated it irrevocably. But, even though the last of the quartet was published in 1933, the series has never been forgotten. At least two of the four books not only rank very near the top among Queen's own early novels, but are among the supreme specimens of American mystery fiction of any period.

At the center of the quartet, aged but erect, is Mr. Drury Lane, the world-renowned Shakespearean actor driven by total deafness from the stage and moved by his love for Shakespeare's universe to create an Elizabethan village community on his estate above the Hudson. The village is dominated by Lane's own towering moated castle, The Hamlet, and is inhabited by down-and-out theatrical people who live on Lane's bounty, wearing period costumes and Shakespearean names. But, unsatisfied with having recreated the world in which Shakespeare lived, and knowing that he cannot create dramatic worlds such as the master created, Lane turns to intervening in, and thereby in a sense rewriting, the dramas of real life. "From obeying the jerk of the master's strings, I now have the impulse to pull the strings myself, in a greater authorship than created drama." Clearly the driving motive in Lane's life is the love of power: the power to stir audiences with his performances; the power over the lives of his villagers, down to their very names; the power to change the outcome of life-and-death dramas by his presence.

The first novel of the quartet, *The Tragedy of X* (1932), opens with a biographical sketch of Lane, and his letter to the New York City police offering the solution to a baffling murder case in the city.[1] When the solution turns out to be astoundingly correct, Inspector Thumm and District Attorney Bruno pay a visit to The Hamlet to meet and thank Lane, and to solicit his help on an infinitely more bewildering murder case that faces them.

It had begun four days before, on the afternoon of Friday, September 4, when Harley Longstreet, an aging, lecherous and sadistic stockbroker, threw a cocktail party to celebrate his engagement to musical-comedy star Cherry Browne. His deeper purpose in having the celebration is to exercise power, to make his guests squirm. Those whom Longstreet has pressured into attending include his browbeaten but relatively honest brokerage partner, John DeWitt; DeWitt's wife, who had been Longstreet's mistress, and his daughter, whom Longstreet would like to make his mistress; and the daughter's fiance, who works for the brokerage. Among the uninvited guests are a former lover of Cherry Browne and a market-playing politican who blames his brokers for his recent ruinous losses. After the cocktail hour, Longstreet insists that the entire assemblage, uninvited guests included, accompany him to a dinner party at his New Jersey home.

But just before the group reaches the street, a sudden and vicious thunderstorm erupts, jamming the avenues with frenzied crawling traffic and making it impossible to secure a taxi for the ride to the ferry. Instead the party crowds into a passing 42nd Street crosstown trolley, struggling through a mob of soaked commuters and past the impassive conductor into the center of the rumbling electrified box. The packed streetcar is lurching westward towards the ferry slip when Longstreet reaches into his pocket for his glasses and suddenly collapses dead in the aisle, his hand pricked and bleeding in a dozen places. Instant panic breaks out in the stifling cage. An off-duty police sergeant orders the motorman to drive straight to the nearest carbarn, and sends the conductor out to phone Headquarters and get a homicide team over to the barn.

Inside the echoing shed, Inspector Thumm quickly locates the object in Longstreet's pocket that caused the multiple pricks: a ball of cork riddled with dozens of needles, each one coated at both ends with pure nicotine poison. Relentless questioning establishes that the lethal ball must have been slipped into Longstreet's pocket on the streetcar itself (for just before boarding he had reached into the same pocket with no ill effects), and that virtually everyone in Longstreet's party had not only motive but, in the shoving crowd, ample opportunity to slip the ball into the victim's coat. Since no one had entered or left the streetcar after the Longstreet party had boarded it (except, of course, for the conductor, who had returned in a few moments with a policeman), the murderer must still be in the carbarn. But the police fail despite microscopic investigations to uncover any leads. Nevertheless, when Thumm and Bruno finish relating these facts to Drury Lane, the actor announces that he believes he knows the murderer. But for his own reasons, based partly on his analysis of the facts and in at least equal part on his desire to exercise power in the case, he refuses at the moment to say more.

The next day Thumm receives a note from the conductor of

the fatal streetcar, requesting a secret meeting that night at the Weehawken, New Jersey, ferry terminal, and promising vital information; but the expected informant is thrown from the upper deck of the ferry as it pulls into its moorings, and is crushed to pulp between the ferry and the pilings. And among the boat's passengers happens to be John DeWitt. A spectacular murder trial, an uncannily disturbing conversation aboard a New Jersey local train, a third murder carried out within a few feet of Lane himself, and a towering number of criminous possibilities are experienced before Lane takes one more train ride and unmasks the murderer.

The Tragedy of X must be ranked among the supreme untouchable masterpieces of the Golden Age. The plot is staggering in its complexity, stunning in its ingenuity, and dazzling in its complete fairness, employing for the first time in Queen's career two devices of which one became the hallmark of the author's first period and the other was to become his distinctive province during the Fifties and Sixties. A specific description of the first device might spoil several novels for those who haven't read all of Queen's early works; suffice it to say that it rests on the same murderer-murderee relationship that Holmes once unearthed at Birlstone Manor, from which we hereby dub this device the Birlstone Gambit. The second device is, of course, the classic Queenian situation of the Dying Message. While riding in the Weehawken local during the small hours of the morning, Lane and several others, one of whom will die within minutes, discuss the last moments of life—a conversation as central to Queen's work as is the famous locked-room lecture in *The Three Coffins* to the understanding of John Dickson Carr. The discussion culminates in Lane's words: "There are no limits to which the human mind cannot soar in that unique, god-like instant before the end of life."[2]

That statement reflects the fact that beneath the surface of this magnificent formal problem Queen is seriously preoccupied with the phenomena of power and the love of power. These themes recur in the novel in several forms: the murderer's silent intimate relationships with his victims over the years it takes him to shape their destruction; Longstreet's sadistic desire for power over the men and women in his milieu; the motives behind Lane's own investigations; the godlike power of the dying.

The large number of sharply etched characterizations, the superb vivid evocations of time and place (especially of the three today-all-but-extinct transportation networks: the streetcar, the ferry, and the New Jersey short-line passenger train), the integration of the milieus into the plot and of each of the plot's thousands of details into a rationally harmonious mosaic—these are so many more reasons why *The Tragedy of X* must appear in any listing, however short, of the supreme achievements of crime fiction, and why it will be read with awe long after our grandchildren are dust.

The Tragedy of Y (1932) is the equal of *X* in the dazzling perfection of its structure and technique, and in addition is an attempt more sustained and organic than in *X* to integrate the deductive problem with "serious" literary intent. The book's central themes can be traced back to the plays of Eugene O'Neill and through him to Greek tragedy, and apparently exerted marked influence on such later works as Raymond Chandler's "The Curtain," William March's *The Bad Seed*, and Hitchcock's *Psycho* which itself influenced Queen when in 1963 he reshaped some elements from *Y* into *The Player on the Other Side*.

The book opens on the afternoon of February 2, 19- -,[3] when a fishing trawler off the Atlantic coast discovers the shapeless eaten body of a man who is identified as York Hatter, who had vanished from his wife's house on Washington Square North four days before the previous Christmas. A suicide note, handwritten in indelible ink, is found inside a waterproof tobacco pouch on the body; but the autopsy proves that the cause of death was not drowning but poison. The body is identified, without hesitation and without a tear, by Emily Hatter, the iron-willed, ruthless millionaire beldame who made her inoffensive unworldly husband's life one long hell throughout thirty-seven years of marriage. But, there being no evidence incompatible with the theory of suicide, the case is soon dropped.

The Hatter household had long been the focus of madness and perversion. As a young woman Emily had been divorced under hushed-up circumstances from Tom Campion, her first husband, who later died mysteriously. The child of that marriage, Louisa Campion, had been born blind, dumb, and with an incipient deafness which became total on her eighteenth birdtday, "as a sort of birthday gift from the dark gods who seemed to rule her destiny." The fact that Tom Campion had had a completely normal son by a previous marriage had made it monstrously clear that there was something evil in Emily's blood which had put this curse on her child. Soon after Tom's death, his son had dropped out of sight, and Emily had married an impoverished but brilliant young research chemist named York Hatter.

Now, thirty-seven years later, the three children of Emily's second marriage live with her in the Washington Square mansion: Barbara, the brilliant avant-garde poetess; Conrad, the hopeless alcoholic; and Jill the vicious, frigid playgirl and "a worthy younger edition of her mother." Martha, Conrad's meek and beaten wife, is forced to live in the big house with Conrad and their two sons: thirteen-year-old Jackie, wild, willful, precocious and sadistic, and the inevitably imitative four-year-old Billy. Like her father-in-law York Hatter until death released him, she has become "a lost soul in the Inferno." Louisa Campion also exists in the house, sleeping in the same bedroom with her mother, hated by most of the household because she is the only person Emily (whom they hate in any event) cares for. In the household but not of it are the various servants and employees, including Louisa's permanent nurse and the children's tutor. Captain Trivett, the one-legged retired shipmaster who lives next door, frequently visits the house to sit with Louisa and hold her hand. The family doctor, Emily's attorney, and Conrad's business partner are occasionally seen within the mansion.

During the afternoon of Sunday, April 10, two months after the recovery of the body identified as York Hatter, the nightmare begins. The customary afternoon egg-nog prepared for Louisa

Campion is snatched from the dining-room table and partially drunk by the mischievous Jackie—who at once falls to the floor, screaming. Little Billy's dog wanders into the room, laps up some of the spilled drink, shudders and twitches convulsively, then lies still. The egg-nog contains enough strychnine to kill a dozen people; some strychnine tablets are found to be missing from York Hatter's private laboratory, which had been locked up since his disappearance. Inspector Thumm solicits the advice of Drury Lane, who warns him that the poisoner will probably try to strike at Louisa again.

Two months later, on Sunday, June 5, Lane is summoned to Washington Square North by a call from Thumm: during the night someone had taken York Hatter's mandolin from its glass case in the library downstairs and with it had bludgeoned Emily to death in her bed. A hypodermic syringe is found among the dead woman's bedclothes, and a poisoned pear in the fruitbowl on the night-table separating Emily's and Louisa Campion's beds; and it was well known that Emily detested pears. It is clear to the police that Emily caught the poisoner trying to slip the pear into the bowl, and paid with her life; but what kind of poisoner would carry a mandolin to the scene of his crime?

The fact that Louisa Campion was a witness to the murder—that she testifies (through a braille board) that she touched the intruder's nose and cheek and smelled a flavor of vanilla on the person—leads the police nowhere. Nor do the box of spilled talcum powder, the tiptoeing footprints, or the smears on the poison shelves of York Hatter's laboratory. But they seem somewhat more meaningful to Lane, who however keeps his own counsel and follows his own paths.

The long and microscopically detailed investigation bristles with intellectual excitement and unearths possibilities pointing in every direction, while at the same time it evokes a growing sense of the senselessness and imbecility of these most carefully worked out crimes which matches our growing understanding of the rot and perversion eating away at the Hatters. For this doom-haunted family does not exist merely as the locus of a detective novel.

Queen invests it with qualities that transform it into a paradigm of American society, all of its members except the unworldly poetess rotting with greed, sadism and inertia, consenting for the sake of expected legacies to be dehumanized in love-hate relationships with each other and with the bitch goddess of wealth and property that rules the roost. But the family does not represent merely some aspect of American or capitalist society that is magically curable by socioeconomic revolution; on a deeper level, the sickness in the Hatter blood is not some naturalistic venereal disease but a sickness of human nature and the human condition, the gift of a dark god. "Good God," Bruno gasps, stunned at the identity of the murderer. "Not a very good God," Lane replies. "Not to that poor. . .creature."

The Tragedy of Y is one of the most stunningly brilliant formal deductive problems ever written, easily ranking among the ten finest flowers of the Golden Age. In its deeper aspects, it has had a long and fruitful influence; its black design may well have helped to shape the nightmare stories of Cornell Woolrich (the vision of the dark power), and Hitchcock's *Vertigo* (the interweavings of fiction/illusion and reality) and *Psycho* (the stance at once of compassion and loathing towards the murderer, the horrific shock at the revelation of the truth, the matriarch as a metaphysically evil being, the relation between the mother's and the descendant's perversions). Rooted in a form that has traditionally been oriented to order, reason and optimism, *Y* evokes depths of tragic despair and a sense of meaninglessness that are virtually unparalleled in the deductive genre and to which Queen would return, in a different vein, in his great novels of the late Forties.

Although a minor effort compared with *X* and *Y*, *The Tragedy of Z* (1933) is a highly intriguing and rewarding successor in its own right. The impersonal and somber narrative of the earlier tragedies is replaced by the sprightlier first-person storytelling of a newcomer to the Lane milieu. Miss Patience Thumm, the Inspector's beauteous and brainy daughter, who had spent her childhood and adolescence in Europe, returns to New York ten years after the events recounted in *X* and *Y*,[4] and takes up residence with her father, now retired from the force and running his own detective agency. Patience is herself gifted with no mean deductive abilities, and on being taken to meet and to help celebrate the seventieth birthday of the Drury Lane of whom her father had told her so much, she astonishes not only Lane but her father and former District Attorney Bruno, now Governor of New York, by deducing instantly that Lane is composing his memoirs.

The Thumms' birthday-party excursion to Lanecliff is only a detour on their way to Leeds, the county seat of Tilden County in upstate New York; for the Inspector has been retained by the half-owner of the local marble quarry to find out whether the fact that his partner's brother is a state senator has any connection with the inordinate number of state building contracts the quarry has been awarded. But not too long after the arrival of father and daughter on the scene, the investigation is interrupted by the fatal stabbing of the senator in his study. The case is a complex one, involving such phenomena as a part of a carved toy chest, a footprint trodden in ashes, a jagged scratch on a forearm, and a blackmail demand from a convict just released from the state prison outside the city. It is this convict, a one-eyed, one-armed friendless derelict named Aaron Dow, whom the police seize upon as the obvious murderer. Despite Patience's insistence that, properly interpreted, the evidence proves Dow's innocence, the local District Attorney, who stands to gain considerable political advancement by the senator's death, proceeds to put the haggard wretch on trial for murder. At this point Patience returns to The Hamlet to enlist Lane's aid in saving Dow's life.

The race against time is complicated by a prison break, a second murder (whose victim also received a section of a carved toy chest before being stabbed to death), and a chain of events originating in Vietnam at the turn of the century. The novel culminates in one of the most chilling denouements in the history of crime fiction, as Lane reconstructs the case and unmasks the killer in the execution chamber of the prison only seconds before the electrocution of Aaron Dow is to take place.

Z cannot be included among Queen's greatest achievements,

for as a whole it is less dazzlingly full-bodied than the master-works of the Canon. Lane is kept offstage (except for one brief scene) until almost halfway through the book, and the presence and first-person narration of Patience Thumm are interesting but inadequate substitutes.[5] Compared with what Queen proved himself capable of in 1932, the plot is both simplistic and flawed (it presupposes, for example, that a dedicated and incorruptible warden discovers a message-smuggling system in operation within his prison and does absolutely nothing about it, not for any intrinsic reason but because the plot requires the system to be still operational at a later point in the book). But even if the novel had many more faults than it does, they would be more than made up for by the bone-chilling bizarrerie of the two sequences in the death house, and by the unobtrusively brilliant planting throughout the book of clues to be collated by Lane at the denouement. Though not one of Queen's most distinguished novels, Z is a well-crafted and rewarding work that repays more than one reading.

The last of the Barnaby Ross tetralogy is the single early Queen novel that one might wish had remained unwritten. *Drury Lane's Last Case* (1933) contains some excellent ideas but is flawed by haste, lack of organization, coincidence, artificiality, incredible motivation, and a (for Queen) staggering number of holes in the plot.

The rather Oppenheimish prologue takes place on Monday, May 6, 1934,[6] when a mysterious man sporting a blue and green beard visits Inspector Thumm's detective agency and pays the Inspector one thousand dollars for holding a manila envelope in which the client claims there is a clue to a secret worth millions. He arranges to call Thumm on the twentieth of each month, in order to establish that nothing has happened to him; only if he fails to call on a twentieth is Thumm to open the envelope, and then only in the presence of Mr. Drury Lane.

The body of the book opens on Tuesday, May 28. Fisher, a sightseeing-bus driver, asks Thumm's help in locating a mutual acquaintance named Donoghue, who retired from the police and took a job as guard at the Britannic Museum, a small but distinguished repository of Elizabethan culture on Fifth Avenue near 65th Street. Donoghue unaccountably disappeared from the museum on the previous afternoon while a group of vacationing Indiana schoolteachers were being given a guided tour by the curator. Fisher believes that the guard's disappearance is somehow connected with the fact that, whereas he drove nineteen people to the museum in his sightseeing bus, only eighteen returned with him. But Thumm's investigation of the Indiana party soon discloses an even stranger fact: there are only seventeen schoolteachers in the group. Thus there were two extra men aboard Fisher's bus, one of whom returned and one of whom didn't. And a visit to the museum adds more fuel to Thumm's frustration; for evidence indicates that the nineteenth man broke into a glass case, removed an extremely valuable edition of Shakespeare, replaced it with another that is absolutely priceless, and next day returned the stolen edition to the museum.

By this time Drury Lane, a financial patron of the Britannic, is in the case alongside Inspector Thumm, Patience, and a young Shakespeare scholar named Gordon Rowe who has fallen in love with Patience at first sight. They continue to unearth conundrums—another snatched-and-returned Shakespeare, a stolen sheet of library stationery—but it is not until June 21, and the failure of Thumm's initial client to put in his call, that they discover that the man with the dappled beard and his envelope are also involved in the strange doings at the Britannic Museum. Although murder doesn't rear its head until the final quarter of the book, there is so much intellectual puzzlement throughout that one is hardly aware of the lack.

Unfortunately not all of the puzzlement is dissipated at the end. We never learn how the museum thief learned of the unscheduled bus trip to the Britannic; how the man who followed Lane on June 21 knew that Lane was coming to New York, and why he wanted to follow Lane in the first place; how an extension phone got into Dr. Ales' garage; how the planter of the time bomb got into Ales' house undetected; or why a fugitive from French justice would carry a priceless Shakespeare folio with him in his flight. Moreover, when explanations are provided they are all too often absurd. (The antics of the bibliomaniacal Sedlar brothers are prompted by some staggeringly far-out motivations; the failure of the Tarrytown police, on their first visit, to search Dr. Ales' cellar, where a body and a bomb are lying, does not say much for their or their creators' thoroughness.) Equally damaging to the book is the disastrous decision of the authors to put almost the entire deductive burden on Patience Thumm, who sometimes gives one the unpleasant impression that "she" is really Ellery Queen in drag (especially when she addresses her ardent swain in such Elleryesque periods as: "But the only thing that differentiates us from the lower primates is the power of reasoning, and I don't see why the mere fact that a woman is biologically different from a man should prevent her from cultivating her mind.") Finally, the climactic Shakespearean revelations are not as brilliant nor the identity of the murderer as staggeringly original (though it is both surprising and fairly clued[7]) as Queen apparently supposed. It is not discreditable that out of eight novels in two years, including three or four of the finest works in the genre, one should misfire; but it is unfortunate that the two finest sequences in the book— the deductions from the Saxon Library notepaper and the matter of the ax-wielder and the alarm clock—were not instead incorporated into additional short-story-length *Adventures of Ellery Queen*.

We have spent enough time with one of Queen's awesomely rare weak books. Let us return to Ellery and his father, and to the most involuted, brain-crushing, miraculously well-constructed and intellectually rewarding deductive novel published in the United States during the Golden Age.

NOTES

[1] For some unaccountable reason, these introductory elements are missing from the otherwise superb revival under the Queen byline of Lane's first three cases, *The XYZ Murders* (Lippincott, 1961).

[2]The Vienna dying-message story which Lane tells his companions on the train was reworked by Queen twenty-odd years later into the short story "A Lump of Sugar."

[3]Although the decade in which the novel is set is unspecified, the York outline in Act III Scene 2 indicates that the story occurs at a time when both Hercule Poirot and Ellery Queen are universally known as fictional detectives. Thus the time must be around 1931-32. The importance of this point will become clearer when we discuss the alleged temporal setting of *The Tragedy of Z*.

[4]The addition of Patience was clearly not in Queen's mind when he wrote *X* and *Y*; for as Patience herself points out in *Z*, there is not the slightest hint in the earlier books that Thumm ever had a daughter. The supposed ten-year hiatus between the prior cases and *Z* is another obvious afterthought, since *X* and *Y* not only give no indication of being set in the early 1920's but contain innumerable details that prove their setting to be contemporary: e.g., the reference in Act II Scene 9 of *X* to George Arliss' screen portrayal of *Disraeli* (1929), and the allusion in Act III Scene 2 of *Y* to the fictional detective Ellery Queen, who of course did not debut until 1929.

[5]However, Queen must be credited with uncommon boldness for his sustained attempt to get inside a woman's consciousness—a feat which less than a handful of male mystery writers have ever attempted. The only other examples that spring to mind are Selwyn Jepson's Eve Gill novels and Cornell Woolrich's *The Black Angel*.

[6]Though published in 1933, the book is set in the near future.

[7]In fact, one clue is planted as far back as *The Tragedy of Z*. The exact passage cannot be specified here lest we spoil *Drury Lane's Last Case* for those who haven't yet read it; but it appears on page 492 of *The XYZ Murders*.

MORE ON AUTHOR AND SUBJECT

Francis M. Nevins Jr. received his Doctor of Law degree from New York University School of Law and is a member of the New Jersey Bar, but seems to spend quite a bit more time teaching, writing and editing than in a law office. He has published articles on such subjects as the films of Alfred Hitchcock, the constitutional rights of conscientious objectors, the writings of Cornell Woolrich, and the wacky world of Harry Stephen Keeler. The preceding essay comes from a book-in-progress on Ellery Queen.

Those who are interested in further in-depth treatments of Queen may want to check into The Queen Canon Bibliophile, edited by Rev. Robert E. Washer (80 East Eighth Street, Oneida Castle, New York 13421), the quarterly in which the above article first appeared.

†Being an attorney myself, I felt this book would not be complete without some consideration of the late Erle Stanley Gardner; and one of the contributors to the present book, Prof. Donald A. Yates, happened to know of two pieces that he thought would fit. We decided that Mr. Robbins' companion piece, "The World of Perry Mason," should go into Prof. Yates' own forthcoming anthology of crime fiction commentary (of which more later), while I would take the following delightful survey of Gardner's second most famous world.

The Firm of Cool and Lam
by Frank E. Robbins

Those characters of fiction who happen to live in Los Angeles are fortunate in one respect. Should they in some fashion or other attract the unfavorable attention of the homicide squad there are an unusual number of first-class detectives whom they may consult with confidence that they themselves will emerge from their difficulties unscathed, though there may be a few more casualties among their less desirable acquaintances before their troubles are over. Philip Marlowe, for instance, will do the job for a reasonable fee, and so will Lew Archer, though he has not been in business quite as long and is a somewhat rougher diamond. The old reliable Perry Mason comes higher; we count him as a detec-

136

tive though he is really a lawyer, but with Della Street at his side and Paul Drake's agency to do the legwork he is sure to get the customer off. And then again if one goes to the firm of Cool and Lam, Confidential Investigations, and particularly if he secures the personal services of Donald Lam, the junior partner, the job will be done to the client's ultimate satisfaction.

Mr. Mason's doings, thus far, have been chronicled in thirty-eight volumes and are favorably known to millions of readers; the exploits of Bertha Cool and Donald Lam have filled only thirteen volumes to date, and the protagonists are by no means so famous, but yet they deserve the serious attention of those who like that sort of thing, and apparently very many people do. Both Perry Mason and the Cool and Lam partnership are the creation of the same extremely ingenious man, Erle Stanley Gardner, who uses the pseudonym A. A. Fair when he writes about Donald and Bertha; nevertheless, though they walk the streets of the same city and have a number of characteristics in common, Bertha and Donald seem never to have heard of Perry, nor Perry of Bertha and Donald.

This engaging pair first came before the public in 1939, in the story *The Bigger They Come,* and, as in the case of Perry Mason's chronicles, while the tales themselves seldom give any indication of their exact dates, they have every appearance of being contemporary with the year of publication and the few dates which are mentioned support this assumption. For example, in *Bats Fly at Dusk,* a 1942 production, Harlow Wilbers' will is dated January 25, 1942, and Donald Lam's telegram in Chapter 13 was sent on August 29, 1942; comparable instances in two other books can be cited. The complete list, as it stands today, is *The Bigger They Come,* 1939; *Turn on the Heat* and *Gold Comes in Bricks,* 1940; *Spill the Jackpot* and *Double or Quits,* 1941; *Owls Don't Blink* and *Bats Fly at Dusk,* 1942; *Cats Prowl at Night,* 1943; *Give 'Em the Ax,* 1944; *Crows Can't Count,* 1946; *Fools Die on Friday,* 1947; *Bedrooms Have Windows,* 1949; and *Top of the Heap,* 1952. Altogether they present a considerable amount of biographical material concerning the two chief characters.

The elder, Mrs. Bertha Louise Cool, went into the "confidential investigation" business when her husband died in 1936 or thereabout, that is, three years before the time of *The Bigger They Come*. Her married life had not been without its irritations, but she had managed to make satisfactory adjustments to its drawbacks. Seemingly she was always one of those women who will put on weight at the slightest encouragement; she put in ten years, she says, dieting and wearing girdles and brassieres to catch a husband, and during the first part of her married life she continued to deny herself the cream, sugar, and butter that she dearly loved. Henry Cool, her husband—"an average specimen"—did not have to deprive himself in order to keep his figure, or perhaps he did not care; at any rate he kept on indulging in the rich foods that Bertha craved, and she discovered that he indulged himself in other ways too. Finally, when he announced that he had to go to Chicago on business, Bertha hired a detective and discovered that he had taken a trip to Atlantic City with his secretary. Thereupon Bertha issued an ultimatum; if Henry was going to take that peroxided hussy to Atlantic City over week-ends and make her like it, she would eat what she pleased and make him like it, and she did. She let Henry carry on with his secretary until the latter tried to blackmail him, but then she went down to the office and told the girl off in no uncertain language. Henry's next secretary was a "good-looking little trick" picked out for him by Bertha herself, one that she had so much on that the girl didn't dare to blackmail him. Thereafter, under those arrangements contrived by Bertha, everything went well until Henry died. This ultimate hand-picked secretary, incidentally, was Elsie Brand, who stayed with Bertha when she opened her own office and is a fixture in the firm of Cool and Lam.

Bertha, you will understand, is a strong-minded woman well able to take care of herself. She is also a big woman; for years, after abandoning her diet, she weighed about 275 pounds, and it took an attack of flu and pneumonia in 1941 to reduce her weight by 100 pounds to 160. More recently it has remained at 165 pounds, and is mostly bone and muscle, for since her illness Bertha has taken up fishing, which has given her a fine tan and presumably helps to keep her in condition, although she still likes her sugar and cream and enjoys loafing in her apartment on a lazy Sunday. When she and Donald were in New Orleans in 1942 she ate three pecan waffles for breakfast and scandalized a waiter by putting catsup on her steak.

Aside from her heft, Bertha has flowing white hair which gives her a deceptively motherly, or grandmotherly, appearance, and little glittering gray eyes. She uses bifocals, and likes to wear loose clothes. She has a peculiarly effortless way of walking and even in her fattest days didn't waddle. She is a cigarette smoker—brand not specified, uses a long carved ivory cigarette holder, and wears diamonds on her left hand.

But though Bertha's physical characteristics are striking e-nough her habits of speech and her mental attitudes are even more so. She is probably the most profane person in the detective business; in fact almost the only profane person in that line of work, as they are described to us by the masters of detective fiction. Even the hard-boiled lads, like the Continental Op or Philip Marlowe, scarcely ever utter as much as a damn, but that is one of the commonest words in Bertha's vocabulary, and she makes free use of others too which you won't hear used even in a political campaign and much less in the bosom of the family. As she puts it, she likes profanity, loose clothing, and loose talk.

Bertha is also a realist, which in her case chiefly means that she has a high regard for money. Her doodling when she interviews a client in the office is apt to concern the amount she thinks the client is good for; her tips hardly ever exceed a dime, and she voices strenuous objection to Donald's including "Regards and best wishes" in a collect telegram. One brief conversation, in which Bertha is the first speaker, goes like this: "You mean she turns down money?" "Exactly." "I don't get it." And she does-n't; if there is money to be had she is hot on its trail, and if there is money in the office it is kept in the locked cash drawer of Bertha's desk and doled out with marked reluctance. She makes a good many investments, some of them safe and bringing good returns, some of them gambles, and she is quick to bet on a horse race when she thinks that Carl Keetley's system of handicapping has presented her with a sure thing.

How old is Bertha? That is a question hard to answer. When he first met her, in 1939, Donald placed her "somewhere in the sixties," which would make her, in her latest appearance thirteen years later, somewhere in the seventies. But in *Bats Fly at Dusk* (1942) Bertha is described as "somewhere in the fifties," and in *Crows Can't Count* (1946) Donald confesses that he doesn't know her age and says that she looks about the same as she always has. Certainly she has not yet begun to show the signs of advanced age, and perhaps it is safest to take the lower estimate and assume that Bertha is now somewhat over sixty years old.

Donald Lam's age is much easier to figure; when he entered Bertha's employ, in 1939, he was twenty-nine years old, so that he would now be forty-two; but like Bertha he gives no indication of diminishing energy in spite of sundry beatings-up, a year in the Navy, a bout with malaria or some similar tropical infection, and thirteen years as a detective.

Back in 1939 Donald was in the hardest of hard luck. He was a college graduate, but his course had been calculated to give him "an appreciation of art, literature, and life" rather than to fit him to earn money. Seemingly he had also gone through a law school, for he had been admitted to the bar, but he couldn't practice because his license had been revoked for a year. The year was up, but Donald had no money to furnish and open an office; his father had died two years ago, and he had just ten cents in his pocket when Bertha gave him a job.

The reason for his being in such a fix was that he was too smart. He thought up a way to commit a murder in such a fashion that nobody could do anything about it; his mistake was that he spoke about it to a client and offered to bet on it; the client turned out to be a gangster, was arrested that night, and babbled to the police that for $500 Donald was going to show him how to murder with impunity. This the Grievance Committee decided was unethical.

On his first job, however, Donald had the opportunity to demonstrate his theory. He goes to Yuma, Arizona, opens a bank account, buys a car, pays for it with a check on the wrong bank, and drives back to California. The indignant car-dealer has him stopped by the California police; he is forcibly haled back to Yuma, protesting vigorously. There he soon shows that it was all a harmless mistake; the proceedings are dropped, and an agreement to that effect is signed by all concerned, including the sheriff and the deputy district attorney; but Donald doesn't simply get up and leave, he says he has something on his mind—he is the man who killed Morgan Birks, and he tells how he did it. Arraigned at a habeas corpus hearing before Judge Raymond C. Oliphant, with a California murder warrant and a writ of extradition hanging over him, Donald manages his own case and easily shows that he is not in Arizona of his own free will but was dragged there by force and consequently is not a fugitive from justice and cannot be extradited as such. Furthermore, he cites legal precedents to support his contention. The judge is astounded; the whole history of the case, he says, "indicates that the petitioner is possessed of an astute legal mind, which, unfortunately, is not balanced by a corresponding sense of legal ethics." However, after a thirty-minute recess Judge Oliphant regretfully concludes that there is nothing he can do about it and discharges Donald. (Of course Donald wasn't actually guilty of the murder; his "confession" was intended merely to flush the real murderer.)

Alva Johnston, in *The Case of Erle Stanley Gardner,* tells about the late Dean John H. Wigmore's comments on this legal dodge. He could not agree that the accused was not really a fugitive from justice, though after Mr. Gardner submitted an "exhaustive brief" on the subject he admitted that the case was a better one than he had at first supposed. He warned, however, that the courts have a way of reversing themselves from time to time and it would not be safe for a real murderer to put his trust in Donald's procedure.

Donald indeed has an "astute legal mind" and it is at least not weighed down by considerations of ethics. Like Perry Mason,

he constantly ventures onto thin ice if it seems necessary in order
to complete his case successfully, but while Perry's sense of loyalty to his client is the chief motivating force, Donald seems to take
chances simply because of the urge to beat the opposition and
come out on top. Furthermore, while he is wiry and durable, he
is far from impressive physically; he weighed only 127 pounds
when he applied to Bertha for his first job and only 140 after
steady employment and a lucrative partnership had permitted him
to eat regularly and well. Consequently, both as a boy and as a
man, he has had to rely upon brain rather than brawn to overcome opposition and his methods are indirect and devious. This
does not imply that he suffers from an inferiority complex—far
from it—or that he lacks courage; he is, as Bertha puts it, "a pint
sized parcel of dynamite with the nerve of a prizefighter and a
punch that wouldn't jar a fly loose from a syrup jug." His
"nerve" gets him well beaten up in *The Bigger They Come* and
Turn on the Heat, and his willingness to take chances results in
his being at least wanted by the police in all the firm's cases except the two which Bertha managed—with some remote control
from Donald—while he was in the Navy. In four of them—*The
Bigger They Come, Give 'Em the Ax, Fools Die on Friday,* and
Bedrooms Have Windows—he is actually arrested, and he escapes
in *Owls Don't Blink* only by enlisting in the Navy. Just as it is the
rule for Perry Mason to risk disbarment and solve his case at the
very last moment in the courtroom, so one can confidently expect
Donald to place his license in jeopardy and not to elucidate the
situation until he is handcuffed and on the way to jail—or at least
on the verge of apprehension.

Bertha, in general, recognizes and values Donald's ability,
though she is not infrequently irked by his daredevil methods of
operation when they threaten the welfare of the firm. In *Top of
the Heap,* when Donald is hiding from the San Francisco police
and accused of blackmail and other misdemeanors, she goes so far
as to dissolve the partnership, scratch his name from the door,
cancel the partnership's bank account, and clear his desk of personal belongings—only to take it all back when Donald returns

with a $5,000 fee from his client and $40,000 that he has made on a mining stock deal. She does, however, have two standing complaints against her partner; he spends money like water and he is a pushover for women. There really isn't sufficient evidence to support either of these allegations. In comparison with Bertha Donald is indeed liberal with money, but he is hardly a spendthrift. He likes a good suit of clothes and he will occasionally bet on a horse or try out a slot machine; he raises Elsie Brand's salary, but she deserves it; he buys a big over-stuffed chair for Bertha's office, and pays $125 for it, but clients will relax in it and loosen up. As for the women, undoubtedly he likes them; a pretty client with a good figure always commands his best efforts, and furthermore the women like him, but he hasn't completely lost his head over any of them thus far—Alma Huntley, Helen Framley, Billy Prue, Ruth Otis, Marian Dunton and the rest are pleasant memories, Shirley Bruce's kiss may still be hot on his lips, and Dona Grafton's painting hangs in his office; but Donald is still a bachelor without regrets.

Physically Donald is on the small side. Esther Clarde, who tends the cigar counter at the hotel in which the gambler Jed Ringold was killed, describes him as about twenty-seven years old, five feet six inches tall, weighing about 125 pounds, with clean-cut, finely chiseled features, an engaging voice, and lots of personality. In view of Donald's undoubted attractiveness to women this may be colored slightly in his favor—apparently he looks younger than he really is, for one thing—but it is much closer to the truth than the description given by Markham, the night clerk at the same hotel, who told the police that he was shifty-eyed, nervous in manner, and emaciated, and that he looked like a dope fiend. Markham was prejudiced.

In 1940 Donald was living at Mrs. Eldridge's rooming house, but more recently he has favored apartments, and one of Bertha's complaints is that he drifts from one apartment to another and never has a listed telephone number. Outside of his girl friends, Donald has no close pals—and this seems to be the case with Bertha, too. He gets too much exercise and amusement out of his business to make golf, club life, horse-back riding, and such like attractive, but for professional purposes he has learned how to box from Louis Hazen and jiujitsu from Tokamura Hashita. Both of these skills he puts to good use, to knock out Parker Alfman on one occasion and to throw Marco Cutler over his shoulder on another. He has also attended Frances G. Lee's seminar on homicide investigation.

It is Donald who makes the Cool-Lam combination successful. Before he came, Bertha had worked on minor assignments which other agencies wouldn't touch—divorce cases, automobile accidents, and the like; but after his arrival and when his reputation for getting results was noised around, the establishment found itself attracting more important and lucrative—and more risky—cases. For two years Donald worked for the agency as an employee; then, right in the middle of the *Double or Quits* case, he served an ultimatum, a full partnership or he leaves. It took three days for Bertha to make up her mind that she could not do without him, but she eventually met his terms. In fact, Bertha realizes Donald's value so keenly that in 1942, when his uneasiness made it clear that he wanted to join the armed forces, she cooked up a defense work project for the firm which would exempt him from military service. Donald would have no part of this and entered the Navy. His service there lasted nearly two years and made him a hero; his ship was sunk by a mine, and he saved the men who were with him on a liferaft by improvising a mirror out of mercury from fever thermometers and the bottom of a bucket, so that they could signal a destroyer. Discharged in 1944, he brings home with him the remains of an infection caused by "tropical bugs," and the injunction to take it easy for a while, live in a cool climate, and not get too excited, a rather difficult prescription for a member of the firm of Cool and Lam to follow.

While Donald was away Bertha had to carry on as best as she could. Elsie Brand stayed, though she could have made more money with an airplane factory, but out of loyalty to Donald she wanted to do what she could to hold the business together in his absence. For a while Bertha managed well enough, but as time went on things grew worse; clients wouldn't do things her way and she couldn't do them Donald's way. Two cases of this period are recorded, *Bats Fly at Dusk*, which Donald broke during a short leave, and *Cats Prowl at Night*, which Bertha blundered through by herself, surviving the most amusing episode of the entire history, her encounter with Imogene Dearborne. This "estimable young lady" became enraged at Bertha for calling her a "little twirp," and sued for damages. Bertha got cold comfort from her lawyer, but more substantial help from Sergeant Frank Sellers, of the Homicide Squad, who demonstrated that Imogene made more or less of a racket out of such suits.

The firm of Cool and Lam has its offices in the Drexel Building, somewhere in downtown Los Angeles. The nucleus is the outer office, presided over by Elsie Brand, from which one enters Bertha's large room with her creaking swivel chair and big desk, together with several filing cabinets, a table, a book-case, and some chairs, including the $125 item bought by Donald. This was the complete lay-out until two years after Donald's release from the Navy; then, in the middle of the *Crows Can't Count* case, by arrangement with the building manager, he arranged to take the adjoining suite for his own, cutting a communicating door through the wall and establishing Elsie Brand in the outer room as his personal secretary. But Donald is not one who spends much time in an office.

Elsie Brand is the Della Street of the firm, but without Della's self-assertiveness and ability to take responsibility. She does not run the office, as Della so efficiently does for Perry Mason. Bertha wouldn't allow her to do so. In fact, Bertha has her completely under control, insists that she keep the typewriter going every minute of the day, and gives her an endless stream of form letters to write, mostly to lawyers, soliciting business. This probably accounts for her taciturnity, for she has very little to say for herself. Elsie had been Henry Cool's secretary, selected by Bertha (who "has something on her"), and has been with Bertha ever since Henry's death. Donald's advent is a fine thing for Elsie; they like each other and Elsie becomes about as much devoted to him as Della Street is to Perry Mason, but in a more platonic way. She does a few shadowing jobs for him not too successfully, hides him in her apartment when the police are after him; trustfully poses as his wife at a motor court; wires him her savings, $350, when he is in trouble in San Francisco; and for his sake does not leave the firm while he is away fighting. On the other hand Donald raises her wages $10 a week just as soon as he becomes a partner; makes $13,000 out of her $350 by a smart deal in mining stock, and annexes her as his own secretary when the office is enlarged. For the rest, Elsie has straw-colored hair and though she has taken care of her face and figure is beginning to show her age, which is not far from Donald's own. In the office she is extremely neat and efficient, but her apartment is a mess.

If Elsie is Donald's Della Street, Sergeant Frank Sellers, of the Homicide Squad, who first appears in *Bats Fly at Dusk*, is his Lieutenant Tragg and Sergeant Holcomb. Sellers, however, is not as smooth as Tragg nor as vindictive as Holcomb; he is a big, heavy-handed police officer who puts his feet on the desk and is not averse to reading other people's letters. He almost has a romance with Bertha—kisses her in the *Bats* case and in *Crows Can't Count* avers that she would make someone a good wife. Donald is more of a trial to him; he takes him into custody three times—briefly, because Donald always produces the right answers at the last moment; but it is Sellers upon whom Donald calls to get a quick passport for Colombia in the *Crows* case. At that time, incidentally, Sellers is a captain and off Homicide, but in the two following cases he is again a sergeant on his former assignment.

While the firm ordinarily operates in Los Angeles, circumstances, or Donald's reputation, have brought it five cases which have taken it afield, and a sixth, mentioned but not recorded, had a Florida locale. *Turn on the Heat* is mostly concerned with Santa Carlotta, a nearby city described as graft-ridden; *Spill the Jackpot* takes Donald and Bertha to Yuma and other parts of Arizona; the *Owls* case is laid in New Orleans; the *Crows* case necessitates a trip to South America, and Donald is in San Francisco for the greater part of the *Top of the Heap* case. The firm's adventures also introduce them—and their readers—to a variety of *curiosa*, such as the inward workings of a slot machine (*Spill the Jackpot*), the habits of street beggars (*Bats Fly at Dusk*), the emerald trade (*Crows Can't Count*), the real estate business and horse-race handicapping (*Fools Die on Friday*), the difference between accidental death and death by accidental means (*Double or Quits*), how to beat the Blue Sky law and how to salt a gold mine (*Gold Comes in Bricks*), the methods of night-club photographers (*Bedrooms Have Windows*), and the delights of Creole cookery (*Owls Don't Blink*). Furthermore, the firm's cases have the habit of getting delightfully complicated, as you will realize if you undertake to write down an outline of *Top of the Heap*, for instance, and dovetail together the schemes of John Carver Billings, Gabby Garvanza, George Tustin Bishop, and Hartley Channing. Donald sees through it and you will eventually; and it is this complication of plot and variety of scenery and subject, coupled with Donald's monumental nerve and unfailing resourcefulness, that make it profitable for the reader to follow the fortunes of the firm of Cool and Lam.

MORE ON AUTHOR AND SUBJECT

Frank E. Robbins received his Ph.D. from the University of Chicago in 1911, came to the University of Michigan as an instructor in Greek the following year, and remained associated with the University, later becoming assistant to the university president and director of the University Press. Despite his many academic and administrative duties, he was an avid reader of mysteries and (as the preceding essay attests) an especially avid reader of Erle Stanley Gardner. Mr. Robbins died in 1963.

The standard work on Gardner, though long out of print and outdated, is Alva Johnston's The Case of Erle Stanley Gardner *(Morrow, 1947). Mr. Robbins' "The World of Perry Mason," a companion piece to the above essay on the Cool & Lam novels, appeared in the* Michigan Alumnus Quarterly Review *(now* The Michigan Quarterly Review*), Summer 1950. A relatively recent* and extremely relevant work is Charles Morton's "The World of Erle Stanley Gardner" (Atlantic Monthly, January 1967).

†The mystery writer need not write with words but may instead use pieces of film; and the name that is synonymous with film of suspense is, and has been for over forty years, Alfred Hitchcock. But a new generation of film critics—one of the most articulate of whom is Robin Wood—has come to see in Hitchcock far more than the sardonic fat man who makes you pay to shudder. The younger writers stress that beneath the master of suspense is a penetrating and serious artist whose tragic vision, as given form in his best films, rivals that of Camus. It is from this standpoint that Wood now studies Hitchcock's most famous work.

Hitchcock's Psycho
by Robin Wood

. . .function
Is smother'd in surmise, and nothing is
But what is not.
               (Macbeth)

But if you look at the matter from a theoretical point of view and ignore this question of degree you can very well say that we are all ill, i.e. neurotic; for the conditions required for symptom-formation are demonstrable also in normal persons.
(Freud, *Introductory Lectures on Psycho-Analysis*)

149

> You have to remember that *Psycho* is a film made
> with quite a sense of amusement on my part. To
> me it's a *fun* picture. The processes through
> which we take the audience, you see, it's rather
> like taking them through the haunted house at the
> fairground. . .
> (HITCHCOCK, interview in *Movie 6*).

Psycho opens with a view of a city. The name of the city appears, followed by a precise date and a precise time, as the camera swings over the rooftops and apartment blocks. It hesitates, seems to select, tracks in towards one particular block, hesitates again before all the windows, seems to select again, then takes us through one slightly open window into a darkened room. Arbitrary place, date and time, and now an apparently arbitrary window: the effect is of random selection: this could be any place, any date, any time, any room: it could be *us*. The forward track into darkness inaugurates the progress of perhaps the most terrifying film ever made: we are to be taken forwards and downwards into the darkness of ourselves. *Psycho* begins with the normal and draws us steadily deeper and deeper into the abnormal; it opens by making us aware of time, and ends (except for the releasing final image) with a situation in which time (i.e. development) has ceased to exist.

The scene we witness between Marion Crane (Janet Leigh) and Sam Loomis (John Gavin), while carefully and convincingly particularized in terms of character and situation, is ordinary enough for us to accept it as representative of "normal" human behaviour. A leading theme emerges, unexceptional both in itself and in the way in which it is presented, though it subtly pervades the whole scene: the dominance of the past over the present. The lovers cannot marry because Sam has to pay his dead father's debts and his ex-wife's alimony; "respectable" meetings in Marion's home will be presided over by her (presumably) dead mother's portrait. From this "normal" hold of past on present, with its limiting, cramping effect on life (the essence of life being development), we shall be led gradually to a situation where present is entirely swallowed up by past, and life finally paralysed. That the lovers are meeting surreptitiously, doing things that must be concealed from the outer world, provides a further link (still within the bounds of normality) with Norman Bates. And in both cases the "secrets," normal and abnormal, are sexual in nature.

Everything is done to encourage the spectator to identify with Marion. In the dispute between the lovers we naturally side with her: Sam's insistence on waiting until he can give her financial security annoys us, because it is the sort of boring mundane consideration we expect the romantic hero of a film to sweep aside, and we are very much drawn to Marion's readiness to accept things as they are for the sake of the relationship. This is in fact the first step in our complicity in the theft of the 40,000 dollars. It is Sam's fault that Marion steals the money, which has no importance for her. It is simply the means to an end: sex, not money, is the root of all evil. Indeed, the spectator's lust for money, played upon considerably in the early stages of the film, is aroused only to be swiftly and definitively "placed": the fate of the money, after the shower murder, becomes an entirely trivial matter, and Hitchcock by insisting on it evokes in us a strong revulsion.

Our moral resistance is skilfully undermined during the office scene. The man with the money—Cassidy—is a vulgar, drunken oaf, he has plenty more; his boast that he "buys off unhappiness," that his about-to-be-married "baby" has "never had an unhappy day," fills us with a sense of unfairness even as we realise how far his boast probably is from the truth: whatever he is, Cassidy does not strike us as a happy man.

The whole fabric of the film is interwoven with these parent-child references: even Marion's fellow office-girl has a prying mother, and Marion's room is decorated with family photographs which look down on her as she packs. Cassidy's relationship with his "baby" takes us a step into the abnormal, because it is highly suspect: she will probably be better without the $40,000 house, which is clearly a symbol of her father's power over her. That Marion will also be better without it is a reflection we do not allow ourselves, any more than she does. By minimizing our moral opposition to the notion of stealing 40,000 dollars, Hitchcock makes it possible for us to continue to identify with Marion, involving ourselves in her guilt as easily and unthinkingly as she herself becomes involved. There is no clear-cut moment of decision: she takes the money home, changes, packs her suitcase, but the money lies on the bed and she constantly hesitates over it: her actions tell us that she has committed herself, but she doesn't consciously accept that commitment. We are able to commit acts we know to be immoral only if we inhibit our conscious processes: Macbeth never really knows why he "*yields* to that suggestion whose horrid image does unfix his hair. . .", but the yielding itself involves the paralysis of his conscious moral faculties. So it is with Marion: the decision having gripped her (rather than been taken), she necessarily forfeits her powers of conscious will. She drifts helplessly, and we drift with her.

Her inability to control her actions rationally is illustrated in numerous incidents. As she drives, she imagines voices, conversations: Sam, her boss, Cassidy. She knows Sam will be horrified, will reject the money (she cannot finish the imaginary conversation with him); yet she drives on. Her boss notices her as her car is held up by traffic-lights, and she sees him notice her; yet she drives on. Everything she imagines stresses the impossibility of getting away with it and the uselessness of it anyway; yet she drives on. A suspicious policeman sees her changing cars, and she knows that *he* knows what her new car looks like, and what its number is, and that she is throwing away an irretrievable 700 dollars quite pointlessly; yet she goes through with the exchange. Throughout the journey Hitchcock uses every means to enforce audience-identification—the staging of each scene, the use of subjective technique, the way in which each subsidiary character is presented to us through Marion's eyes, Bernard Herrmann's music and Hitchcock's use of it, all serve to involve us in Marion's condition. With her, we lose all power of rational control, and discover how easily a "normal" person can lapse into a condition usually associated with neurosis. Like her we resent, with fear and impatience, everything (the policeman, the car salesman) that impedes or interferes with her obsessive flight, despite the fact that only interference can help her; just as, two films later, Marnie will be helped only by events that are entirely contrary to her wishes, everything she wants being harmful to her. As Marion drives on (after the exchange of cars) we share her hopelessness and her weariness. The film conveys a sense of endless journey leading nowhere, or into darkness: as the imagined voices become more menacing, darkness gathers. Driving through darkness, she imagines Cassidy learning of the theft of the money: "I'll replace it with her fine soft flesh": Marion's verdict on herself, hideously disproportionate to the crime, will find its hideous enactment. Rain begins to fall on the windscreen before Marion—before us. She pulls up at the Bates Motel, which seems to materialise abruptly out of the darkness in front of her. She has by her actions penetrated the shell of order, and like Macbeth plunged herself into the chaos-world, which finds here its most terrifying definition.

The confrontation of Marion and Norman Bates (Anthony Perkins) is in some ways the core of the film: the parallel made between them provides the continuity that underlies the brutal disruption when Marion is murdered. It is part of the essence of the film to make us feel the continuity between the normal and the psychotic behaviour of Norman Bates. In the "parlour" behind his office, surrounded by Norman's stuffed birds and paintings of classical rapes, they talk about "traps." Marion is brought face to face with the logical extension of her present condition. Norman tells her, "We're all in our private trap. We scratch and claw, but only at the air, only at each other, and for all of it we never budge an inch": he is defining the psychotic state, the condition of permanent anguish whence development becomes impossible, a psychological hell. The parallel between the two is clinched when Norman says to her, "We all go a little mad sometimes. Haven't you?"

It is her perception of Norman's condition that gives Marion her chance of salvation, which she takes. In answer to his question, she says, "Sometimes just one time can be enough. Thank you." She decides to return the money the next morning. The decision this time is clearly made: she has regained her freedom of will, her power of rationality. The scene prepares us for the transference of our interest from Marion to Norman. We see Marion under the shower, and her movements have an almost ritualistic quality; her face expresses the relief of washing away her guilt.

It is not merely its incomparable physical impact that makes the shower-bath murder probably the most horrific incident in any fiction film. The *meaninglessness* of it (from Marion's point of view) completely undermines our recently restored sense of security. The murder is as irrational and as useless as the theft of the money. It also constitutes an alienation effect so shattering that (at a first viewing of the film) we scarcely recover from it. Never—not even in *Vertigo*—has identification been broken off so brutally. At the time, so engrossed are we in Marion, so secure in her potential salvation, that we can scarcely believe it is happening; when it is over, and she is dead, we are left shocked, with nothing to cling to, the apparent centre of the film entirely dissolved.

Needing a new centre, we attach ourselves to Norman Bates, the only other character (at this point) available. We have been carefully prepared for this shift of sympathies. For one thing, Norman is an intensely sympathetic character, sensitive, vulnerable, trapped by his devotion to his mother—a devotion, a self-sacrifice, which our society tends to regard as highly laudable. That he is very unbalanced merely serves to evoke our protective instincts: he is also so helpless. Beyond this, the whole film hitherto has led us to Norman, by making us identify with a condition in many ways analogous to his: the transition is easy. After the murder, Hitchcock uses all the resources of identification technique to make us "become" Norman. He is a likeable human being in an intolerable situation, desperately in need of help and protection yet by the very nature of the case unable to obtain it. As he cleans up after his mother's hideous crime, the camera becomes subjective; they are our hands mopping away the blood. At the same time we cannot forget Marion; the intense anguish aroused in the spectator arises, as usual, from a conflict of responses. Our attention is directed repeatedly to the last lingering trace of Marion which Norman almost overlooks: the money, become now a mere squalid bundle of paper, an ironic reminder of her life, her desires, her relationship with Sam.

Psycho is Hitchcock's ultimate achievement to date in the technique of audience-participation. In a sense, the spectator becomes the chief protagonist, uniting in himself all the characters. The remainder of the film is an inquiry into the sources of the psychological hell-state represented by Norman Bates: a descent into the chaos-world. The other characters (Sam, Lila, Arbogast), perfunctorily sketched, are merely projections of the spectators into the film, our instruments for the search, the easier to identify with as they have no detailed individual existence. Each stage in the descent adds to the tension within us: we want to know, and we dread knowing, we want the investigators to find the truth and put an end to the horrors, yet we have involved ourselves in those horrors through our identification with Norman. One is struck (bearing in mind the care with which Hitchcock always selects his players) by close physical resemblances between certain characters. That between Vera Miles and Janet Leigh can be easily explained: they are sisters: but what of that, still more striking, between Anthony Perkins and John Gavin? As they face each other across the counter of Norman's office, we have the uncanny feeling that we are looking at two sides of the same coin; and the scene in question, which seemed at first mere suspense, useful only in its plot context, becomes one of the most moving of the film. The two men look at one another, and we look at them, and we realise suddenly that they are interchangeable: each seems the reflection of the other (though a reflection in a distorting mirror), the one healthy, balanced, the other gnawed and rotted within by poisoned sex. Similarly, Vera Miles is the extension of Janet Leigh, and what she sees is, potentially, inside herself. The characters of *Psycho* are *one* character, and that character, thanks to the identifications the film evokes, is us.

Lila's exploration of the house is an exploration of Norman's psychotic personality. The whole sequence, with its discoveries in bedroom, attic and cellar, has clear Freudian overtones. The Victorian *décor*, crammed with invention, intensifies the atmosphere of sexual repression. The statue of a black cupid in the hall, the painting of an idealised maiden disporting herself at the top of the stairs, a nude goddess statuette in the bedroom, are juxtaposed with the bed permanently indented with the shape of Mrs. Bate's body (the bed in which, we learn later, she and her lover were murdered by Norman), the macabre cast of crossed hands on her dressing-table, the stifling atmosphere of stagnation: one can almost *smell* it. The attic, Norman's own bedroom, represents the sick man's conscious mental development: strange confusion of the childish and the adult, cuddly toys, grubby unmade bed, a record of the "Eroica" symphony; the unexplained nature of all this carries the suggestion that what we see are mere superficial hints of underlying mysteries, a suggestion confirmed by the clasped, untitled book that Lila never actually opens (a Bates family album?). Consequently we accept Norman more than ever as a human being, with all the human being's complex potentialities. The cellar gives us the hidden, sexual springs of his behaviour: there Lila finds Mrs. Bates. It is a *fruit*-cellar—the fruit is insisted upon in the mother's macabre joke about being "fruity": the source of fruition and fertility become rotten.

Our discovery of the truth, of course, partly changes our attitude to what has gone before. It adds, for example, many complexities to our understanding of the shower murder, which we see now as primarily a sexual act, a violent substitute for the rape that Norman dares not carry out, and secondarily as the trapped being's desire to destroy a woman who has achieved the freedom he will never achieve: a point that gives added irony to the fact that it is her awareness of Norman that gives Marion that freedom. What it cannot do is remove our sense of complicity. We have been led to accept Norman Bates as a potential extension of ourselves. That we all carry within us somewhere every human potentiality, for good or evil, so that we all share in a common guilt, may be, intellectually, a truism; the greatness of *Psycho* lies in its ability, not merely to *tell* us this, but to make us experience it. It is this that makes a satisfactory analysis of a Hitchcock film on paper so difficult; it also ensures that no analysis, however detailed, can ever become a substitute for the film itself, since the direct emotional experience survives any amount of explanatory justification.

The effect of forward tracking-shots in the film (from the opening right through to Lila's exploration of the house) is to carry us always further inside or into darkness. All the time we are being made to *see*, to see more, to see deeper: often, to see things we are afraid to see. Hence the insistence on eyes, into which the camera, our own eyes, makes us look, to see the dark places of the human soul beyond. And hence the dark glasses of the policeman: he is the only character whose eyes we never see, because it is he who is watching Marion, and hence ourselves. By the end of the film, Hitchcock has placed us in the policeman's position: we watch Norman Bates as the policeman watched Marion, and he is as conscious of our gaze as Marion was of the policeman's. On the other side of the cinema screen, we are as inscrutable, hence as pitiless, as the policeman behind his dark glasses. We may recall Norman's remark about "institutions" in the dialogue with Marion: ". . .the cruel eyes studying you." Norman is finally beyond our help. Much of the film's significance is summed up in a single visual metaphor, making use again of eyes, occurring at the film's focal point (the murder of Marion): the astonishing cut from the close-up of the water and blood *spiralling* down the drain, to the close-up of the eye of the dead girl, with the camera *spiralling* outwards from it. It is as if we have emerged from the depths *behind* the eye, the round hole of the drain leading down into an apparently bottomless darkness, the potentialities for horror that lie in the depths of us all, and which have their source in sex, which the remainder of the film is devoted to sounding. The sensation of vertigo inspired by this cut and the spiralling movement itself, are echoed later as we, from high above, watch Norman carry his mother down to the fruit cellar.

The cellar is another clear sex symbol. And what Vera Miles finds there at the end of the quest are once again eyes: the mocking "eyes" of a long-dead corpse as a light-bulb swings before its face: the eyes of living death, eyes that move without seeing, the true eyes of Norman.

The psychiatrist's "explanation" has been much criticized, but it has its function. It crystallises for us our tendency to evade the implications of the film, by converting Norman into a mere "case," hence something we can easily put from us. The psychiatrist, glib and complacent, reassures us. But Hitchcock crystallises this for us merely to force us to reject it. We shall see on reflection that the "explanation" ignores as much as it explains (the murder as symbolic rape, for example). But we are not allowed to wait for a chance to reflect: our vague feelings of dissatisfaction are promptly brought to consciousness by our final confrontation with Norman, and this scene in the cell, entirely static after the extremes of violence that have preceded it, is the most unbearably horrible in the film. What we see is Norman, his identity finally dissolved in the illusory identity of his mother, denounce all the positive side of his personality. "Mother" is innocent: "she" spares the fly crawling on Norman's hand: it is Norman who was the savage butcher. Thus we witness the irretrievable annihilation of a human being. The fly reminds us of Marion, who wasn't spared: the act constitutes a pathetic attempt at expiation before the pitiless eyes of a cruel and uncomprehending society. For a split second, almost subliminally, the features of the mother's ten-year-dead face are superimposed on Norman's as it fixes in a skull-like grimace. The sense of finality is intolerable, yet it is this that makes our release possible: we have been made to see the dark potentialities within all of us, to face the worst thing in the world: eternal damnation. We can now be set free, be saved for life. The last image, of the car *withdrawing* from the dark depths of the bog, returns us to Marion, to ourselves, and to the idea of psychological liberty.

*   *   *

Psycho is one of the key works of our age. Its themes are of course not new—obvious forerunners include *Macbeth* and Conrad's *Heart of Darkness*—but the intensity and horror of their treatment and the fact that they are here grounded in sex belong to the age that has witnessed on the one hand the discoveries of Freudian psychology and on the other the Nazi concentration camps. I do not think I am being callous in citing the camps in relation to a work of popular entertainment. Hitchcock himself in fact accepted a commission to make a compilation film of captured Nazi material about the camps. The project reached the rough-cut stage, and was abandoned there, for reasons I have not been able to discover: the rough-cut now lies, inaccessibly, along with vast quantities of similar raw material, in the vaults of the Imperial War Museum. But one cannot contemplate the camps without confronting two aspects of their horror: the utter helplessness and innocence of the victims, and the fact that human beings, whose potentialities all of us in some measure share, were their tormentors and butchers. We can no longer be under the slightest illusion about human nature, and about the abysses around us and within us; and *Psycho* is founded on, precisely, these twin horrors. For Hitchcock it was a "fun" picture, and a streak of macabre humour ("Mother. . .what is the phrase?. . . isn't quite herself today") certainly runs through it. Is it, then, some monstrous perversion? Many have found it so, and their reaction seems to me more defensible than that of those (must we include Hitchcock himself?) who are merely amused by it (". . . make us think twice about stopping at any building looking remotely like the Bates motel. . ."). David Holbrook, for example, remarks (presumably with *Psycho* in mind, since his book appeared in 1962), "Of course, if we live in the world of detective stories and Hitchcock films we may take all this sordidness in a light-hearted spirit as a snuff-like piece of stimulation. But if we are responding to poetry and drama our senses should be sharpened. . ." (*Llareggub Revisited*). Yet this seems to me a short-sight-ed and insensitive verdict: if one is responding to *Psycho*, one's senses should be sharpened too. No film conveys—to those not afraid to expose themselves fully to it—a greater sense of desolation, yet it does so from an exceptionally mature and secure emotional viewpoint. And an essential part of this viewpoint is the detached sardonic humour. It enables the film to contemplate the ultimate horrors without hysteria, with a poised, almost serene detachment. This is probably not what Hitchcock meant when he said that one cannot appreciate *Psycho* without a sense of humour, but it is what he *should* have meant. He himself—if his interviews are to be trusted—has not really faced up to what he was doing when he made the film. This, needless to say, must not affect one's estimate of the film itself. For the maker of *Psycho* to regard it as a "fun" picture can be taken as his means of preserving his sanity; for the critic to do so—and to give it his approval on these grounds—is quite unpardonable. Hitchcock (again, if his interviews are to be trusted) is a much greater artist than he knows.

MORE ON AUTHOR AND SUBJECT

Robin Wood first came to prominence as a member of the group of young British film critics whose journal was the film periodical Movie. *He has taught at London University and has published studies of Howard Hawks and Ingmar Bergman in addition to his work on Hitchcock. He is presently teaching at Queen's University in Ontario.*

The literature on Hitchcock has grown to immense proportions over the past decade. John Russell Taylor includes a reliable survey of the director's work in his Cinema Eye, Cinema Ear *(Hill & Wang, 1964). A monumental (but to me terribly misleading) interview with the filmmaker is the subject of François Truffaut's* Hitchcock *(Simon & Schuster, 1967). For another essay specifically on* Psycho, *see Raymond Durgnat's "Inside Norman Bates," in* Films and Feelings *(MIT Press, 1967). A new and expanded edition of Wood's own classic 1965 study* Hitchcock's

Films *has recently been published, by A. Zwemmer Ltd. in England and A.S. Barnes in this country.*

†The literature on crime films is already considerable and constantly growing, although it is read more by film enthusiasts than by mystery lovers. Unfortunately, this neglect on the part of those who delight in written crime fiction has led to a general (and completely false) impression that the crime film rarely if ever gets beyond the Bulldog Drummond in Las Vegas *level so common in the early Forties. Mr. Richie, a specialist in the Japanese cinema, here shows how a first-rate Oriental director transformed an American police procedural novel into a framework for his own vision of the nature of man and the world.*

High and Low
by Donald Richie

The Story

The story, with major revisions, is taken from a novel by Ed McBain. Gondo (Toshiro Mifune) is production head of a shoe company who, having trouble with the directors, is planning a coup whereby he will gain control of the stock and thereby the company. He mortgages his home and belongings to get enough money to make the initial payment. Just then he receives word that his son is kidnapped and the criminal asks for an exorbitant amount—very near that which he has just raised. A bit later the boy returns and it is discovered that his playmate, the

162

chauffeur's son, was the one who was kidnapped.

The question becomes: is a chauffeur's son worth as much as an industrialist's?   At first Mifune says no, refuses, particularly when the kidnapper calls, admits the mistake, but insists that he be paid anyway.   After much thought the industrialist, upon the advice of the police, agrees to pay.   The rendezvous is on a speeding express train.   The money is handed over, the boy is returned and the first half of the film is over.   Mifune is ruined but now the police start trying to get back the money.   This occupies the second half of the film.

One clue leads to another, and eventually a young intern, Takeuchi (Tsutomu Yamazaki), is implicated.   He is also guilty of selling heroin to addicts and, eventually, of killing his accomplices in the kidnapping.   He is captured, confesses and in the final scene in the prison asks to meet Mifune.

Yamazaki: Ah, Mr. Gondo, thanks for coming. You look very well. What are you doing these days?

Mifune: Making shoes, just as I always have. It's a small company but they've been kind enough to put me in charge of production. I hope someday to be able to build something even better than National Shoes was.

Yamazaki: Why do you keep *looking* at me like that? In a few hours I'm going to die but don't think that frightens me. It doesn't. And don't think I called you here because I wanted your pity. . .why should I spend the last few moments of my life listening to slop like that? You see, I'm concerned with the truth, no matter how ugly. . . But, how about it—now that I'm going to die, are you happy?

Mifune: Why do you talk like that? Why are you so convinced that it is right that we hate each other?

Yamazaki: I don't know about that. . .it is just that. . .from my dirty little room, too cold to sleep in the winter, too hot to breathe in the summer, I could see your house and it was like looking up at heaven. I looked up at your house every day and somehow began to hate you. After a while it was hating you that kept me going.

And you know something? I found out that people like me can have a lot of fun making people like you miserable.

Mifune: Were you that miserable?

Yamazaki: Want the story of my life? Not a chance. Your sympathy doesn't interest me, Mr. Gondo, and I really don't have that much time. . . It will soon be over and I'm glad of it.

Mifune: If that is the way you feel why did you send for me?

Yamazaki: I didn't want you to think that I died begging for mercy. . .

He suddenly clutches the wire-screen, his hands shaking.

You think my hands are shaking because I'm scared. Look—I've been in solitary for two weeks now—it is a common physical reaction. When a man is taken out of solitary he starts to shake—that's the truth. A death sentence means nothing to me. I've been living in my own private hell for a long time. So I'm not afraid of going to hell.

He stands up, anguished, shouts:

Now, if someone were to tell me I was going to heaven, then I guess I'd really start to shake, wouldn't I?

He begins to cry, to laugh, to shout. The guards rush in and take him away. The iron shutter falls over the glass and wire between them. Mifune is left sitting alone in front of the closed prison shutter, and the film ends.

Treatment

The title of the film in Japanese is *Tengoku to Jigoku* (or *Heaven and Hell*) and this suggests an extreme opposite that merely *High and Low* does not. The first half of the picture takes place in heaven—that is, in Mifune's apartment, high on a bluff in

Yokohama and visible from most of that section of the city. Even the background for the credit titles is scenes of Yokohama taken from high up. These include the harbor, Chinatown, the trains and factory chimneys which later become important to the action, and all are seen as Mifune himself sees them—from above. The second half of the film takes place in hell—in Yokohama itself, and eventually descends to the lowest circle: the alleys around Chinatown where in a warren of cheap hotels and bars the heroin pushers are found.

Formally, the film is designed to break into two. At the end of the first, the ostensible story is over—the boy is back, we are consequently no longer emotionally involved. The second half is an elaborate hunt and our interest becomes intellectual. As in *Stray Dog* we are presented with a puzzle and then watch it worked out, step by step. As in the 1948 film (and oddly, *Un carnet du bal*—a film much admired in Japan) the audience is given evidence bit by bit.

Kurosawa plainly shows what *he* thinks is important. It is not the kidnapping itself (done off screen) nor the fate of the small victim (the return is purposely done in extreme long-shot as though to rob it of all emotion), nor is it Mifune's moral dilemma. It is the search, the capture, and the confrontation. The form would indicate this—or else why have the boy returned half way through the film?—and so does the way in which the two parts are filmed.

If the first half is statement and exposition, then the second half is development and conclusion; if the first is theory, then the second is practice.

The first half—it takes one hour and five minutes—not only takes place entirely in Mifune's apartment, but the action is so static that it is very close to theater. Several cameras are used but the takes are enormously long—some run to ten minutes and would probably have run longer but this was the capacity of the camera's magazines.

I was present during the filming of the early morning scene where the detectives have stayed the night: Mifune comes in, opens the windows, is asked to close them, eventually refuses to pay and goes out. During the rehearsals one of the lights fused. It was an arc simulating early morning sunlight outside the window from which Mifune was to pull the curtain. Even though it was only a rehearsal Kurosawa said: "Let's wait until they fix the light. . .we might as well do it right."

This is typical of the meticulousness which went into these static-appearing scenes. We know they are static, even feel a mild claustrophobia, but we are never bored, we remain interested. And when things happen, they happen fast: the chauffeur comes in with a sweater for his son, asks for him, the wife goes to look in the garden, the telephone rings, it is the kidnapper, and we get the first close-up: Mifune on the phone.

There are only three indications of passing of time in the first half. They are all wipes. The first is the second phone call, the detectives already there, wipe/the next scene is everyone listening to a taping made by the police some time after. The second leaves the chauffeur pleading with his employer, in full obeisance on the floor, with Mifune walking out of the room, wipe/next morning Mifune coming downstairs. The third is the call, wipe/the family listening to the taped call while in the background the detectives are following the kidnapper's taped instructions, putting the money into briefcases—cause and effect included in the single shot. There are many other short-cuts used in this first half. "Is that the police?" asks the wife. "No," says the chauffeur, "only a department store truck." "Funny time for it to come," says Mifune and instantly the chauffeur is announcing the police, and there is not another word explaining that they came disguised as truckers.

The train sequence, which is the visual center of the film, is given the amount of time it would actually have taken, about four minutes—but four minutes of an action so furious that after the stillness of the first hour, the effect is overwhelming.

The second half begins at once and here the leisurely method of the story-telling chronicle is abruptly changed—using the freely-cut train sequences as link—to an essay-like, analytical narration (a bit like that in *Ikiru*) where past and present are seen at the same time. First, however, Kurosawa makes certain that we understand we are now in hell. Detectives are checking phone boxes. They look up and there is Mifune's house. One says to the other: "Looking up at his place from here it *does* sort of seem he's looking down his nose at everyone." The camera looks at the scummy canal and in a distance the radio is heard playing the theme and variations movement of Schubert's *Forellen* quintet, the camera pans up and follows a new character, a young man. He is followed through alleys until he reaches his room, turns on the radio, starts searching the newspapers. It is the kidnapper.

Here, Kurosawa purposely throws away mystery and suspense. Not only do we know that the boy has been returned, we also know what the kidnapper looks like, which is more than anyone else does. We are forced to become as analytical as the detectives. We can savor their getting nearer and nearer because we now know what the criminal looks like and we discover something about his life.

We are not allowed to look too long, however. At once we are taken on the chase which includes almost every technique in the cinematic repertoire.

> First we see the eight millimeter shots taken from the train, then a blow-up of a single frame, there is a man with a cow. It was he who says he saw a man running with two briefcases and driving away. From this they get tire-marks and some paint scrapings. The little victim has in the meantime drawn a picture of what he saw: Mt. Fuji and the sea. At police headquarters they are checking all pay phones from which Mifune's house is visible (since the kidnapper said he could see it, and wondered why—when the police were there—the blinds were drawn)—they find three and we have already seen them do so. The kidnapper said it was hot—the police discover that one of

them is in the sun at the hour the call came. It turns out the little boy was given ether to keep him quiet. The car model is identified and there is a glimpse of the police stopping a car. The police discover an abandoned car (seen) and its license number tallies with the number of a stolen car. The attendants on the freeway remember seeing a boy asleep in the back of a car—we see detectives talking with them; in the meantime the police have been trying to find a place where both Fuji and the sea are visible (and a short scene shows this). A detective in replaying the tapes hears the sound of a cable-train in the background. He starts to investigate: a short scene of his talking with train men, their identifying it. They find the house and the dead accomplices, they also find a note (seen in blow-up in the laboratory) saying they intend to spend the money unless they get more dope. In the meantime we know that the briefcase is still with the kidnapper and that it contains chemicals that color smoke if they are burned. Again a shortcut is used. The criminal sees a picture of the briefcase in the paper. Cut to the child having drawn a picture of the kidnapper. Cut to the children racing into the room to say some funny smoke is coming from a chimney.

This last, as are all other successful clues, is accompanied by a fanfare on the sound track. And, like it, all of these tiny scenes are imbedded in the larger scene of policemen making separate reports to their superiors. While they explain we see them doing what they are talking about. Very often past and present are there at the same time, cause and effect are made practically one, a number of false leads are followed but, through elimination, the cops get warmer and warmer. One detail is piled on top of another, each one significant, some very witty. A cop looking through binoculars from a window is accompanied by a distant record playing a song the lyrics of which are: "I can see your lovely eyes;" when the police move in through the moonlight a radio plays *O sole mio*. This telescoping, and the technical brilliance of the exposition makes this section, about thirty minutes, the shortest half hour in all of Kurosawa's cinema.

Then the detectives decide to arrest, and in this climax of the hunt Kurosawa presents a kaleidoscope which must be compared with the night-town sequences of *Ikiru* for sheer visual exhilaration. One marvelous scene after another: the cops disguised as toughs in a Yokohama dance-hall; the villain walking through Chinatown, his glasses reflecting the lights; the head-cops in a car which is speckled with passing neons; a very exciting scene where the ruined Mifune is walking accidentally in the same neighborhood (looking at shoes in a store window) and the kidnapper, recognizing him, asks for a light and then looks curiously at him for a second. The hunt comes to an abrupt end when they snap the handcuffs on him at the deserted house overlooking the sea where they found the murdered couple. Then comes the coda and the confrontation.

In his depiction of contrasts Kurosawa follows Dante. Heaven is a measured place of muffled crisis where things as they are are insisted upon; hell is a chaos, wildly exciting, quite dangerous. The disguised cops move through this hell like demigods, or angels, always alert, always watching. Mifune moves through this world like Dante himself, oblivious even when confronted with the evil that has wrecked his life. Only the head detective, his brow furrowed, worries, invisible but watching over him, Virgil-like. The parallel need not be labored, there is no doubt that Kurosawa is surely on the side of the angels. In this film there is not the slightest sympathy for the villain nor for the world that is his. The police are true protectors, the villain is truly black. Morally, it would seem to be the most black and white of all of Kurosawa's films because its eventual ambiguity is not one of character.

Characterization

Though there are many characterizations of others in the film (the wife is in kimono throughout except in the final scene at the house where, in Western dress, she faces eviction; each detective is given his own little quirk; the head detective is obviously and wholly benevolent), there are really only two fully-drawn characters: those of Gondo, the unfortunate; and Takeuchi, the bringer of misfortune.

Gondo is a completely ordinary man—he could be almost anyone. He has gotten where he is in the world through hard work, yet he has never sacrificed his integrity and this integrity is that of a workman who will not produce shoddy goods. This is fully established in the opening scene, a quarrel between him and the other directors of the shoe company based on just this point. Yet, at the same time, he has lived enough in the world to know how to take care of himself. When his son and the chauffeur's boy are playing outlaw and sheriff, Gondo calls out: "Running away from the sheriff won't help. Hide and then let him have it. Don't you run, let him run. It's kill or be killed. . .don't forget." This advice is precisely that which he himself is following in buying out the stock. It will ruin the other directors who are set on getting control themselves. He is therefore no better than they—though he has our sympathy because he has a kind of integrity which they do not. And this he shows, when, in the midst of his misfortunes, he sits down on the floor, calls for his tools—which he obviously has not used for years—and begins taking the leather briefcase apart to put in the smoke capsule. "In my day shoemakers made briefcases too. I never thought my days as an apprentice would be so valuable. Yet here I am, starting from scratch again." And he laughs—in the very face of his troubles. There is a cut to the train (the beginning scene in that sequence) where the head detective reinforces our own impressions with: "You know, I really admire that man."

He is admirable but as the film continues it becomes clear that this admirable quality is mainly that of his being able to tolerate the idea of beginning again, of his being willing to accept a meaningless disaster for which he could in no way be considered responsible, of his finding the strength to continue, his ability to believe in himself.

It is here that *High and Low* reveals itself as having the same ideological basis as the majority of Kurosawa's films. Like Watanabe in *Ikiru,* like the girl in *One Wonderful Sunday,* like the detective in *Stray Dog,* like the young hero of *Red Beard*—Gondo has the ability to believe and the will to continue.

The character of Takeuchi, the kidnapper, seems at first a complete contrast. It would seem that he is plain bad just as Gondo is plain good. Even the looks of the actors suggest this. Mifune is, of course, a good, even noble-looking man. On the other hand, Tsutomu Yamazaki (a stage actor whose first big film part this was) looks, at least in this part, untrustworthy, twisted, faintly repellent. This is the way the characters appear, but here we might remember Sanjuro's advice: You cannot tell what a person is like by how he looks.

Yamazaki certainly *acts* different from Mifune. He is compulsive, he is a man running away, and the police call him a maniac. While not that, he *is* one of life's dissatisfied. Unable to love, he finds pleasure—as he brags at the end of the film—in hating. This man, then, has chosen to be evil—just as the criminal in *Stray Dog* chose. And we remember Detective Shimura's words in that film: "Look, *my* knapsack and money were stolen too. I felt outraged. I knew that this was a dangerous point in my life. But what did I do? I chose this work." Evil, then, is merely the wrong choice at the moment of truth.

His choice of Gondo seems completely gratuitous. He has no motive other than the pleasure of hate, and that Gondo's house is so grand. Evil is non-selective and Gondo's first reaction is an outraged: "Why me?" When the kidnapper calls on the phone (always being careful to call him "*Mr.* Gondo" with an obsequiousness which cannot hide the joy he is feeling at the irony of his, finally the man in power, calling the other, the fallen, *Mr.*) Gondo's reaction is not anger so much as incomprehension.

We watch Gondo's attempt to escape from the consequences of the actions of the other. There is no reason why he should pay. It is that he cannot *not* do it. At first he refuses absolutely. Then he attempts to explain why he is refusing. Finally, he agrees to say he will pay. Next he agrees to take the money from the bank, but says he won't hand it over. It is only as he himself pushes it from the train window—in that one dazed second—that he realizes what has happened and says: "It is my life."

Both police and press think well of this action. They think it is socially desirable, civic-minded, even brave. He is a wonderful man, they tell each other. But his being thought a wonderful man will not get back his life for Mr. Gondo.

He, who has always taken full responsibility for his life (and prided himself in it) is suddenly no longer responsible for it. First, the kidnapper takes over his life and, second, the police take it over. These two things are equated in a curious and meaningful way. It is both kidnapper *and* police who make it impossible for him to work. The first has a certain power over him—if Gondo does as he says the boy may be returned; but the second has a like power—if he does what they say the money may be returned. In either event he can no longer do any work—and he apparently takes to wandering (an action which cannot have been habitual to him) and it is on one of these walks that he first, unknowingly, meets the criminal.

The world is indeed a fine place if things like this can happen to such a good-hearted man, such a well-intentioned man as Mr. Gondo. But (as Kurosawa never tires of pointing out) the world is just like this. It is indeed a hell (as we have been told in *Rashomon,* in *Record of a Living Being,* in *The Lower Depths,* and now here). But it is not a private hell. We are all in it—so is the kidnapper.

He is a man to whom things have happened all of his life and so, just for this once, he decides to make something happen to someone else. He is "oppressed" and so he will oppress an "oppressor." There is something noble in his resolve in that it takes a kind of bravery and considerable courage. At least he is not going to sit back and let life batter him over the head. The flames of hell will not get him without a struggle. So he makes his plan.

However, the same thing happens to him that happens to Gondo. First, he becomes responsible—he must see his crime through to some kind of conclusion. Second, he too becomes responsible to the police. He might have been caught with the boy; now he might be caught with the money. We are much more familiar with this process in the bad man than we are in the good because so many stories and movies have shown us how one "evil" action leads to the next, and so on. Very rarely, however, have we been shown—and shown so clearly—that by the end the bad man has become thoroughly *subject* to those very actions through which he sought to free himself. He and Gondo have become rather alike—neither can work, both are given to wandering. They can be identified with each other.

Camera

Reality is heightened in this film not so much through story, as in *Ikiru,* or form as in *Rashomon,* as through the eye itself. The references to seeing in the film are many and varied. The kidnapper can see into Gondo's house, the policemen, in turn, use binoculars to peep out; many in the cast wear glasses; the kidnapper wears dark glasses at night and their surface reflects what he sees; devices for seeing—still pictures, motion pictures, drawings, are constantly used; there are many mirrors in the picture—the wall mirror in the Yokohama dive, rear view mirrors in cars; there are all kinds of reflections, from reflections on water to reflections on the shiny surfaces of automobiles; a kind of paranoia is felt—someone is always *watching*—and in the confrontation scene it is reflections on a sheet of glass which give the film its final and profoundly ambiguous meaning.

Kurosawa's camera—never self-effacing—has almost never been so prominent. But, as always, it is completely to the point. Throughout the picture there is an insistence that the camera view-point be either high or low. The opening credits are from high above Yokohama; the kidnapper in his room is from below. Scenes in Gondo's house are taken from chest level. Scenes in the dope-dens are taken from a lower angle, around hip level. At the same time—particularly in the first half of the picture—there are many rising/falling shots which insist, accompanying risings and sittings of the actors, upon high and low. This kind of movement is particularly important in the first half because the scenes in themselves are static, as they must be if the second half is to have its full impact.

The way in which these static scenes were vivified is interesting. For the main set, Gondo's apartment was created twice—there were two major sets, identical. One was at the Toho studio, the other was overlooking Yokohama; in other words, Gondo's house was, in part, built. Scenes showing the family against daylight Yokohama were actually filmed there. The night scenes from ostensibly the same location were filmed from yet a third set which had a complete miniature set of Yokohama at night (the real one did not photograph well enough) outside the window. The main body of the first half (all scenes with the curtains drawn) was filmed at the Toho studio.

This set was made much like a stage with no proscenium—a room with the fourth wall missing. Kurosawa's cameras were outside this missing wall and tracks were laid in various positions. The camera itself was rarely taken into the set—close-ups being obtained through long-distance lenses.

For the morning scene mentioned above, the tracks were laid in an inverted V-shape with the two free ends meeting the corners of the set. On one track was a dolly with a camera equipped with long-distance lenses. On the other was another dolly with a small elevator attached. The third camera was hidden in the hallway leading from the far end of the room and was likewise equipped with a telescopic lens. The method of filming was something like that used in TV with different cameras using different lenses, changing position from time to time. The entire operation had been thoroughly practiced, the actors' movements had been worked out, the camera's movements (both dolly cameras moving continually, the elevator following the motions of the actors) and the cues for changing lenses—everything had been choreographed. The three cameras were run simultaneously and the take was repeated twice, which meant one hour of film for a ten minute scene. The sequence was then put together in the cutting room.

The effect is one of complete freedom within a very constricted area and the camera work alone is responsible for the fact that this half, though over an hour in length, seems so very much shorter. Yet this very restraint also assists the visual explosion of the train-sequence—one of the most exciting five minutes in Japanese film.

Here the camera is hand-held or it is bolted to the train floor to make it jump, or put into the cab of the engine, or held out of the window. Nine cameras were used for this sequence including the eight-millimeters which took the scenes later projected at the police headquarters. In the edited version the continuity is superb: one is never lost nor do any of the tiny reactions (Mifune's expression when he lets go the money) escape. At the same time the sense of crisis, of excitement is completely captured.

In the latter half of the film so much is happening that one has to look hard. The cops passing notes back and forth (the machinations of the police force would have delighted Dr. Mabuse); the crowded scenes in the dance-hall with only the flick of an eye to identify the fuzz; the fascinating juxtaposition of seeing what they did while they tell about doing it; the fantastic telephoto shots with people all jammed into a single plane; the bravura of throwing away breathtaking shots with Fuji in the distance. Just as the cops must remain completely alert, forever searching, so must the spectator.

At the same time the camera continuity is so swift that to lapse is to miss. An example of this is the way in which the kidnapper is finally identified. The kidnapper is looking through the newspapers again. The following is all one shot, the camera hand-held but rock-steady, shooting from a relatively short distance with a 75 mm. telescopic lens:

His face, extreme close-up looking at papers, looks startled, pan to paper, picture of briefcase, pan up to him, he drops paper, turns; door opens, extreme close-up, no telling what it is; he pulls things out of closet (it must have been the closet door); finally gets briefcase, holds it open,

*camera swings to see it just before it disappears
into cardboard box; his hands in close-up, they
find twine; pan to box, twine, up to enormous
close-up of face, pan down to hand to show—for
the first time, but only for a second, the cut on
his hand which will eventually identify him.*

This shot of the most controlled brilliance and the most
supernal difficulty lasts about 30 seconds.

*Cut to Gondo's house. They are looking at the
picture the child drew of the kidnapper and all
notice that he has drawn one hand bandaged |
cut. The boys run in and say to come look at the
smoke | cut. Color shot (very brief) of police,
family, Yokohama in distance, red smoke coming
out of chimney. Fanfare on sound track.
Cut to the bottom of the chimney, a policeman
talking to the man who burns the refuse. Discovers that the briefcase came from an intern.
Cut to the waiting room of the hospital. Cops
are there. The kidnapper in his intern smock
comes by. He stops on the stairway. They see
the cut on his hand. They react. Fanfare.*

What the picture insists upon is the reality of what is happening but, at the same time, it is so extraordinarily concerned with
the ways in which reality is counterfeited—mirrors, cameras, binoculars, even eyes—that it is almost equally concerned with illusion. The police are obviously trying to separate, for their own
purposes, illusion from reality—that is what a police hunt is. As
in *The Bad Sleep Well*, Kurosawa is here much concerned with
illusion-making machines. In the former film there is the magical
scene of the man looking at his own funeral service while listening
to a tape which shows him how his death was to have been contrived. In *High and Low*, too, the tape recorder is again used, as
are films—ghost machines both.

That the picture is concerned not only with theory and
practice but also with illusion and reality is wonderfully brought

out—and the two are brought together—in the final scene, the confrontation. Yamazaki is in the death-cell and Mifune comes. Mifune is outside; Yamazaki is inside. They are separated by wire mesh and by a plate of heavy glass. Their conversation begins and the photographic method is, at first, the classic one-two shot: first a close-up of Mifune, then one of Yamazaki. But here we notice something strange. The close-ups of each are taken from the side of the glass opposite that on which he is sitting so that over each close-up is the reflection of the other. As their conversation continues, the set-ups move back further so that, for example, Mifune will be on one side of the screen and Yamazaki on the other but Mifune's reflection will appear in the middle. Over their talk the camera set-ups shift in such a way that the image of the one more and more precisely coincides with the other's reflection.

"If that is the way you feel, why did you send for me?" Mifune asks, and their images coincide. The tears in Mifune's eyes appear to be swimming in the dry eyes of the kidnapper.

In *Stray Dog* the cop and the robber roll fighting in the mud and at the end of the picture they are indistinguishable: cop and robber are one. At the end of *High and Low* something of the sort occurs but much more subtly. We know they are not one—they are good and evil; they are opposite poles. This is what we have been led to believe, this is what we *must* believe. Yet, here, slowly but inexorably, Kurosawa is showing us something entirely different. He is suggesting that, despite everything, good and evil are the same, that all men are equal.

"I am not afraid of going to hell," shouts the kidnapper but it is Mifune's reflection which seems to shout, just as it is the kidnapper's reflection which seems to weep. Good and evil are made to coincide; they are made identical. In *Stray Dog*, the men merely *look* alike. Here they are made to seem to be *giving* each other attributes of themselves. Precisely: they seem to be sharing an identity.

There is no longer any question of a hero or a villain, or heaven or hell, of high or low, of good or of bad. We have already seen that, since the kidnapping, they have come more and more to resemble each other. Having initially hated each other, they are now close to accepting each other.

Mifune, then, has truly had his sense of responsibility tested. He wants to be responsible to himself and make good shoes; his company directors disagree and so he feels right in trying to take over the company in order to continue making good shoes. When the boy is kidnapped a less central sense of responsibility is tested for he is asked to ruin himself for a reason he cannot accept. This, however, he does—and this already indicates how extraordinary he is. Now, at the very end, his sense of responsibility is given its most severe test—he is asked to take responsibility for the actions of the very man who has wronged him. And the indications are that he will.

Yamazaki is just as much a victim as Mifune is though it is more difficult to assess him because he falls into that convenient and meaningless category of "the victim of society." Actually, however, he falls victim to the actions of Mifune no less than Mifune falls victim to his. If Mifune had not made his grand house on the bluff none of this would have happened. You cannot realize yourself in this world without hurting something. Mifune wants to realize himself and builds the house which hurts the kidnapper; he, in turn, wants to realize himself, and takes the child which hurts Mifune.

There is one great difference, however. Yamazaki is going to die and he knows it. It is with horror, then, that he sees the awful alternative of going to heaven rather than to hell. Awful, because—accepting hell as hell—he has identified himself with it, acted as though he belonged there. If he goes to heaven what will become of *him*. Perhaps that is the reason he asked to see Mifune. He wanted to find hate in those eyes, he wanted this reassurance that he was evil, that he was at least this much, that he was at least something.

And the irony is that Mifune will not, cannot. It is no longer a question of compassion nor forgiveness. It has become interior. Mifune must accept responsibility for the criminal's actions. It is

easy enough to understand them (the cop in *Stray Dog* completely understood the criminal), it is a bit more difficult to accept them (though the hero of *The Bad Sleep Well* is very near
that), but to accept these actions as your own, that is the most
difficult of all.

And this—as Dostoevsky has pointed out—is necessary. The
free man is he who accepts his own actions and accepts those of
others as though they were his own. The reflections of the two
men coincide and Yamazaki says: "You see, I'm concerned with
the truth, no matter how ugly. . ." Which is just what Mifune is
most concerned with at this very moment. He asks, and it is
though he is asking himself: "Why are you so convinced that it is
right that we hate each other?"

The question hangs, almost palpable, between the two men
as one is led away, the iron shutter clangs shut, and one remains
behind. After the screen darkens and the film ends, one may
imagine Mifune still sitting there, the question before him, the
question before us.

MORE ON AUTHOR AND SUBJECT

*Donald Richie was born in Lima, Ohio, in 1924, graduated
from Columbia University, and has resided in Japan during most
of the years since the end of World War II. He has directed a
number of films and written film criticism for the* Japan Times,
*but is best known in this country for two loving and monumental
studies of the cinema of Japan:* The Japanese Film *(with Joseph
L. Anderson) and* The Films of Akira Kurosawa. *He is presently
serving as Curator of Film at the Museum of Modern Art in New
York City.*

*Those who would like to learn more about Kurosawa's
criminous films (such as the Simenonian* Stray Dog *and the richly
acclaimed* Rashomon*) will find no better place to begin than
Mr. Richie's books above mentioned.*

†As a further step in persuading you of the infinite variety of the best movies in the crime genre, I am happy to offer this selection of notes by one of the foremost film historians alive. You will notice that Everson, like Wood and Richie and virtually every other film commentator of note, presupposes that the primary creator of a film is the director, not the screenwriter as too many casual filmgoers too often assume. Everson's comments may lead you to scrutinize more carefully the old movies screened by your local film society (if you're lucky) or TV station (if you aren't).

Six Mystery Movies and Their Makers
by William K. Everson

I. Fritz Lang

Fritz Lang was born in Vienna in 1890, entered the German cinema at the end of World War I, made his finest films in the 1920's, emigrated to Hollywood in the middle Thirties and there enjoyed his most elaborate and prolific period. His characteristic heroes and heroines were normal, everyday people, often to the point of being quite colorless compared to the far more interesting and spectacular villains. But there was nothing normal about the characteristic Lang milieu, which is consistently grim, even macabre, constructed of stylised sets and stressing scenes of night or artificial darkness. His best films, both German and American, evoke this uncompromisingly threatening world, almost totally devoid of warmth or humor; and he demands that you believe in this world totally.

> DR. MABUSE DER SPIELER (Decla-Bioscop, Germany, 1922). Distributed by UFA in two parts of ten reels each: "Dr. Mabuse der Spieler: Ein Bild der Zeit" and "Inferno: Menschen der Zeit." Directed by Fritz Lang. Scenario by Thea von Harbou from the novel by Norbert Jacques. Camera: Carl Hoffmann. Sets and design: Otto Hunte, Stahl-Urach. Costuming: Vally Reinecke. Music: Peter Schirman. Players: Rudolph Klein-Rogge (Dr. Mabuse), Bernhard Goetzke (von Wenk), Aud Egede Nissen (Cara Carozza), Alfred Abel (Count Told), Gertrude Welcker (Countess Lucy Told), Paul Richter (Edgar Hull), Lydia Potechina (Russian woman), Karl Huszar-Puffy (Hawasch), Forster Larrinaga (Spoerri), Hans Adalbert von Schlettow (chauffeur), Georg John (Pesch), Grete Berger (Fine), Julius Falkenstein (Karsten), Julius Bergmann (Schramm).

Many rediscovered "primitives" (and despite its 1922 date *Dr. Mabuse* is a primitive in relation to other Lang works) turn out to have amazing vitality and beauty; such has certainly proven the case with the early serials of Louis Feuillade. *Mabuse* on the other hand might disappoint a little if one takes the attitude that it is only four years prior to Lang's *Metropolis*. However, this is rather like being disappointed in D. W. Griffith's *Judith of Bethulia* because it is only two years before *The Birth of a Nation*. The emphasis surely is wrong; rather one should be astounded at the mastery achieved in the later films over such a short period. On its own merits however, *Dr. Mabuse* is a fascinating work, not only because of its clear ties to the ultra-detailed novel of mystery and detection, and for roots which obviously derive from ' ᵕ early serial films, but also because here one can see at the source so many of the themes, characters, incidents and even individual shots that were to permeate Lang's later films, most specifically *Metropolis* (1926), *Spione* (1928), and the two Mabuse sequels: *Das Testament des Dr. Mabuse* (1932) and *Die Tausend Augen des Dr. Mabuse* (1961). Lang's criminal world was always a dark and nightmarish one, but here in the first *Dr. Mabuse* the world is grey rather than black and dream-like rather than nightmarish, with all of the characters, good and bad, seeming to glide through the cold empty rooms in a kind of somnambulistic trance.

What is most surprising of all is Lang's comparative playing-down of melodrama. His later films had tremendous pace, and here his sequences of action and chase are interspersed method-ically, dropped in where they will do the most good, but never sustained for too long. Possibly Lang, not yet too sure of himself, was carefully following a formula which he knew was acceptable. His too-frequent use of the iris device further slows the physical pace of the film. Of course, Lang liked the long film as a matter of policy, not only because he enjoyed that kind of framework, but also because, as he remarked in 1963, and in all seriousness: "If my films were long they couldn't put anything else on the bill, and I got all the money!"

But if Lang's vigor is somewhat diluted in *Mabuse,* there are still ample signs of the glories that were to come. The sets in the first half particularly, with their bizarre and semi-surrealist design, are often superb. The whole sequence in the Stock Exchange gets the film off to a fine start, and Lang's talent for suddenly turning the everyday into an unreal world of terror is beautifully dis-played in the card game sequence where the hideous face of Mabuse suddenly surges forward out of a totally black screen, like some evil spider on an invisible web. There are welcome moments of humor, but somehow they always manage to stay outside the main plotstream, so that one is never encouraged to regard any of it with anything but the utmost seriousness. And when Lang does swing into his action and chases, he builds them by surprisingly simple and unexpected devices, in which movement usually occurs on two planes. Thus as Wenk pursues Mabuse's car in part one, the doctor's auto goes under a railroad bridge and to the right. Almost simultaneously (and this is an optical effect, confirming that Lang did it quite deliberately) the wheels of a train are seen crossing the bridge going left. This is the kind of device that Lang was to use more and more; here of course it is not done by editing, but in *Metropolis* the same pace-building effect is created by a direct cut—from Klein-Rogge falling outward and down to the right of the frame (from the cathedral roof) to the crowd below surging forward from right to left of frame.

Lang himself claimed that his major interest in making *Mabuse* was that it enabled him to attack the shocking conditions of crime and perversion that were rampant in postwar Germany. It is true that none of Mabuse's victims are very sympathetic. Most of them are society parasites living empty, useless lives. Mabuse feeds on them like a wolf on a dying carcass, not from necessity but because playing with human destinies is the only exciting game left in a decadent world. For the most part, the socialites look and behave like debauched sleepwalkers, and even the virile Hull, ostensibly the hero in part one, stirs so little sympathy in Lang that he allows him to be killed off casually, in a long shot; his death has to be confirmed by a later subtitle. A sign of the times perhaps is that here Mabuse is contemptuous of modern art and expressionism, considering them merely time-killers for the rich; later Lang villains were often presented as decadent partially *because* they had become collectors of modern art. But the sociological content of *Dr. Mabuse* plays a distinct second fiddle to the melodrama. Lang claims that he wasn't "allowed" to make the film the way he wanted, but one wonders. In all of the films where he had a message, alleged or actual—*Metropolis, Fury* (1936), *You Only Live Once* (1937)—one has the feeling that he really doesn't give a fig for social comment, and that he's much happier playing around with his lights and cameras on macabre scenes of suspense and thrill. For all of the implied degeneracy in *Mabuse* (the very first title refers to drug addiction, and there's a delightful all-purpose club where different code-words can produce a variety of vices), the impression is not so much of a debauched Germany in the 1920's as of a vintage Robert Louis Stevenson or Bram Stoker novel somehow brought up to date with automobiles and night clubs. Sometimes indeed one forgets entirely that this is a modern story, and it is quite a shock to see an automobile emerging from the shadows. It must have seemed even less contemporary in 1922, when the real thing surrounded it on all sides. The new musical score added to some recent prints of the film helps to re-establish period with some very authentic German jazz of the Twenties, and a great deal of Kurt Weill flavoring.

More so than in *Spione* and the later Mabuse films, Mabuse is here really the "hero" in the sense that the parallel villain Fu-Manchu was the hero of the Sax Rohmer novels. Rudolph Klein-Rogge, Lang's favorite villain, was a kind of composite of Boris Karloff and Lon Chaney. Oddly enough, he was also the first husband of scenarist Thea von Harbou, who later became Mrs. Lang. His marvelous face, handsome and sinister at the same time, is here used to excellent effect in some first-rate disguises which—rare in this kind of film—convince and work so well that the audience doesn't always realise right away that it is Klein-Rogge beneath it all. (Mabuse spends so much time donning disguises and being in the right place at precisely the right time that one wonders where he ever found the time to run the rest of his huge operation.)

Perhaps because of the influence of the original novel, far more emphasis is placed in the first *Mabuse* on the personal titanic struggle between the doctor and the rather humorless but dogged policeman, Wenk. The hero of *Spione* was a carefree James Bond blueprint; Inspector Lohmann from *M* (1931) and *Das Testament des Dr. Mabuse* a more human but not very active opponent. Wenk in the present film assumes the Sherlock Holmes or Nayland Smith role, and is far more dedicated personally and more involved in the proceedings. Mabuse too, like Moriarty, leaves less to his organisation and takes up the fight in person. His aims are less ambitious than in his later films, but his motivations are more clearly spelled out, and he emerges as a more human (and thereby slightly less menacing) opponent because of it. Sometimes he is even human enough to give way to rage and frustration, something that the later master criminals were always too self-assured to do. Mabuse has his vast organisation, his band of blind counterfeiters, his autos fixed up with gas chambers, and a laboratory full of snakes, but it is his own dynamic personality that holds his empire together, and after his total triumph in part one it is rather sad to see him brought to heel in part two.

Curiously, although part two has more basic action than part one—the hypnotic drive to the quarry, the gun battle and round-up, Mabuse's impressionistic descent into madness—it is slower-paced and generally a little less stylistic than part one. It is as though Lang had spent part one in establishing Mabuse, and had used all the serial-like twists to that end. In part two, he seems more concerned with telling and concluding his story in a wholly serious vein. But be assured that the second part is mildly disappointing only in relation to part one. On its own it is still an exciting and absorbing work.

Lang never intended that the film be shown complete in one sitting: his original German audience saw the first half one week and the second a week later, after the manner of serials. Some sort of intermission is necessary when the film is run entirely in one evening. Even if the spectators settle for brushing away the cobwebs in the fresh air in lieu of stronger stimulants, they'll enjoy part two the more for it.

II. Roland West

One of the great silent pictorialist directors, Roland West—whose name usually meant more to the box office than those of his stars—is all but forgotten today. None of his great silent films are known to have survived, and while his three talkies do exist, only the last of them, *Corsair,* is currently available. His career came to a sudden end in the early Thirties when he was suspected of the never-solved murder of Thelma Todd, his leading lady in *Corsair.*

CORSAIR (Roland West Productions-United Artists, 1931). Produced and directed by Roland West. Screenplay by Roland West and Josephine Lovett, from the novel by Walton Green. Camera: Ray June. Music: Alfred Newman. Players: Chester Morris, Alison Lloyd (Thelma Todd), Fred Kohler, Ned Sparks, Frank McHugh, Mayo Methot, Frank Rice, Emmett Corrigan, Gay Seabrook, Al Hill, Addie McPhail, William Austin.

The third of West's trio of films starring Chester Morris (*Alibi* and *The Bat Whispers* preceded it), *Corsair* doesn't make it easy on its audience. As in all of West's films, the development is far from straightforward and the motivation far from simple. Many of the movie's strongest plot elements are not present at all in the original novel, a fairly routine bootlegging yarn written by Walton Green, a prohibition inspector. At a time when so many talkies were just talkies, *Corsair* is all movie, with a reliance on the same technique that distinguished all of West's pictures: stylish pictorial elegance, dramatic lighting and closeups, superbly smooth moving camera shots, use of shadows and silhouettes, and often stylised, deliberately unrealistic sets, plus some lovely night exteriors. (How many times did they have to take that lighthouse shot to get the gull flying past at just the right moment?) Considered old-hat and passé at the time, this pictorial virtuosity gives the film a staying power quite missing from the average stagy and prosaic crime film of the early Thirties. As part of that crime cycle, *Corsair* has something in common with *The Finger Points* and *Night Nurse* in its casual acceptance of crime and total lack of any kind of "moral compensation"; for crime definitely does pay here, and even murder goes unpunished.

III. Alfred Hitchcock

The classic Hitchcock situation is that of nice, normal young people caught up in nightmarish adventures played out against everyday backgrounds, with the villains often perfectly likeable and even civilised. As long as the spell is maintained for the duration of the film, Hitchcock doesn't concern himself with logic or plausibility. The effectiveness of his thrillers depends not so much on credibility or realism as upon the full utilisation of all the tools of cinema—sound, color, editing, camerawork, writing, and only lastly upon actors, for whom he has always had a kind of genial contempt. Even his weakest films are meticulously constructed in advance and directed with superb visual flair. He is simply one of the most valuable directors the cinema has yet seen.

> NUMBER 17 (British International Pictures, 1932). Directed by Alfred Hitchcock. Executive producer: John Maxwell. Scenario by Alma Reville, Alfred Hitchcock and Rodney Ackland, from the novel by J. Jefferson Farjeon and the play as produced by Leon M. Lion. Camera: John Cox and Bryan Langley. Assistant director: Frank Mills. Music by A. Hallis. Edited (picture and sound) by A. C. Hammond. Players: John Stuart, Leon M. Lion, Anne Grey, Donald Calthrop, Garry Marsh, Barry Jones, Ann Casson, Henry Caine.

Hitchcock has always repudiated *Number 17* as being totally unimportant, and has bracketed it together with *Jamaica Inn* (1939) as a film he never wanted included in Hitchcock retrospectives—although the stricture was academic, since until recently the film wouldn't have been available anyway. In a way, it's easy to see why today Hitchcock repudiates it, just as Lang repudiates some of his best work. It's all style and no content, and certainly has nothing to "say." Everything is admittedly on the surface; but what a wonderful surface it is, especially if one exercises a little patience in the admittedly too measured first half. The last of Hitchcock's B.I.P. melodramas—only *Waltzes from Vienna* (1933) stood between it and *The Man Who Knew Too Much* (1934) and the start of his great Gaumont period—*Number 17* is admittedly a shoestring production, with budget seriously curtail-ed. And if *The Man Who Knew Too Much* seems a spectacular stride forward over a mere two-year period, it is not least because of the much greater freedom in casting, locations, etc. that its more liberal budget made possible. But *Number 17*, even as is, is a remarkable discovery, and not only a vigorous and imaginative lit-tle film, but one which, even this early in Hitchcock's career, is already a kind of spoof of his own speciality.

Most of the Hitchcockian trademarks are here: the mixing of melodrama with urbane comedy, ultra-civilised villains, a smatter-ing of piquant sex (the two leading ladies are regularly and thor-oughly searched), even such standard Hitchcockian situations as the hero and heroine shackled together. The opening is typical of Hitchcock's contempt for logic if it serves no purpose. It's a mar-vellously stylistic opening—howling wind, a hat blown away, feet running after it, hat and owner coming to rest outside a mysteri-ous mansion, and curiosity drawing the man inside. Within a few moments, and with no time wasted, the plot is under way, visually and excitingly. What matter if, five reels later, we find out that he was going to the house anyway?

Based on a dull and unreadable novel by Jefferson Farjeon, the film is immediately transposed into a fascinating exercise in style. Its first half, all mood and shadows and suspense, shows just how much Hitchcock had learned from his association with the German film: moving camerawork, distorted shadows, bizarre lighting, and photographic composition which turns even the com-monplace into the nightmarish. When a trapdoor is lifted, steam from a railway train below floats menacingly upwards; a simple flight of stone steps, so lit that one sees neither top nor bottom, suggests that Hitchcock remembered and improved on one of the atmospheric crypt sets in Tod Browning's film of *Dracula* (1931). It is as well that there is so much photographic elegance to dwell upon, for the mystery element in the earlier portions of the film just isn't strong enough to hold an audience's attention on its own. Then, in the middle portions, it comes to life with some fast-paced serial-like melodrama, and then launches itself into one of Hitchcock's very best and most exciting chase climaxes. Climax is perhaps too tame a word, since it takes the last third of the picture—and incidentally is a sequence not present in the original novel at all. The chase, between a motor coach and a train, builds beautifully, tacks on a spectacular wreck as an unexpected bonus, and is splendidly edited. Admittedly it makes generous use of table-top and miniature work, and goes far beyond the use of miniatures as mere cutaways or establishing scenes as Hitchcock used them in *The Secret Agent* (1936) and *The Lady Vanishes* (1938). Here some of the most impressive scenes involve the prolonged use of miniatures, incredibly photographed in long sweeping tracking shots and with extremely complicated camera movements, all intercut most effectively with the lifesize vehicles. One wonders what ever happened to these elaborate miniature sets and trains, and what lucky studio executive's son inherited them.

If there is a major flaw in *Number 17*, it is the excessive footage given to the cockney comedy relief, Leon M. Lion, who also gets top billing in the cast. Not that he has any long comedy setpieces; it's just that he seems in the way all the time, and his cockney dialect is sometimes quite hard to decode, given the rather harsh sound recording of the day. The explanation is that Lion was not only an actor but a notable theatrical impresario of the day, and had money and a production hand in this film. He had produced *Number 17* on stage, and in 1932 had taken over the Garrick Theatre in London, where he had a considerable success in presenting a series of John Galsworthy plays, headed by *Escape* and *Justice*. So presumably one must give him credit for being a more creative gentleman than his work in this film might suggest.

Apart from the measured pacing in the earlier portions, *Number 17* doesn't really date, and in fact it is often surprisingly slick technically. It's rare to find such an effectively atmospheric musical score in an early British talkie; and there is one splitscreen effect, in which the wheels of an authentic train are linked with studio-shot footage of the villains clambering over the train's top, that is so good it passes almost unnoticed. *Number 17* is by no means a masterpiece, but it's certainly much more than an academic milestone in Hitchcock's career, and, however many signposts it may have to his later work, it remains a thoroughly entertaining thriller in its own right.

IV. Michael Curtiz

Michael Curtiz' career (initially as an actor-director) began in the Scandinavian cinema prior to World War I and continued without pause until his death in 1962. Yet, probably because he amiably and expertly turned out such an astonishing variety of work in the Thirties and Forties, he is regarded primarily as just a Warner workhorse of a director, with everyone applauding his showmanship and expertise but no one thinking to take him seriously. Curtiz switched effortlessly from comedy to spectacle, from heavy drama to horror film, applying an appropriate style—particularly the style of the right camerawork and lighting—to whatever film he was making, without borrowing that style from another director. He was too good a showman to sneer at the obvious and yet too good a craftsman to use the obvious lazily. His long string of films testifies to his always solid and often very creative craftsmanship; it's high time that they—and he—were recognized for what they were.

> THE KENNEL MURDER CASE (Warner Brothers, 1933). Directed by Michael Curtiz. Screenplay by Peter Milne and Robert N. Lee, from the novel by S. S. Van Dine. Camera: William Reese. Players: William Powell, Mary Astor, Eugene Pallette, Ralph Morgan, Helen Vinson, Jack La Rue, Robert McWade, Frank Conroy, Paul Cavanagh, Robert Barrat, Arthur Hohl, Henry O'Neill, Etienne Girardot, Spencer Charters, Charles Wilson, James Lee, Wade Boteler, George Chandler, Milt Kibbee, James Burke, Leo White, Paul Panzer.

The Kennel Murder Case, the fifth film to be based on a Philo Vance novel, is one of the very best films of its genre, and William Powell, flawlessly cast as Vance, was by far the most satisfactory of the ten players who took on the role between 1929 and 1947. The beauty of the film is that it succeeds despite the limitations of its breed, and without really departing from a formula which was then popular but which would today date the film very badly were it not for its superb style. Van Dine's novel is beautifully constructed, and unlike many movie adaptations, this one follows its parent novel to the letter. Although the film is inevitably talkative, it manages to avoid the static, ponderous quality which had marked the earlier films of *The Canary Murder Case* and *The Greene Murder Case* (because of their undue length) and which was to mark many later Vance films (because of their lack of imagination). From its impressive opening titles, *The Kennel Murder Case* has real zip and pace. Potentially slow scenes are broken up via camera movement, interesting lighting, and a stress on low angles which seem to put the audience in the position of being an eavesdropper. There are some unusually good miniatures of the adjoining houses which figure so prominently in the action, and Curtiz frequently resorts to swish-pans to keep the tempo lively. The foreground dialogue is suave, polished and informative, as it should be in these mystery circles, while the background dialogue, all but thrown away, is both naturalistic and crackling. The first reel, with its marvelous collection of suspects, positively works overtime in setting up motives for the murder, since the victim-to-be never seems to open his mouth unless it is to renege on a deal, issue a racial insult (the Chinese have quite a rough time of it in this picture), or befoul the path of young love. If the identity of the murderer is all too obvious even before the killing has taken place, it's only because the man with his position, besides being the least likely suspect, has almost never failed to be revealed as the guilty party in the last reel of this type of film. However, in 1933 his perfidy was less well known, so this hardly constitutes a weakness of the picture, which has not only an unusually intriguing mystery but a logical and well-arrived-at solution too. Typical of the upper-crust mystery tales in which everybody lives in mansions but modestly calls them houses, *The Kennel Murder Case* should delight whodunit aficionados, and entertain anybody who likes a good well-turned-out movie.

V.   Edgar Ulmer

Early in his directorial career Ulmer made one fine film, *The Black Cat,* then worked for a while in the Yiddish cinema, then in the Forties turned out a string of low-budget films for Producers Releasing Corporation, concealing the cheap sets with atmospheric lighting. For his PRC output certain French critics have heaped accolades upon him; but, as much as I love *The Black Cat,* it is very difficult indeed to share—let alone understand—the enthusiasm of the French for Ulmer's work as a whole, or to avoid the conclusion that Ulmer was strictly a one-picture director. But what a splendid film his one masterpiece is!

> THE BLACK CAT (Universal, 1934). Directed by Edgar G. Ulmer. Screenplay by Peter Ruric and Edgar G. Ulmer suggested by Edgar Allan Poe's short story. Camera: John Mescall. Producer: E. M. Asher. Players: Boris Karloff, Bela Lugosi, David Manners, Jacqueline Wells (Julie Bishop), Lucille Lund, Egon Brecher, Anna Duncan, Albert Conti, Henry Armetta, André Cheron, Harry Cording, George Davis, Alphonse Martell, Tony Marlow, Paul Weigel, Albert Polet, Rodney Hildebrant, Paul Panzer, John Carradine.

The first of three bona fide Karloff-Lugosi co-starring vehicles (they often appeared together later, but never in such showcase films, and usually with Lugosi in a lesser role), *The Black Cat* was easily the best, and the only one of the trio in which both stars had equal opportunities. Although allegedly based on the Poe story, the film has no relationship to it whatsoever, drawing its inspiration far more (as did several other horror films) from the career and personality of the notorious satanist Aleister Crowley. However, its mood and its oppressive, claustrophobic and generally unhealthy atmosphere do evoke a very definite Poe feeling. The film is slow and stately, its macabre story of devil worship imbued with a sense of death and decay which is furthered by some extremely literate and well-delivered dialogue. In a way, it may be considered one of the most successful attempts to transfer Poe to the screen, even though it transfers a mood and not a plot.

Karloff's performance in *The Black Cat* is one of his finest; he clearly respects the film and his role, and gives his best to both. With his black costume, Satanic haircut, and beautifully modulated and accented lines, his Hjalmar Poelzig is a marvelous incarnation of evil for its own sake. And Lugosi too—never as good an actor as Karloff, but capable of extremely good things at times— rises to the occasion with one of his best performances, as the vengeful Dr. Verdegast. It is Karloff's and Lugosi's show all the way, and supporting players matter but little. Henry Armetta's comedy bit is unnecessary but brief, and David Manners is a typically useless hero, but there are some interestingly depraved faces among the devil-worshippers.

The modernistic sets, the striking quality of eroticism, the lighting and the slow gliding camerawork of John Mescall are all helped in their creation of mood by a quite brilliant musical score that draws heavily on the classics (as did so many early horror scores), and particularly on an imaginatively orchestrated arrangement of Liszt's B Minor Piano Sonata and Schumann's Quintet in E Flat Major, Op. 44—with a few chunks of Tchaikovsky here and there. Incidentally, the story-line is both a sadistically "sick" and a complicated one. Unless I have the family trees mixed up, Karloff, who marries both Lugosi's wife and his daughter, winds up as Bela's father-in-law. Thus Lugosi's ultimate revenge is not only medically drastic but also paternally tactless to say the least.

Since *The Black Cat* runs a mere 65 minutes, I suppose it is technically a "B" film, although quality rather than length was always the deciding factor in a film's billing status in the early Thirties. What a pity that it is no longer possible, in view of the current economic structure of the business, to make such short and thoroughly stylish films today. All in all, *The Black Cat* is almost certainly the best film of that interesting but over-rated director, Edgar Ulmer.

VI. Rowland V. Lee

Rowland V. Lee is one of the most curious and unjustly ignored of all film directors. He has perhaps only one really great film to his credit—the lovely and long unseen *Zoo in Budapest*— but he has made a large number of incredibly varied and tremendously interesting lesser films.

Lee had a useful knack of endowing cheap pictures with apparent production value. He also had unquestioned versatility, turning out with ease anything from horror films and comedies to swashbucklers and melodramas. Perhaps because he tackled anything and everything, he never developed much personal style, unless it be a recognisable "penny dreadful" and overly gory approach to subjects of seemingly greater stature. There always seemed something just a little shoddy and lurid about Lee's melodramas. He certainly isn't one of the great unsung masters of the cinema; but he is a good deal more interesting than many of his far more highly acclaimed confreres.

> LOVE FROM A STRANGER (United Artists, 1937). Directed by Rowland V. Lee. Screenplay by Frances Marion, from the play by Frank Vosper and the story ("Philomel Cottage") by Agatha Christie. Associate producer: Harry Eddington. Music: Benjamin Britten. Camera: Philip Tannura. Players: Basil Rathbone, Ann Harding, Binnie Hale, Bruce Seton, Jean Cadell, Bryan Powely, Joan Hickson, Donald Calthrop, Eugene Leahy.

Lee made four films with Basil Rathbone, and the two made almost as felicitous a team as John Ford and John Wayne. Lee was especially adept not only at controlling Rathbone's tendency to overact but also, as in this film, at exploiting that tendency for scenes of nervous hysteria. *Love from a Stranger* is one of the best of that select theatrical group of wife-terrorised-by-husband thrillers of which *Gaslight* is in a sense the prototype, even though not the first. Based on a play by Frank Vosper (who enacted the lead on the London stage, and himself disappeared mysteriously aboard ship, a presumed murder victim or suicide), the film is by now basically familiar stuff, but is so tautly done and splendidly acted by its two stars that it maintains suspense still. Perhaps because Ann Harding isn't the mousy little wife type, the battle of wills between wife and husband gains considerably in dramatic value. Rathbone too is exactly right all the way: debonair and charming at first, then suddenly and shockingly insane when one least expects it. There isn't too great an attempt to hide the movie's stage origin, but the film moves constantly, and at key moments there are bizarre camera angles which may be theatrical in themselves but which work well in emphasizing the tension and hysteria. Altogether, for a stage adaptation made in England at a singularly dull period, *Love from a Stranger* holds its own surprisingly well today, and hasn't dated a whit.

MORE ON AUTHOR AND SUBJECT

William K. Everson was born in England in 1929 and has been associated with various aspects of cinema since 1944. He came to the United States in 1950, worked as foreign publicity manager for Allied Artists, then left the business side of films to concentrate on film history. He has taught at New York University and The New School for Social Research, and is president of the Theodore Huff Memorial Film Society. His books include The Western *(with George Fenin; Orion Press, 1962),* The Films of Laurel & Hardy *(Citadel Press, 1967), and* The Art of W. C. Fields *(Bobbs-Merrill, 1967).*

A bibliography of the writings on the crime film is long overdue, and regretfully there is no place for it here; but devotees should keep a sharp eye out for Mr. Everson's A Pictorial History of the Detective Film, *to be published by The Citadel Press.*

PART II.

TAXONOMY

†If there is a purely American subgenre within the overall category of crime fiction, it is the hard-boiled story that we associate with Hammett and Chandler. Prof. Durham's survey of this whole school of "tough guy" writing is a magnificent piece of historical and critical analysis, well calculated to drive one into the stacks of moldering old pulps in the nearest secondhand bookstore.

The Black Mask School
by Philip Durham

When Henry L. Mencken and George Jean Nathan began publishing, in the early spring of 1920, the *Black Mask*—one of their three pulp magazines—they could not have known that they were creating a medium which became a vehicle for the "hard-boiled" writers, those writers whose heroes acted as rugged individualists while they brought justice to the deserving. The heroes were violent, but their violence was not merely that of sensationalism. It was rather a kind of meaningful violence, sometimes symbolic of a special ethical code or attitude, sometimes an explicit description and implicit criticism of a corrupt society. Thus, in one of America's unique magazines, the *Black Mask* School was created.

The early *Black Mask*, featuring "mystery, detective, adventure, western, horror, and novelty," was patterned along the lines of such first rate pulps as *Argosy*, but the original contributors rarely measured up to the stature of those writers found in the better-known *Argosy*. In those days, however, pulps were money makers, and editors Mencken and Nathan sold *Black Mask* after six months for a nice profit. Under the subsequent editorship of such capable men as Phil Cody and Harry North, *Black Mask* began to take on a specific character, and within two or three years a version of the heroic knight emerged; the Private Investigator was poised and indestructably ready to clean up the cesspools of crime in New York City.

The two heroes who played a major role in the development of *Black Mask* were Race Williams and the Continental Op in tales by Carroll John Daly and Dashiell Hammett. In November 1926, the *Black Mask* acquired a new editor, Captain Joseph T. Shaw, who during a full decade molded the magazine into a medium which made a unique contribution to American literature. Characteristics of daring, courage, egotism, artistry, and appealing personality combined to place the new editor in a position where his stable of writers began to look to his approval as a panegyric.

A descendant of Roger Shaw, one of the New England immigrants of the 1630's, Joseph Shaw graduated from Bowdoin College, where he specialized in athletics, and then went to work for the American Woolen Company. When he published *From Wool to Cloth* (1904), Shaw was destined to become a literary man. His next work, *Spain of To-day; A Narrative Guide to the Country of the Dons, with Suggestions for Travellers* (1909), indicated broader interests. In the meantime he had begun to specialize in the handling of the sword, eventually winning the national championship in sabers and the president's medal for the championship in all three weapons, foil, epée, and saber. After World War I the captain stayed in Europe to serve for five years with the Hoover mission in Czechoslovakia, completing the experiences he was to find useful for an editorial and literary career. That Joe Shaw had writing ambitions can be inferred from his numerous short stories and half dozen novels in the field of mystery, detection, and adventure. It was not in fiction, however, that his talent lay. His novel *Danger Ahead,* for example, begins with the hero executing "graceful motions" with the saber; but the story is a stilted Jamesian imitation without grace or style. Cap Shaw was an editor, as his magazine and many of its contributors will testify.

From the vantage point, of twenty years, Shaw looked back, in 1946, to the time when he first came to *Black Mask.* He had meditated then, he later wrote, on the possibility of creating a new type of detective story, different from the one established by Poe in 1841 and so consistently followed right down to the 1920's: the tale of ratiocination, of clues, of puzzles, the locked closet had-I-but-known sort of thing. In the pages of the *Black Mask* he singled out the stories of Dashiell Hammett as approximating what he had in mind: "simplicity for the sake of clarity, plausibility, and belief." Shaw wanted action, but he "held that action is meaningless unless it involves recognizable human character in three-dimensional form." With the work of Hammett as the model, the editor began to search for the stories of those men who wrote in a similar vein; the July 1927 issue carried the statement "We are constantly looking for new writers who have the *Black Mask* spirit and the *Black Mask* idea of what a short story should be." The result became known as the Hard-Boiled School or the *Black Mask* School of Detective Fiction, with such chief practitioners as Dashiell Hammett, Raymond Chandler, Raoul Whitfield, Paul Cain, Lester Dent. The characters which the writers created were, admitted Shaw, hard-boiled, but the authors' "style and treatment were something else again." Modern critics identify the style and treatment as objective realism. Shaw was explicit in pointing out that his writers observed a cardinal principle—"in creating the illusion of reality"—by allowing their characters to act and talk tough rather than by making them do it. Instead of telling the reader how infallible the actors were, the authors allowed their heroes to demonstrate their abilities. By achieving ever greater restraint and by carefully avoiding incredibility, the *Black Mask* boys, thought Shaw, "wrote convincingly."

Eventually the cover of the *Black Mask* dropped such previously used terms as mystery, adventure, western, horror, and novelty; and over the objections of some of the authors but with the approval of many, the magazine retained only one exciting challenge—SMASHING DETECTIVE STORIES.

Those writers who did not agree with the literary theories of Shaw drifted away, or at least their stories did, to other pulp magazines. Some of those who remained, however, confused him with George Bernard. One of the latter was Lester Dent, who after thirty-five years of publishing fiction still thought Shaw the "finest coachwhip I ever met in an editor's chair." Cap convinced his boys that they were not pulp hacks, but rather he inspired them to believe in themselves as writers with great futures. *Black Mask* in Cap Shaw's hands, said Dent, "was akin to a writer's shrine." That was in the twenties and thirties, that "brief and wonderful time when American literature was endowed with the most effective training ground in all history—the pulp magazine." The writers whom Shaw published, continued Dent, "were sort of automatically endowed with a hair shirt that they wore with pride and some dubiousness, because where writers got together you were pointed out as a *Black Mask* man; not a *Post* writer, a *Colliers* writer, or *Doc Savage* writer, but a *Black Mask* writer."

Joseph Shaw gave dignity to *Black Mask* magazine by his constant reference to it as "the book." He refused, also, ever to use the word "pulp." One wrote either for his "rough paper book" or for a "smooth paper" magazine. There was a difference. Raymond Chandler once wrote a story, "I'll Be Waiting," for the *Saturday Evening Post* and was sorry about it until his death twenty years later because in the smooth paper attempt he felt he had given in to slickness. It was Chandler's work, incidentally, which Shaw frequently used as a model to illustrate what could be done with style. A writer sitting across the desk from the editor would suddenly find in one hand a paragraph from Chandler and in the other a blue pencil and the Captain would be saying, "Would you cut that somewhere. Just cut a few words." The idea, of course, was that there was no wordage fat. One could not cut. Every word had to be there.

When Shaw became the editor of *Black Mask* it contained, as Erle Stanley Gardner has pointed out, a type and a style. The type was well known through the stories of Daly, but it was left to Hammett to combine the type and style. Short on style though Daly was, one would have a difficult time finding a more effective hard-boiled hero than was his Race Williams, whom the readers did not examine but merely swallowed in great quantities. One of the earliest, latest, and most prolific of the *Black Mask* contributors, Daly turned out Race Williams stories and novels by the score. According to Gardner, editor Harry North once said that when he put Race Williams on the cover, the *Black Mask* sales jumped fifteen per cent.

In both the June, 1923, and April, 1927, issues of *Black Mask* the editors reported interviews with contributor Carroll John Daly, an assured and somewhat flippant writer, who described his hero, Race Williams, as thirty, five feet eleven and one half inches, one hundred eighty-three pounds, with dark brown hair and black eyes. There was nothing "soft-boiled" about the man who admired a clever woman and respected a good one—"when he finds her." He was a Private Investigator, in the business for thrills and money. Here was the original hard-boiled detective, the private eye who, during the next forty years, moved in fiction across the country—from New York to Chicago to San Francisco to Los Angeles. At times he changed into the clothes of a police detective, newspaper man, camera man, undercover man for the Racing Commission, insurance investigator, good-guy gambler, or just plain knight, but he was always, essentially, the same hard-boiled hero. Some of these men were more attractive than Race Williams, although they were like him: indestructible, fearless, courageous; he was violent, often brutal, a dead-shot, killing when he thought it necessary; he was a celibate admired by women and feared by men; he had his own sense of right and wrong by which he lived, meting out his individual concept of justice that more often than not was contrary to the accepted mores or to the law, which was restrictive and too slow. With supreme confidence in his own judgment, this individualist did not think it necessary to play by the book—one who did was often thought naive. In addition to what he said and did, he frequently administered justice by what he did not do: letting a murderer go free if he exhibited an extra measure of guts, or allowing a girl—who had just put a bullet from a small Colt automatic through a two-timing skunk— to escape because she had been victimized, had a good heart, and meant well. The private eye was always on the side of right, but it was his own personal interpretation and definition of "right."

In "Knights of the Open Palm" Race Williams, always the first person narrator, stated his position: "I'm what you might call the middle-man—just a halfway house between the dicks and the crooks. . .But my conscience is clear; I never bumped off a guy who didn't need it." This credo was elaborated on throughout his heroic career. In *The Snarl of the Beast,* for example, Race restated his position, adding that "right and wrong are not written on the statutes for me, nor do I find my code of morals in the essays of long-winded professors. My ethics are my own. I'm not saying they're good and I'm not admitting they're bad, and what's more I'm not interested in the opinions of others on that subject." Williams, in "The Amateur Murderer," promised readers that if anything happened to the girl he would "pop" off the offender, and he followed the assurance with his philosophy: "Not good ethics? Not right thinking? Maybe not. We won't go into that." The fact that he was on the side of right in the spirit of individualism justified almost any act. As he threw terror into all evil-thinking men, Williams' reputation became a symbol which allowed his problems to remain comparatively simple as long as he followed his slogan: "I trusted myself. That was what counted."

Opinions on patriotism, nativism, altruism, communism, and politics were all within the scope of Carroll John Daly. With an eye to public sentiment in the 1920's, Daly had Williams speak on the uselessness of senators, from whom one gets nothing at all. A congressman was a little better, for one can at least get garden seeds from him. When in *The Third Murderer* Florence Drummond—The Flame, the good girl with the criminal mind—complained to Race of the state of society by saying "Honesty—the one thing that the rich leave for the poor to fatten on," Race replied, "You didn't bring me here to fill me up on Communism." "No," Flame said, "Communism is a hatred of the poor for the rich—not simply an envy." Appealing to Williams as a "staunch citizen" was the wrong approach, for he did his work only at the right price. Like the big shoe manufacturer and Henry Ford and John D. Rockefeller, with Race Williams it was a business. They did not give away shoes, cars, or oil, but they gave generously to charity. Foreigners from all of Asia and most of Europe were villains per se, and because they were so frequently arch criminals they made excellent antagonists for Race. He favored patriotic Americans, born and raised, unlike Count Jehdo, on American soil. Yet in "Murder Book" when Race acquired the document which might have saved our country and prevented a war, he returned it for the life of The Flame who was being tortured after having been caught acting as an agent of the government. Williams' personal sense of justice, integrity, and loyalty came first.

Daly was not one to miss the value of "reckless courage" even in the villains; he could say admiringly of Mark Yarrow—the number two bad man of "Murder Book"—"He passed out tough." And there was Purdy Young in *Tainted Power* who represented the "new school" of racketeering because he wore a hundred and fifty dollar gray business suit instead of a sweater and cap—"Purdy Young had guts." Daly saved his unstinted praise, however, for the show of guts in the good guys, including one cop: "Good old Sergeant O'Rourke. He had the guts to live no matter what the consequences." The guttiest of them all was, of course, Race Williams himself, admirably summed up by The Flame.

> "You made use of just what you always
> make use of. It's not your head; it's the ani-
> mal in you. The courage in you; the thing that
> drives you on. You're licked—licked a dozen
> times, over and over. Everybody knows it but

you! No, it's not your head."
"If it isn't my head, what is it?"
"Just guts, I guess," she said. "Just guts."

Clichés and sloppy writing characterized Daly's work. He was a "he don't" writer who had Williams say, "I shoved a butt into my face, gave it heat." Williams identified a bad guy on a foggy, dark night by his bloodshot eyes and yellow teeth. Daly employed brutal death in the tough manner: "Joe Gorgon jumped sort of in the air, half spun, fired wildly, and I laid my next bullet smack between his eyes. Just a little round hole, ever growing larger. Joe Gorgon waved his hands once. His right foot came slowly up, like a lad in the slow motion pictures. Then he pitched forward on his face." Some of his most extravagant prose Daly saved for Williams in "I'll Tell the World": "Both my guns had spoken—both roared out their message of death—and, so help me God, but a single hole appeared in Lutz's forehead. I've done a deal of shooting in my day—mighty fine shooting, but never anything like that." Mr. Daly had been reading Dime Novels.

Carroll John Daly was a careless writer and a muddy thinker who created the hard-boiled detective, the prototype for numberless writers to follow. Race Williams was a popular literary hero in the 1920's and 1930's, but no different from the rugged individualists of any other decade who could say with Race,

> "I'm a man of action but I can think occasionally."
> "I'm sorry if I appear hard boiled or cold blooded. . .but them that live by the gun should die by the gun."
> "I'm all for justice and fair play."

Within a few months after the stereotyped, single-minded Race Williams first appeared in *Black Mask,* a relatively complex hard-boiled hero began his career in the pages of "the book": The Continental Op, a far more imaginative character than Race Williams, was created by Dashiell Hammett, who became one of the most successful of all *Black Mask* contributors. After a varied career which included a period of several years with the Pinkerton Detective Agency, Hammett—who knew a man who once stole a Ferris-wheel—began to turn his experiences into stories. With an eye to style and literary effectiveness, he experimented with techniques. Although he was credited with being the leader of the hard-boiled school of detective fiction, and although his hero had the basic characteristics found in the traditionally tough hero, it is no good trying to make Hammett all of a piece; the idea is too simple and his writing is too subtle. The good writers of Hammett's group, as do good writers in any group, experimented with writing techniques in order to determine what was most useful and effective for their own individual expression. They worked with plot, trying to keep it from becoming too obviously stereotyped; they created a character in their developing short stories who would later stand up in longer works of fiction; they agreed on the theme of the rugged individualist righting the social wrongs; they tried both the first and third person to see which would make the style more objective; and they concentrated on their hard-boiled style, hoping to make it as action-packed as possible. Hammett did all of these things and a bit more. Although he may not have been the smoothest and most consistent stylist, throughout his decade of prolific writing, he changed viewpoint and modified his hero several different times in trying for maximum literary results.

Nicely written though it is, there is but little in such an early Hammett story as "The Green Elephant," which appeared in *The Smart Set* in 1923, to draw unusual attention to the writer. Joe Shupe, whose fault was "that he was an unskilled laborer in the world of crime, and therefore had to content himself with stealing whatever came to hand," was suddenly and accidentally the possessor of a quarter of a million stolen dollars. Unable to cope with so much money, Joe walked the streets, couldn't sleep nights, and changed hotels every day. Only after his suspicious actions caused him to be picked up and jailed by prohibition officers could Joe become "his normal self again, both physically and mentally."

There was no hero, let alone a hard-boiled one, in this story without even any tough writing, and tales of this kind did not bring for Hammett the acclaim he later received.

Dashiell Hammett soon, however, acquired a reputation, and among the many who eventually gave him unstinted praise for his writing ability, few were more succinct in expressing praise than Raymond Chandler. He realized that Hammett continually viewed violence as an act of human courage, and therefore admirable. Violence, according to Chandler, did not dismay the Hammett characters, "it was right down their street." Furthermore, Hammett was writing for "people with a sharp, aggressive attitude to life." It was in the matter of style, however, that Chandler was most critically aware. Hammett had a style, "but his audience didn't know it, because it was in a language not supposed to be capable of such refinements." The "style," which Chandler held did not belong to Hammett or to any particular individual because it is "the American language," could say things that Hammett did not know or feel the need of saying. Hammett "was spare, frugal, hard-boiled, but he did over and over again what only the best writers can ever do at all. He wrote scenes that seemed never to have been written before." The idea that style is the American language—discovered independently by several writers in the hard-boiled genre—is unquestionably one of the most significant aspects of the evolving hard-boiled tradition. Style, then, is where you find it: not restricted to the drawing room or study, but equally discoverable in the alleys. Stephen Crane went down into Rum Alley, and in *Maggie* produced a first-rate novel; but "tattered gamins" making a "furious assault" on their "antagonist," while they were "swearing in barbaric trebles," is neither alley style nor American style. Hammett went to the American alleys and came out with an authentic expression of the people who live in and by violence.

Although the early *Black Mask* story "House Dick" contained brutality and four killings, it was only a warm-up for what was to come in later works. The Continental Op did not figure in much of the violence, being rather just simply a thoughtful, fearless man, doing his job. As his creator had done before him, the Op carefully and thoroughly checked his evidence, for "from any crime to its author there is a trail. It may be—as in this case— obscure [but] finding and following such trails is what a detective is paid to do." There was in this story, however, early evidence of clipped prose, that which was to become a Hammett trademark: "Picked him up when he got his mail yesterday afternoon." "Got an apartment on Van Ness Avenue." "Packing a gun under his left arm." The statements imply—although the economy of expression purposely controls—action, violence, and excitement. Perhaps the most important contribution of an early *Black Mask* story such as this was the presentation of the nameless fat man with an age varying between thirty-five and forty (based, said Hammett later, on James Wright, Assistant Superintendent of Pinkerton's Baltimore Agency, under whom Hammett worked); the detective performed through dozens of Hammett's pieces for the Continental Detective Agency's San Francisco office. In these short stories Hammett developed his style and prepared his character, the Op, for the novels which were to come.

In "The Tenth Clue," at the beginning of 1924, the Op con- tinued his patient pursuit of evidence and details, but he threw in a little detection hint: "There are many, many murders with never a woman in them anywhere; but seldom a very conspicuous killing." An unusual Hammett story for these years appeared in the middle of January, unusual because of the setting and the switch to third person. In "The Man Who Killed Dan Odams" the Montana scene was vital, and the Odams woman and her son were like the determined, worn, brutal West of which they were a part. The people and the landscape were immeasurably strong, but the strongest of all was Silence. By the spring of 1924 in "Zigzags of Treachery" the Op was an efficient, dependable detective, but as yet not much given to heroics. He did not like eloquence because "if it isn't effective enough to pierce your hide, it's tiresome; and if it is effective enough then it muddles your thoughts." He was not "a brilliant thinker," yet he had "flashes of intelligence." He was a man of action, really, who liked his jobs to be "simply jobs—emotions are nuisances during business hours." Not yet legendary, he accounted for some of his feats after shooting a gun out of Jake Ledwich's hand: it "looks like a great stunt," the Op told the reader, "but it's a thing that happens now and then. A man who is a fair shot (and that is exactly what I am—no more, no less), naturally and automatically shoots pretty close to the spot upon which his eyes are focused." Unlike Race Williams, whose shooting was calculated to overshadow that of Davy Crockett, the Op simply maintained that when a man goes for his gun you shoot at *him* and if you are looking at his gun you might hit that; if you do, it looks impressive.

It was not long, however, before an accent on violence became pronounced in Hammett's stories, although at first the hero observed it with detachment and only later performed it with virtuous reflection. In "The Golden Horseshoe" the story started slowly with "thumbnail gouging into eye," and a head hanging "crookedly, dangling from a neck that had been cut clean through to the bone." The tempo stepped up when Gooseneck fired at Kewpie at the moment she threw a knife at him. Kewpie "spun back across the room—hammered back by the bullets that tore through her chest. Her back hit the wall. She pitched forward to the floor." Gooseneck was in similar trouble as he stopped shooting and tried to speak, while the haft of the girl's knife protruded from his throat. "He couldn't get his words past the blade. He dropped one gun and tried to take hold of the protruding haft. Halfway up to it his hand came, and dropped. He went down slowly—to his knees—rolled over on his side—and lay still." Hammett was beginning to succumb to the literary tricks used by writers trying to squeeze out the full value of violence but who resorted to artificial means for the effect. The knife in the throat, along with the ice pick in the chest, became a common device for increasing the intensity· of the narrative, restricting natural movement, and hindering speech. Although it was not dwelt upon with as much pleasure, it was hardly more ingenious than hand-stomping in the Western story.

The Continental Op soon became physically and personally involved in violence, getting smashed up thoroughly in "One Hour." It was not long, as in "Women, Politics and Murder," before he thought violence was sheer pleasure. "I began to throw my right fist into him. I liked that. His belly was flabby, and it got softer every time I hit it. I hit it often." And the mood continued in "Dead Yellow Women" where the Op observed Dummy Uhl, who with "all the middle of him gone—slid down to the floor and made more of a puddle than a pile there." As the Op continued down a hall, "cracking everything" that got in his way and being "cracked" back, he began to enjoy the violence which was technically accentuated by one sentence paragraphs.

> When he crouched above me I let him have it.
> My bullet cut the gullet out of him.
> I patted his face with my gun as he tumbled down past me.

The violence-is-fun technique which Hammett so thoroughly explored in his short stories of the middle 1920's was soon to reach its apex in his first novel.

In the meantime, however, Hammett had not forgotten the complete role his hero was playing in the tradition. In "The Gutting of Couffignal," for instance, the Op's intelligence was questioned because he refused to cut himself in on a big take. He stopped long enough to explain his role and concept of right and wrong: in addition to his honesty and sense of loyalty, he was a detective because he wanted to be one and because he liked the work. He knew he could make a great deal more money doing something else, but "liking work makes you want to do it as well as you can. Otherwise there'd be no sense to it." But being loyal to himself and his employer did not obviate his commenting on social situations. Couffignal was an island owned and ruled by "well-fed old gentlemen who, the profits they took from the world with both hands in their younger days now stowed away at

safer percentages, have bought into the island colony so they may
spend what is left of their lives nursing their livers and improving
their golf among their kind. They admit to the island only as
many storekeepers, working-people, and similar riffraff as are
needed to keep them comfortably served." Hammett had a social
conscience which Carroll John Daly never dreamed of.

The knightly role aspect of the hard-boiled or *Black Mask*
tradition was developed in "The Scorched Face," a story otherwise notable for its brutality and smashing tempo—both in content and style. The Op and Pat Reddy, a good young cop, moved
in to clean up one of the California "mystical" cults which
victimized naive, wealthy women. The cult operated by first
taking compromising photographs of its victims and then controlling the susceptible women through threat of blackmail.
Murder was done before the Op and Pat Reddy cleaned out the
cesspool. As a policeman Reddy was obligated to turn over the
murderer and all evidence, according to law; as an independent
detective the Op took a more liberal view, according to his conscience. Because of his obviously higher law, the Op was able to
persuade Reddy to cover the whole thing up, to destroy the evidence and let the murderer off—this prevented more suicides and
protected womankind.

That Hammett was continuing to explore among literary
techniques during the middle twenties can be inferred from
"Ruffian's Wife," in which he worked with third person narration—the viewpoint used in *The Maltese Falcon*—and in which he
introduced Leonidas Doucas, a fat man who suggested Casper
Gutman of *The Maltese Falcon*. Created also in "Ruffian's Wife"
was an unusual version of the tough guy. Guy Tharp was "hard-
boiled, hard-nerved, to whom violence was no more than addition
to a bookkeeper." But under the fat man's pressure, Tharp's
image dissolved into weakness; for his wife, the "red wolf of a
husband" became only an illusion, and all she had left was his
"callous brutality."

The individualistic attitude toward law was made specific in
"Corkscrew," wherein the Op, by going from San Francisco to the

Arizona desert town of Corkscrew, found himself in the nine-teenth-century West. Upon arrival, the Op was warned by the "better element"—which included Miss Janey, the false-toothed, sour-faced school teacher—against the violent element which in-cluded both the good and bad guys. The Op, who was not much of a rider, was tested by being given an unrideable horse. Prefer-ring, obviously, the violent element to the better element, the Op attempted to prove himself worthy of his chosen group by con-tinuing to mount the horse as long as his battered body could draw itself into the saddle. Having become accepted by his courageous display of guts, the Op was ready to enlist admirers. One of the most individualistic of these was Milk River, who was willing to work with the Op if he did not have to become a deputy; Milk River would not put himself in a position where, as he said, "I'll have to enforce no laws I don't like." In this "hard neighborhood" where the inhabitants were "hell-bent on proving to everybody that they're just as tough as the next one," the Op found himself a worthy antagonist and explained to the reader the joy of physical contact as he "smacked both hands into his body, and felt happy when the flesh folded softly around them." Not to be outdone, Milk River was "grinning" while he shot another contestant out of the saddle.

This was a different kind of philosophic attitude toward violent death from the one Stephen Crane had expressed a generation before in "The Blue Hotel." In Crane's story the Easterner explained to the cowboy how in every murder there are from a dozen to forty women involved, but in the death of the Swede only five men collaborated, including the poor gambler who wasn't even a noun, only an adverb. The cowboy cried out blindly and rebelliously against this "mysterious theory." There is no mysterious event to account for the violence in "Corkscrew;" Slim merely refused to pay for his meal at the Toad's eatery. Milk River summed it all up with his own brand of amoral humor: "Think of all them folks that were killed and maimed and jailed— all over a dollar and ten cents. It's a good thing Slim didn't eat five dollars' worth of grub. He'd of depopulated the State of

Arizona complete!" It was but a short jump from the wild West back across the street to the violence of the big city, and Dashiell Hammett's Continental Op was now finely trained for the biggest criminal affair the country had to offer.

In February and May of 1927 the *Black Mask* carried two of Hammett's long stories—"The Big Knock-Over" and "$106,000 Blood Money"—which together constituted in effect his first novel. One hundred and fifty of the country's finest crooks gathered together in San Francisco where they simultaneously knocked over The Seaman's National and The Golden Gate Trust. During the noisy affair sixteen cops were killed and three times that many wounded; twelve bystanders and bank clerks were killed; and the bandits lost seven dead and had thirty-one of their number taken as bleeding prisoners. In a case of this size it was decided that the Op could use some help in recovering the money, but two or three additional operatives from the agency sufficed. One was Dick Foley whose rule it was never to waste words. Another was Jack Counihan, "full of the don't-give-a-damn-gaiety that belonged to his youthfulness." And then there was the Continental Op at his cold-blooded best, deciding that the most effective way to get to the source and recover the money was to arrange for the hoods to eliminate each other. So within a few hours one house contained fourteen dead, the next six dead, and so on until the St. Valentine's Day Massacre which happened two years later back in Chicago began to look like a teenage tiff. The Op's part in the decimation of the hoods could be thought ethical only in his own eyes; the readers could accept his chicanery and double-cross only after accepting the role of the Op. Among other tricky moves, the Op befriended one of the hoods so he could later shoot him in the back, and at another point he arranged for one of his own operators to be shot. True, the operator had defected, but it was the Op who meted out the justice, with an additional motive of keeping clean the good name of the Continental Agency. Not since the days when eliminating inhuman Indians was a hero's duty had an individual's judgment caused the demise of so many.

If there is such a thing as a poetry of violence, Hammett

achieved it, technically at least, in this novel. At the height of a scene of smashing, slashing, and sudden death, the Op was having the time of his life. As he saw a mouthful of teeth smashed in, a blackjack crunch an arm, a side of a face blown away, the Op got with the rhythmical spirit of the occasion: "It was a swell bag of nails. Swing right, swing left, kick, swing right, swing left, kick. Don't hesitate, don't look for targets. God will see that there's always a mug there for your gun or blackjack to sock, a belly for your foot." Without any perspective shots, the author kept the reader on the scene, and by using diction appropriate to the characters, the narrator was not allowed, except physically, to achieve the superiority which would destroy the unity of effect. From this vantage point the Op delivered one of his most poetic lines: "I swayed and broke a nose where I should have smashed a skull."

Short stories of this period, late twenties, continued to show the Op's various roles as the traditional hero. In "The Main Death" he was a knightly hero who got the murderer and collected his fee for it, but he refused to divulge to his client the knowledge of an affair which would implicate his client's wife. In "Fly Paper" the Op was exclusively the hard-boiled hero, with Hammett working his prose for all the violent effects he could squeeze from it. He could use it tight: "Babe liked Sue. Vassos liked Sue. Sue liked Babe. Vassos didn't like that. Jealousy spoiled the Greek's judgment. He kept the speakeasy door locked one night when Babe wanted to come in. Babe came in, bringing pieces of the door with him. Vassos got his gun out. . .Babe hit him with the part of the door that had the brass knob on it. Babe and Sue went away from Vassos's together." Or Hammett could resort to the smashing paragraphs.

> "I shot his right knee.
> He lurched toward me.
> I shot his left knee.
> He tumbled down."

During the thirty-two months from November 1927 to June

1930, Hammett's four important novels were published serially in
Black Mask: Red Harvest, The Dain Curse, The Maltese Falcon,
and *The Glass Key.* They are critically regarded as his best work,
but they were successful only because he had previously worked
out everything in them in his short stories. The first two continued the Op as the first person narrator, although he changed character somewhat in the second; the third developed the swaggering
Samuel Spade, told in third person; and the fourth created a variation on the character in Ned Beaumont, also with the third person
viewpoint.

Red Harvest, originally a group of separate stories referred to
under the general title *The Cleansing of Poisonville,* revolved a-
round the Op still at his hard-boiled best, although he was much
more concerned with the problems of a collective society than he
had been in his first novel. The Op, completely hardened, played
everyone off against the middle, and by his own count totaled up
one and a half dozen murders. He admitted he could "swing the
play legally," but he decided that "it's easier to have them killed
off, easier and surer." Allowing himself no sexual diversion, the
Op went in only for heavy drinking, the latter presumably because
even he occasionally reacted to piled-up violence: "I've got a hard
skin all over what's left of my soul, and after twenty years of
messing around with crime I can look at any sort of a murder
without seeing anything in it but my bread and butter, the day's
work. But this getting a rear out of planning deaths is not natural
to me."

The slight crack in the Op's armor, barely discernible in *Red
Harvest,* broadened to measurable proportions in *The Dain Curse.*
He was still the efficient operator, but he had become humanized.
The double-crossing and double-dealing were gone. Murder was
still present, of course, but it was not the Op's doing; rather it was
engineered or performed by Owen Fitzstephan, a man with streaks
of insanity. The heavy drinking was cut down to just drinking,
and although other people had realistic sexual experiences the Op
still abstained. In his most humanitarian role so far, the Op began
a benevolent and knightly campaign to save the misused and bru-

tally treated Gabrielle who believed she was suffering from the Dain curse. She doubted her sanity, so the Op soothed her by saying that everyone except the very crazy and the stupid suspect themselves at times. She did not realize that it was her fears, her psychological maladjustment, and her dope habit that rendered her sexually ineffective. The Op consoled her by explaining that there were "a thousand women in San Francisco making the same complaint." As she gradually became convinced that her "differences" were held by other women, and that they could be cured or corrected, Gabrielle still doubted her ability to give up dope. But the Op also scoffed at that thought, saying, "You've been reading the Hearst papers." Well, Gabrielle was rehabilitated, but at what a price. Dashiell Hammett virtually traded a hard-boiled hero for a part-time sentimentalist, a character who could recognize in himself such emotions as might occasionally be acceptable in the traditional hard-boiled hero, but for Hammett it could mean only that his hero had grown old and soft. Long live the Op. He was ready for discard.

With his hero gone soft beyond redemption in *The Dain Curse,* Hammett created a new or at least variant version in *The Maltese Falcon.* Using the third person instead of the first, for a different viewpoint, the author presented Samuel Spade—several years younger than the Op, six inches taller, and looking "rather pleasantly like a blond Satan." Although definitely in the tradition, Spade was a cool hero who was a devil with the women but never called a spade a heart. As the character changed, in part, so did the style. Instead of allowing his hero to act, the author explained the action: "Spade flung his words out with a brutal sort of carelessness that gave them more weight than they could have got from dramatic emphasis or from loudness." This was not Hammett's style at its best, the writing was less objective and the situations too obviously simulated. Spade's role, however, was less impossible and therefore more believable; he was more as the average man romantically imagines himself—brave, heroic, exciting, and irresistible.

Ned Beaumont in *The Glass Key* was another variation of the hero, not a detective but a right-hand man to a big-time racketeer and politician. Perhaps more than any of the Hammett protagonists, Beaumont came the closest to being an amoral character of the kind which was developing in the tradition. Other than for certain loyalties, his motions were mechanical and his emotions were not there. He had a smooth manner and some refinement, but what he did or how seemed not to matter. "I don't believe in anything," Ned Beaumont said, "but I'm too much of a gambler not to be affected by a lot of things." Yet it is difficult for the reader to discover what things affected him. He was smashed to a pulpy mess, won a large amount of money, and became violently ill from too much drinking, without the author giving the reader a clue as to whether any of these acts pleased or displeased the hero. The words Beaumont did not use might have been supplied by Angel Grace who was pulled out of the bay in Hammett's first novel: "Why didn't they let me alone? It's a rotten thing, living."

Some time during the years from 1927 through 1930 Hammett reached his peak—I personally think with *The Dain Curse*—both as a stylist and as a contributor to the tradition of the American literary hard-boiled hero. His stories of the early thirties, published in *Black Mask, The American Magazine, Liberty,* and *Collier's* were quite ordinary. Three of them continued the exploits of Spade, while others were experimental. "Woman in the Dark" presented an unHammett-like hero who although he had chivalry, loyalty, and physical courage was without any of the hard-boiled qualities. Stylistically, a gauzy mellowness was substituted for the clipped prose: "The wind blowing downhill from the south, whipping trees beside the road, made a whisper of exclamation and snatched her scarf away."

There remains little to be said about Hammett's last major effort, *The Thin Man,* which was obviously written under Hollywood influence. The original version of the novel had been planned and begun in 1930, in the style of that period, but only sixty-five pages were completed. The setting was San Francisco and its environs, the viewpoint the third person, and the detective a kind of modified Op. The most interesting aspect of the fragment was the unreal quality that Hammett insisted on attaching to the hero who was referred to as untouchable, as not even a corpse but a ghost, as one with whom it was impossible to come into contact—like trying to hold a handful of smoke. It was three years, one of which was spent in Hollywood, before Hammett returned to his fragment. Unable or unwilling to continue with it he wrote a different novel.

For some, Dashiell Hammett wrote beyond the tradition by specifically expressing the giddy twenties and gloomy thirties. For those readers and critics his private eye spoke for men who had lost faith in the values of their society—during war, gangsterism, and depression. This view, perhaps, can be thought of as analogous to the attitude held by Eric Ambler's protagonist at the end of the thirties; looking at the body of Dimitrios Makropoulos, Latimer "saw him not as a corpse in a mortuary but as a man, not as an isolate, a phenomenon, but as a unit in a disintegrating social system."

After Captain Joseph Shaw, early in his career as editor of *Black Mask,* had decided on Dashiell Hammett as the leader of the writers who had a new kind of compulsion and authenticity, he set about to find a group good enough to follow the leader. He found them by the dozen, the best of whom he thought would "revolutionize" American literature. Among Hammett's colleagues were several good writers who first published their short stories in *Black Mask,* turned to writing novels, and ended up in Hollywood: Frederick Nebel, Raoul Whitfield, Norbert Davis, W. T. Ballard, George Harmon Coxe, Thomas Walsh, and Lester Dent, among others.

Frederick Nebel had a sound working definition of realism which was not at all hindered by his lack of feeling for humanity. As a writer he thought he should not allow himself any indiscriminate sentiment in viewing human derelicts, but rather he should use the ineffectual man, the "stranded flotsam," as a lesson in "understanding contrasts." He was pleased with one of his heroes who was "*born* hard-boiled," but he was almost equally interested in one of his hoods who was a "man of iron." In *Sleepers East* Nebel wrote a novel of murder and intrigue in politics in which the action is governed by the toughness and weakness in men. The theme, not infrequently appropriated by hard-boiled writers, concerns man's inability to control the incidents of life; man cannot really make the grade, but if he gives it a good try he may get some of what is coming to him if only for the wrong reasons. To live as much and as violently as one can—even for a single night— may be the only way.

The Hollywood setting provided color for much of the work of Raoul Whitfield. He had one big, rough, fearless, frontier-type of hero who rushed to meet danger wherever he sensed it, and he had a private eye who was "cold as hell." Whitfield had a habit of trying to make his hero tough instead of allowing him to be tough, but this was often the result of the hero's compelling drive as a reformer. There was a strong feeling for the joy of violence in the stories of Norbert Davis. Relying on his own sense of justice, the hero—"a gunman, gambler, and soldier-of-fortune"—smashed, shot and killed all over town; but he was doing it for "good," and those who were maimed or killed were on the side of wrong. The principal character in the work of W. T. Ballard was a good deal like his counterparts in the stories of Whitfield and Davis. A liaison man for the General-Consolidated Studio in Hollywood, Ballard's hero used violence willingly, but only to combat violence; he was indifferent to human life generally, but he sometimes cared about "little people."

The "number one camera for the *Globe*" stood in lieu of the private eye in the *Black Mask* stories of George Harmon Coxe. Coxe's hero had already become what he told a girl she would be if she insisted on working for a newspaper. To the girl, newspaper work was like having a season ticket for the drama of life, but according to the cameraman she would soon become a "hard-boiled, vindictive, loud-mouthed dame with a cigarette throat; without an illusion or ideal—without an honest emotion left in her system." Thomas Walsh wrote tight, fast-moving, energetic fiction in which he used as hero a "strong, silent, and extremely fortunate man from Chicago," or he did equally well with a plainclothes-man on homicide. In two of his stories Lester Dent presented a private dick who was as tough and violent as any hero who smashed and ice-picked his way through the pages of Black Mask. In his longer fiction, however, he depended on a financially suc-cessful man of violence, a man whose violence became sticky at times because of the sentiment behind it: "A door mat, Molloy believed, is good only to be stepped on. It gets nothing out of life but wear and tear. Therefore, Molloy had always fought viciously for what he considered to be his privileges as a human and an American-born."

There was at least one among the Black Mask boys whose writing contained something different. The wrappers of the first issue of a novel published in New York in 1933 carried the follow-ing statement: "now comes the hardest, toughest, swiftest novel of them all FAST ONE two hours of sheer terror written with a clipped violence, hypnotic in its power." If there ever has been an accurate blurb, this was probably it. Fast One, published in part in Black Mask in 1932, enjoyed, according to its author Paul Cain (Peter Ruric), a "spectacular critical reception but was not so hot at the box office." When it came out in England, however, it sold like "sixty or seventy."

Among the writers of the hard-boiled genre, there had been an ever-growing awareness of the attitude of negation toward life, a feeling of indifference about humanity which appears to have reached a kind of peak in the early depression years. Humanity was still in evidence around the country, but so were rocks. Again it must be remembered that the awareness of negation was not peculiar to the hard-boiled writers; it had appeared in various forms of literature in America, in the plays of Eugene O'Neill, for example. Nor was it new on the other side of the Atlantic, although a culmination of negation was clearly set forth in Journey to the End of the Night by Louis-Ferdinand Céline, published in France the same year that Fast One ran in Black Mask.

Gerard A. Kells, the protagonist of Cain's novel, had the

characteristics commonly found in the hard-boiled hero—the brutal, gutty, fearless man. Yet there was something more in Kells, a factor which gave him his violently "hypnotic" appeal. To account for this, one is tempted to turn to the existentialism of Jean-Paul Sartre. Man cannot, according to Sartre, be exclusively individualistic, for whatever man does for himself he does for all men. The one thing man has is freedom, but having it he must constantly make choices. Having no legislator but himself, man must do all the deciding for himself. Whatever choice he makes is acceptable, for he obviously could not or did not make the other. Because the overruling aim in each choice is freedom, man can choose either of two opposite moralities—in matters of choice they are equivalent. Gerry Kells, who appeared unaware of the existence of anyone but himself, was without doubt his own legislator. He also made choices, although to the reader they generally appear as unconscious acts. It did not, incidentally, occur to Kells that he was choosing between "two opposite moralities," for he was amoral. Yet this was not the amorality of Theodore Dreiser, who felt that because man was the victim of his environment and physical makeup he had no moral choice. Kells was aware of his options and alternatives, but being cognizant only of his own existence, he was indifferent even to choices.

Having acquired in the East two thousand dollars and a reputation for knowing how to play "rough," Gerry Kells arrived in Southern California. His reputation made it possible for him to begin taking over the Los Angeles rackets, which he proceeded to do by playing off one racketeer against another and by eliminating a few himself. Double-crossing, smashing, shooting, and ice-picking were all in the act; it mattered not at all to Kells how things went. He accumulated several thousand dollars and lost all of it but seventy cents, and he did not react to that. Like all memorable hard-boiled heroes, he had, however, points of vulnerability—his pride, some small feeling of revenge, and a tiny touch of loyalty brought about his end. He went as he had come, alone, "Then, after a little while, life went away from him."

About an hour before noon on a mid-October day in the 1930's, Philip Marlowe drove through downtown Los Angeles. The sun was not shining, and there was a "look of hard wet rain in the clearness of the foothills." The shabbiness of Bunker Hill made him think of its days of respectability. Soon he headed west on Wilshire Boulevard, through Westlake Park, across La Brea Avenue; turning to the north at La Cienega, he crossed Santa Monica and Sunset Boulevards and found his way into the hills of West Hollywood, to the home of General Guy Sternwood. As Marlowe entered the Sternwood mansion, he looked up to see, on a stained-glass panel, a knight in dark armor rescuing a lady who was tied to a tree. The lady was without clothes, but she was wearing long and convenient hair.

In this fashion, in *The Big Sleep* in 1939, Raymond Chandler introduced his hero, the hard-boiled detective who was to become the epitome of them all. In seven novels during the following two decades, Marlowe drove through the streets of Los Angeles, and the surrounding towns, looking for ladies to rescue, for the little fellow who needed help, for the big man who deserved a shot of old-fashioned justice. "Down these mean streets a man must go," wrote Chandler, and his story was "man's adventure in search of a hidden truth." From the skilled hands of this writer, one of the best literary portrayals of the *Black Mask* hero evolved.

Although Philip Marlowe was not introduced, by that name, until 1939, he had been developing in Chandler's short stories for a half dozen years. Chandler's original private eye, using the name Mallory, appeared in *Black Mask* in December 1933. From that date through 1939, he performed in twenty short stories, usually as the private eye (fourteen times), but occasionally as a detective lieutenant, narcotic squad under-cover man, or hotel dick. He used ten different names and was twice nameless, but always he was a part of the man Marlowe was to become. In experimenting with viewpoint, Chandler used the first person twelve times and the third person eight. Once created, Marlowe was always a first person narrator; this technique kept him on the scene, involved in the lives of others.

Beginning with his first story, "Blackmailers Don't Shoot," Raymond Chandler established his hero as one good enough to compete in the violence found in abundance in the far western city of Los Angeles. The man was tall, with gray eyes and thin nose, and he had a "jaw of stone." He was tough, honest, loyal; women found him attractive and hoods played him carefully. He was a "business man" who got "paid [very little] for his work," part of which was dealing death to those on the side of wrong.

Raymond Chandler's style, at the outset, showed qualities which were to make him one of the best of the *Black Mask* detective writers. The restrained statements, the colorful similes and evocative images, the city of oil wells and jacaranda trees in bloom, the reliable lonely hero—it was all there at the beginning. The third story, "Finger Man," can serve as an example of the Chandler touch. Using an uncomplicated plot, Chandler developed his theme around the idea that when crooked politicians and crime choke a city's moral life, it takes the private eye to make the corrections. The police were willing and helpful, but because they were so necessarily a part of city politics their hands were tied. Only the free, uninhibited, and tough individual was able to move far enough and strongly enough in the right direction. At this early stage in Chandler's writing career, the hero was adequately noble and hard-boiled, but he was not yet the smooth nobleman that Marlowe was to be. In matters of style, however, one can see the similes and images beginning to take their places. Comments like "As a bluff, mine was thinner than the gold on a week-end wedding ring" were to become a Chandler trademark. But images like "I stopped beside a forgotten drugstore that slept behind two giant pepper trees and a dusty cluttered window" contributed to his reputation as a literary stylist. Yet one cannot overlook the fact that in weaker moments he sometimes used a cliché of the trade: "I saw that Canales had fired at least once, because Frank Dorr had no right eye." In the eyes of the knight, the moll was a lady, so she was allowed to escape. And the hero, who was more and more appropriating the role of the humanitarian, said, "It's a shame how little account some folks take of human life."

"Killer in the Rain," a short story Chandler later incorporated into The Big Sleep, continued the hero's efforts to help those in trouble. The nameless narrator didn't care about the "trash," but basically good people like Dravec, who had a neurotic daughter, deserved to be saved from a "little heartache," even when it meant ignoring legal requirements. The hero, who saw mankind in a melancholy plight, was provided by the author with a subtle mood through which he observed: "I stared at the window, watched the rain hit it, flatten out, and slide down in a thick wave, like melted gelatine. It was too early in the fall for that kind of rain."

Occasionally a Chandler story had a touch of the old West. The hero of "Nevada Gas" was a good-guy gambler helped by a hotel dick who carried a Buntline Special and said "I'm a tough guy. I used to be a Wells Fargo Dick." The cop in "Spanish Blood" covered for a friend, protected the girl (to whom he said, "Life seems to do nasty things to people"), and lost his badge. One infers that he got his badge back because he was honest and human. He could not help thinking, however, that had it been his grandfather—one of the best sheriffs the county ever had—the case would have been handled "with fewer words and more powder smoke."

Throughout the 1930's Chandler continued to dress his man in the clothes of the traditional hero. Mallory, Carmady, Dalmas, whatever his name, grew harder toward the wrong guys and softer toward the little people. Invariably it was the troubled poor who hired him, so he worked for beans he frequently didn't get. His all-American virility increased with a growing, impatient distaste for effeminate men like Lindley Paul—he had a dimple on his chin in which you could have "lost a marble," and he spoke softly "in the manner of a sultan suggesting a silk noose for a harem lady whose tricks had gone stale." He went to those places where a "hard-boiled redhead sang a hard-boiled song in a voice that could have been used to split firewood," and where a torch singer "sang of something very far away and unhappy, in a voice like old ivory." As he went he drank the "racket" beer which was as "tasteless as a roadhouse blonde."

Drawing from several years' writing experience and specifically from four short stories (three of which were in *Black Mask*), Chandler fashioned his first novel, *The Big Sleep*. The hero, theme, and style came together in a highly successful fruition. "To hell with the rich," Philip Marlowe said, "they make me sick." Yet for a small amount of money, most of which was used on the case, he risked his life many times in trying to help the wealthy Sternwood family. Most of Marlowe's sympathy was spent on old General Sternwood, once virile, now sick and helpless: only "a few locks of dry white hair clung to his scalp, like wild flowers fighting for life on a bare rock." The General's two problems were his two daughters, neither of whom had "any more moral sense than a cat." And Carmen, the younger, was hopelessly psychotic. In his knightly role, Marlowe rescued the ladies, who although beautiful were not very fair. In throwing the naked Carmen out of his bed, the hero brooded over his integrity and moral standards: "This was the room I had to live in. It was all I had in the way of a home. In it was everything that was mine, that had any association with me, any past, anything that took the place of a family." He said, as he moved a piece on his chessboard, "Knights had no meaning in this game. It wasn't a game for knights." Yet he played it as a knight throughout, meeting violence with violence, bringing a little peace of mind to a sick old man, and allowing the murderess to go free. The villains included a dealer in pornography, whose house "had a stealthy nastiness, like a fag party," a blackmailer, and a ruthless killer. They, with several others of their ilk, met justifiable deaths. For Marlowe the "world was a wet emptiness," full of violence and inhumanity, yet he moved through it with dignity and integrity, always, however, alone; in the febrile society in which he operated, the hero never deviated from his code. Occasionally, however, the rain stopped, allowing him to look at "the hard pale wild lilac of the California hills."

During the war years Raymond Chandler published three

more novels of high quality in which the hero sought to bring some degree of justice and sympathy to those living in the world of violence. In 1949 *The Little Sister* included a sharp denunciation of Hollywood, and *The Long Goodbye* (1953) insisted on the value of loyalty in society, especially in a superficial society. When Chandler was nearing seventy he published *Playback*, a novel which clearly indicated a lessening of his talents. Feeling sorry for his lonely hero, the author, at the end of the novel, held out the prospect of marriage, although marriage, according to a younger Chandler, was impossible for his detective hero. With Chandler's death, Marlowe escaped a role for which he had never been fitted.

In the pages of *Black Mask* the detective hero contributed to the American myth of the hard-boiled hero. One component of the myth which the *Black Mask* School utilized was a special attitude toward violence which provided both an ethical and an aesthetic justification for its employment.

In England, where an appraisal of popular American literature is often very discerning, Ernest Borneman held the opinion that the old *Black Mask* "was the training ground of such writers as Dashiell Hammett and Raymond Chandler; it established a new tradition of realism in the detective story; and it contributed to the development of what Mencken called 'the American language'—a prose style which, by transcending the limits of the crime story, has become part and parcel of the serious American novel."

MORE ON AUTHOR AND SUBJECT

Philip Durham was born in 1912 in Portland, Oregon, and received his Ph.D. from Northwestern in 1949. He joined the UCLA English faculty in 1953 and became a full professor in 1963. One of his primary fields of interest is American pulp crime fiction, as witness his Down These Mean Streets a Man Must Go: Raymond Chandler's Knight (University of North Carolina Press, 1963), his introduction to the posthumous collection of Chandler stories Killer in the Rain (Houghton Mifflin, 1964), and the above essay.

Those who wish to pursue the Black Mask School further should consult the magnificent bibliography in William F. Nolan's Dashiell Hammett: A Casebook (Santa Barbara: McNally & Loftin, 1969). Particular attention should be paid to the superb work in which the above essay first appeared, David Madden (ed.), Tough Guy Writers of the Thirties (Southern Illinois University Press, 1968).

*†My own view is that there is no necessary antagonism be-
tween the formal deductive problem and realistic crime fiction;
Dashiell Hammett proved over and over that the two are compatible in a first-rank creator's hands. But this anthology is not designed to reflect merely the opinions its editor agrees with, so here
is a frankly (and wittily and joyously) polemical piece, exalting
the one approach and damning the other, by one of the untouchable grand masters of formal detection of this or any other time.*

The Grandest Game in the World
by John Dickson Carr

"Do you solemnly swear never to conceal a vital clue from
the reader?"

"I do."

That is the first article in the oath taken by members of the
Detection Club. The candidate, placing his hand upon Eric the
Skull, swears this with fervency. He swears it with stern looks fixed on him. He swears it while Eric's eyes (thanks to John Rhode)
glow with red electric lights. He swears it even before he promises
to honour the King's English, use legitimate detective methods in
his stories, and refrain from pinching his fellow-members' plots.

And this rule, the *sine qua non* of the profession, must be emphasized at the beginning to explain my choice of stories in *The Ten Best Detective Novels.*

For the once-humble detective novel has come a long way. It has gone up hill, down dale, over the plain and through the sewer. In fifty years it has undergone so many changes, not to say disguises, that sometimes we quite literally don't know what we are talking about. A new novel is praised because it is well written, because the characters are admirably drawn, because it is "tough," because it is experimental in technique, because it is written sideways or upside down: on any grounds, in short, except that it is a good detective story.

If the term means anything at all, it means this:

The detective story is a conflict between criminal and detective in which the criminal, by means of some ingenious device—alibi, novel murder-method, or what you like—remains unconvicted or even unsuspected until the detective reveals his identity by means of evidence which has also been conveyed to the reader.

That is the skeleton, the framework, the Christmas tree on which all the ornaments are hung. If the skeleton has been badly strung, or the tree clumsily set on its base, no amount of glittering ornament will save it. It falls over with a flop. Its fall may create a momentary sensation, especially among children, but adults are only depressed when they see the same sort of thing happen in fiction.

The author of the book hasn't bothered. He has decided that good construction is of no consequence, or that nobody cares anyway. Far from planning in advance every move, every speech, every detail, he has roared ahead on inspiration and trusted to luck. And his attitude is understandable if he is writing a straight thriller, where rapid-fire action swallows up everything. But it becomes merely bad craftsmanship if he thinks he is writing a detective story.

We might postulate, to begin with, that the detective novel at its best will contain three qualities seldom found in the thriller. It will contain the quality of fair play in presenting the clues. It will contain the quality of sound plot-construction. And it will contain the quality of ingenuity.

Ingenuity? Do we start an argument here?

It seems remarkable that this need for ingenuity in the *outstanding* detective novel has been so strangely overlooked. Perhaps the reason is that you cannot turn it into a "must"; you cannot lay it down as a rule of the game. You cannot say to an author, "Look here, sit down and be ingenious." Maybe he can't be. Maybe he doesn't want to be. His interests may lie along other lines, such as the hero slugging the police or (more pleasant to read about) the police slugging the hero.

But, though this quality of ingenuity is not necessary to the detective-story as such, you will never find the great masterpiece without it. Ingenuity lifts the thing up; it is triumphant; it blazes, like a diabolical lightning-flash, from beginning to end.

It is not of intrinsic interest to read that X has been stabbed to death in a hotel room, and that the police—after re-winding the clock, or studying the bloodstains, or any of the stock-tricks in vogue since the time of Gaboriau—have proved the guilt of Y the waiter. This is all very well; it may be competent work; it will serve to be read if we have nothing better at hand. But, in pitting our wits against the masters of the trade, we require something very different.

We require, for instance, the superb explanation of the clock-alibi, in A. E. W. Mason's *The House of the Arrow.* Or the means used to conceal the identity of the criminal, in Agatha Christie's *Murder in Mesopotamia.* Or the reason why the corpse wore its clothes the wrong way round, in Ellery Queen's *The Chinese Orange Mystery.* Or the ironic brilliance of Anthony Berkeley's *Trial and Error,* in which a man who has confessed to the murder tries to prove himself guilty and can't do it.

These writers (with others like them) are the aristocrats of the game, the old serpents, the gambit-devisers and trap-baiters whose strokes of ingenuity make the game worth playing at all.

For what, after all, is the game itself?

It is a hoodwinking contest, a duel between author and reader. "I dare you," says the reader, "to produce a solution which I can't anticipate." "Right!" says the author, chuckling over the consciousness of some new and legitimate dirty-trick concealed up his sleeve. And then they are at it—pull-devil, pull-murderer—with the reader alert for every dropped clue, every betraying speech, every contradiction that may mean guilt.

Nothing, in fact, shows more clearly the difference between the expert craftsman and the novice than his manner of presenting this evidence. The novice, even when he is anxious to include a clue, develops a case of acute self-consciousness about it. He feels naked before the reader's eye. He is much too afraid of being caught with the goods. So he hurls the clue into the story and then runs like a maniac, as though he had thrown a bomb.

The result is that the clue, one or two words at most, will flash past and become lost among sixty or seventy thousand other words. This is painfully evident during the detective's summing-up in the final chapter.

"The whole question of Dagmar Doubledick's guilt," declares the detective, "turns on the kind of necktie he was wearing when we met him that day at Wemmerly Park. Of course you remember it was a green tie?"

To which the honest reader is compelled to answer: "No, I'm damned if I do!"

And then, if he is conscientious, he will turn back through the book to discover whether Dagmar Doubledick's tie really was green. Perhaps he finds this clue, a violet by a mossy stone, half hidden somewhere in the dusky recesses of Chapter Six; perhaps he misses the page and does not find it at all. In either case he is left with a vague feeling of dissatisfaction: as though he has been, if not swindled, at least out-talked.

Now it may be argued, and reasonably, that the author here was playing perfectly fair. He was not compelled to repeat it, or even stress it. Thus when the whole solution of Earl Derr Biggers' *Charlie Chan Carries On* is based on the single word "stuffy," or when Carolyn Wells in *Luminous Face* argues guilt from the thesis that no gentleman would wear a wrist-watch with evening clothes, these novels are at least technically within the rules.

But the masterpiece of detection is not constructed from "a" clue, or "a" circumstance, or one single inconsistency of any kind. Such methods, dubious enough in a short story, become grotesque when they are applied to a full-length novel. It is too reminiscent of those minute-mysteries, vignettes accompanied by paralytic-looking photographs, with which we are so familiar in magazines.

"You stated, Leonard Andreas," thunders the Inspector, "that you drank a scotch-and-soda in the bar-parlour of The Flaming Bishop at nine o'clock, whereas we know the pub ran out of spirits at half-past eight. It proves, Leonard Andreas, that you committed the murder."

Now this is a bit rough on poor old Leonard Andreas, because it doesn't prove anything of the kind. It proves only that the witness told a lie, or that the landlord (as usual) was keeping his whisky under the counter for favoured customers. We are dealing, here, with murder; and we can hardly let a man's life, even that of a character in fiction, depend on such flimsy evidence.

The fine detective story, be it repeated, does not consist of "a" clue. It is a ladder of clues, a pattern of evidence, joined together with such cunning that even the experienced reader may be deceived: until, in the blaze of the surprise-ending, he suddenly sees the whole design.

Your craftsman knows, as Dr. R. Austin Freeman long ago pointed out, that it is not at all necessary to mislead the reader. Merely state your evidence, and the reader will mislead himself. Therefore, the craftsman will do more than mention his clues: he will stress them, dangle them like a watch in front of a baby, and turn them over lovingly in his hands. He will give not only the clue physical, but the clue psychological and the clue atmospheric.

No speech in the book is included just because it sounds mysterious, or because it makes a given character look guilty, or because the author doesn't know what the devil his character does mean and simply throws in the words to fill up space. Not at all.

In turning over the pages afterwards, the reader can see for himself—how rare it is!—just what each character was *thinking* at any
moment.

And the result?

That is why the story pulses with vitality all the way through,
and springs into living vividness at the end. The veil is twitched
away; the masks are removed. Human beings walk here, and no
sawdust dolls, because the author has described voice-inflections,
shades of feeling, as well as Inspector Hogarth's discovery of the
blunted thumb-tack under the sofa. He has not forgotten to study
his characters merely because he is writing about them in reverse.
That turn of the eyes—of course! That momentary hesitation,
when Betty puts her hand on the window-ledge as though to
steady herself—naturally!

Each small detail glitters now with an effectiveness it should
have had, and would have had, if the story had been written
straightforwardly. It is in the mood, in the tempo, an arrow
whang in the gold. And when, in addition to this, we find ourselves flumdiddled by some master-stroke of ingenuity which has
turned our suspicions legitimately in the wrong direction, we can
only salute the author and close the book with a kind of admiring
curse.

There, good friends, *is* a detective story.

But who writes such stories nowadays?

In considering this question, on a terrain where it is to be
feared that bricks are apt to fly, we might do worse than examine
the wide difference which has developed nowadays between the
British and the American type of detective novel.

During the good (or bad) old days twenty-five years ago—
let's speak first of the everyday mediocre practitioners rather than
the great ones—these novels were of much the same kind. Both
sides were content to write the English language, even when they
wrote it badly. Both sides made some mumbling acquiescence in
the matter of rules, even when they broke rules all over the place.

Their plots, too, were the same. Alter the locale from Long

Island to Surrey, substitute "baronet" for "industrial magnate," and the stories were almost interchangeable. This change, in fact, was actually made when the thrillers about Frank L. Packard's Jimmie Dale were published in England, with the redoubtable Jimmie living in Park Lane and battling against an evil, conscience-less gang of robbers called (it is regrettable to state) the Crime Club.

But the pattern of the average detective story ran thus: The victim, on the eve of making a new will, was found murdered in his library. He had been stabbed with an Oriental dagger, cus-tomarily used as a paper-knife on his desk. The whole room was strewn with cuff-links, bus-tickets, lace handkerchiefs, and ciga-rette-ends, in the fine artistry of a paper-chase.

Inspector Brace, summoned hastily to the scene of the crime, found only the beginning of his troubles. The baronet or indus-trial magnate—in addition to his ne'er-do-well son, his rebellious daughter, and his invalid wife—was afflicted with such a household as nobody, even in the days of the servant shortage, would tolerate for five minutes. The butler was a blackmailer, the chauf-feur an ex-convict, the housekeeper a religious maniac. If this were not enough, investigation discloses that no less than eight other suspects, at the time of the murder, were skulking in one long procession past the library windows.

"This situation," says Inspector Brace, "is hopeless!"

And it is difficult not to agree with him, since the various cuff-links and cigarette-ends are proved to have been dropped innocently by one or the other of the suspects, popping at inter-vals in and out of the windows like Box and Cox. Inspector Brace, desperate, is about to arrest the ne'er-do-well son when the latter's fiancée calls in that gifted gentleman, the private detective Reginald Du Kink.

Then we got real business. It is Du Kink who discovers that the established time of the murder is all wrong, due to an effect of ventriloquism or a phonograph-record of a voice, and at a dramatic gathering of suspects he fastens the guilt on the dead man's secretary. The secretary, haggard and foaming, waits only to scream out a confession before he drinks off the contents of a small vial and instantly falls dead.

And that was that.

Now the above, so help me, is not written in ridicule. It is not meant as burlesque. You and I, who have been improving our minds with sensational fiction for so many years, are much too fond of detective stories. We are aware that all the above plot-tricks were used long before 1920, have been used since, and are still in use today—often by the very best practitioners in the business.

Seldom are they lumped together in one story, as was formerly the case, nor is the clue so naive as a broken cuff-link. And the ghost of Dr. Freud haunts everything today. But the old elements remain. The millionaire's home, the threatened disinheritance, the rebellious family, the enigmatic servant, the multiplicity of suspects, the wrongly accused, the wrong time of death—how many novels can you name in which not one of these elements is to be found?

Why, then, do we protest at the adventures of Inspector Brace and Reginald Du Kink? Why do their frenzied activities hover always on the edge of comedy, not to say broad farce?

We don't find them funny because they are what our age likes to call "period-pieces." Far from it. One glance at a list of the detectives who were practising long before them, a list which includes short stories as well as novels, will convince us of that.

There is nothing in the least funny about the great stories of Sir Arthur Conan Doyle. Nobody smiles today at G. K. Chesterton's Father Brown, though the stumpy little priest first appeared in 1911. The same applies to Inspector Hanaud, whom A. E. W. Mason introduced in *At the Villa Rose* a year earlier; and Dr. Freeman set the experienced John Thorndyke to solve his greatest problem, *The Eye of Osiris,* in the same year. E. C. Bentley, in 1913, was a comparative latecomer with his brilliant tour de force of *Trent's Last Case.* On the other side of the Atlantic, an under-rated genius named Jacques Futrelle had created Professor Augustus S. F. X. Van Dusen as early as 1907, whereas Melville

Davisson Post was already an old craftsman when he gave us the classic book of short stories about the far-from-comic Uncle Abner in 1918.

And here we begin to see the explanation of why, as early as the 1920's, the intelligent reader was getting fed up with the adventures of Inspector Brace and Reginald Du Kink.

"Oh!" said the reader. "I'm tired of just guessing who the criminal is. Instead of these sleight-of-hand half-clues, so that it's never properly explained at the end how the detective knew, let's have some real evidence.

"Furthermore," continued this reader, "it's all very well to have your eight suspects parading in their endless ring-around-the-rosebush outside the library. That's fine. But give some sensible reason why they were there. If you must shower the room with bus-tickets, provide a reason for that, too. In other words, construct your story. Your present problem is not to explain the villainy of the guilty: it's to explain the stupidity of the innocent.

"Finally, your 'amazing revelation' at the end was so soggy, so lacking in essential cleverness, that I couldn't care less. Haven't you a new idea tucked away somewhere? Can't you wield even a minor thunderbolt? It was far different, believe me, from that joyous shock when Father Brown unmasked the Invisible Man, or Uncle Abner showed the meaning of the Straw Man, or Sherlock Holmes, in an unforgettable moment, swept the disguise from the Man with the Twisted Lip."

Hola! Wow!

Please pardon these exclamations. It is only that I, who write this introduction, feel warm with pleasure merely to recall, and taste in memory, those great moments of fictional crime. Once more, in memory, we see the gaunt figure of Holmes with the bath-sponge in his hand, and shock-haired Hugh Boone writhing on the bunk. Or Father Brown, under a lurid sky in the waste of snow, with the giant hall-porter between whose very feet runs the straggle of tracks where no man has passed; and out across the snow rings that despairing cry:

"God! The invisible man!"

Such moments, then, aid us in summing up the reasons why an imaginative reader required somebody more enterprising than Inspector Brace or Reginald Du Kink. He required a skillful story told in reverse by a skillful story-teller. He required (need it be repeated?) the quality of fair play, the quality of sound construction, and the quality of ingenuity. And already, at the beginning of the 1920's, this decade saw new writers who possessed just such qualities.

It saw the debut of Agatha Christie in *The Mysterious Affair at Styles,* based on the (then) startling novelty that the person first suspected turns out to be the murderer after all; he has wanted to get himself tried and acquitted so that he can't be tried again—a device later used by so many other writers. It saw Freeman Wills Crofts, with *The Cask* and its grisly contents, inaugurating the new fashion of the Unbreakable Alibi.

It saw John Rhode, in *The Paddington Mystery,* present a victim dead from no apparent cause—while telling us for the first time (and almost the last time) that Dr. Priestley's Christian name is Lancelot. It saw Anthony Berkeley's initial effort take the form of a "locked room" in *The Layton Court Mystery.* It saw Dorothy L. Sayers—with *Whose Body?*—setting an unfledged Lord Peter Wimsey to solve the puzzle of a strange corpse, clad only in a pair of pince-nez, found stabbed in a dry bath.

These 1920's, whatever may be said against them, thronged with sheer brains. What would be one of the best possible settings for violent death? J. J. Connington found the answer, with *Murder in the Maze.* Has anybody ever used the camera obscura, that eerie periscope-device, for witnessing sinister events at a distance? Mr. Connington again, with *The Eye in the Museum.* In the 1920's, too, Philip MacDonald made his notable advent with *The Rasp.* R. A. J. Walling, in *Murder at the Keyhole,* demonstrated how you can force a reader to look literally in the wrong direction. And always with us during those days, cherubic, dependable, and moaning like an animated cream-bun, was H. C. Bailey's Mr. Fortune.

Now look towards the other side of the Atlantic. It must be

acknowledged that America, during the same period, produced only two detective-story writers of the first class.

Regarding those who were not first-class or anywhere near it, there is no need to mention names. Most of them were women, one or two of whom are still writing today. These ladies waltzed gracefully, waltzed well; but they waltzed always in the arms of Inspector Brace or Reginald Du Kink. We have pleasant memories of them all; theirs is the scent of arsenic and old lace. They call to mind coloured frontispieces from their own books: the yellow gowns sweeping the floor, the padded rooms cosy with crime.

But there is one name which must be mentioned, because it belongs to a man who came dangerously near being first-rate and who had more influence on his medium than anyone seems to have realized. That is the name of Arthur B. Reeve.

Arthur B. Reeve, who began in an earlier era—as, indeed, did most of the lady-waltzers—entered the 20's with his once-immense popularity fading away. Nevertheless his tales of Craig Kennedy had been read by hundreds of thousands, praised by Theodore Roosevelt, and turned into early film-serials which held us petrified.

Craig Kennedy was Professor Kennedy of, presumably, Columbia University. Like Dr. Thorndyke, he was the scientific detective. His laboratory flashed with stranger sparks, and bubbled with more weird beakers and test-tubes, than the laboratory of the late Dr. Frankenstein. For each occasion he had some new gadget, guaranteed sensational, to clap on somebody's wrist or wire underneath the chair. Square-jawed Kennedy in his high collar, whom we remember so well from the illustrations in the Harper editions, has marched into limbo with all his gadgets loaded on him. Much of his scientific knowledge, I believe, has been discredited. Nobody reads about him now., And yet. . .

He was first in the field of fiction with the lie-detector, with murder by electrolysis, with radium poisoning, with death from liquid air. He taught writers the use of the Maxim silencer, and neither tears nor prayers nor curses can induce them to give it up.

As a final achievement among many, in a story called "The Dream Detective" and later in a novel called *The Soul Scar*, it was he who introduced the profession to psychoanalysis.

This, in its way, is a solemn thought. For the humble annals of the detective story, it is like Watt studying the boiling kettle or Franklin flying the kite in the thunderstorm. In these days when every other mystery novel depends on a neurosis or a phobia or a fixation or whatnot, we can see now what wild vegetation has grown from that small seed. Psychoanalysis has been the most widely used contribution to the detective story since the days of Poe and Conan Doyle; and we might do worse than remember who planted the jungle in which our contemporaries lose themselves.

Well, never mind. We were discussing the American situation in the 20's.

Shortly past the middle of the decade, S. S. Van Dine published *The Benson Murder Case*, in which Alvin Benson was shot to death under circumstances which suggested the fate of Joseph Elwell the bridge-expert. It was not a reconstruction of the Elwell case, as we can see for ourselves if we read the real-life account of the police-officer in charge of that affair. But it brought forward a new writer who juggled suspects with such dexterity, like whirling Indian-clubs, that we could only stare in admiration; and a new detective, Philo Vance, who said his method was psychology and scorned the cigarette-ends found near Benson's body. Three years later, when a crooked lawyer was poisoned with some villainous new stuff called tetra ethyl lead in *The Roman Hat Mystery*, we saluted Ellery Queen.

Though these were the only practitioners of the front rank, both were so good that they held the scales almost level against their British confreres. It looked, in those far-off days, as though the golden age of the detective story had come. It now played strictly fair. It was adult. It had lost its clumsiness and grown to maturity.

Then came the 1930's. Then came the cleavage. The hard-boiled detective story, which for some years had been lurking in the magazines without anybody suspecting its inherent genius, suddenly blossomed out until it shadowed the whole field. Few writers, even experienced ones who had been dealing with a different type of story, were completely untouched by its influence. Novices rushed to get aboard the band-wagon. And there began, between the school of Sherlock Holmes and the school of Sam Spade, a difference which has been widening for more than thirty years.

Let us consider the hard-boiled type of story.

Whether you prefer this kind of writing is a matter of personal taste. Whether you acclaim it as good, on the other hand, depends on how it is done. If anybody wants to see how "economical, astringent, muscular prose" should really be handled, let him re-read the best stories of Melville Davisson Post. Post was a great master of prose style, whereas most of the moderns are fairly answerable to some other description.

But we are not here concerned with literary quality. We are concerned with the detective story, and what goes into it. Dashiell Hammett has been praised as "a creator of the first rank," belonging among "the small handful of authors who brought something really new to their chosen field of effort," and as one whose "lean, dynamic, unsentimental narratives created a definitely American style, quite separate and distinct from the accepted English pattern."

These are the words of Howard Haycraft, a sound critic, an admirable critic whose opinions we are bound to respect, and whom we can accuse of eccentric or unbalanced literary judgment only when he praises an undeserving hound named Carter Dickson.

But this originality, this glory of breaking fresh ground, again depends on what you do. You could get a finely original effect, for instance, by sending a whole procession of kangaroos across the stage during a performance of *Lohengrin* at Covent Garden or the Metropolitan Opera. You would be, definitely, a creator. You would have brought something really new to your chosen field of work. Or, to be more restrained about it, you could decide that the trouble with musical shows was the use of music, and the thing to do was have the musical show without any music at all; just as you can decide to have the detective story without any clues to follow or any rules to observe.

As we earlier discussed the saga of Brace and Du Kink, let's take a typical American detective novel of the later 30's. Its plot runs something like this:

The hero, Chip Hardstone, is a wise-cracking private detective with an attractive blonde stenographer. To Chip's office, in violent agitation, comes the lean, elderly, aristocratic J. T. Witherspoon, a millionaire with a country house in Sundown Hills.

Mr. Witherspoon's daughter, it appears, has got herself involved with a notorious character called Smooth Ed Spumoni. A priceless crystal flask, with gold-work by Benvenuto Cellini, has been stolen from the millionaire's collection. Matters at home are tense, since -- in addition to his ne'er-do-well son, his rebellious daughter, and his neurotic young wife -- Mr. Witherspoon has further grounds for suspicion in that the butler is a blackmailer, the chauffeur an ex-convict, and the housekeeper a hop-head. What he wants, he says, is to recover the Cellini crystal and free his daughter from the clutches of Smooth Ed Spumoni.

"But no scandal, Mr. Hardstone!" pleads the millionaire. "Above all things, no scandal!"

Already, before going to the country house, Chip has accumulated a lot of information. Practically every character in the story calls on him and tries to retain him. These he first bluffs and then insults -- all except the representative of an insurance company, whom he merely insults.

Arrived at the house in Sundown Hills, Chip finds the "mad family" of earlier fiction now so completely nuts as to require a psychiatrist rather than a detective. The daughter removes her clothes; the wife intimates that she is willing to do so; the son tries to knock Chip's head off on sight. Other friends swing punches at the son, at Chip, or at each other; and Chip, who replies by insulting everybody he has previously missed, is interrupted with the discovery that one of the guests has been found dead ---- his throat mangled ---- in the swimming pool.

(Observe the departure of originality here. The millionaire himself is seldom murdered. He must be kept alive to pay Chip's fee.)

But one of the guests is murdered. No less than eight persons, it appears, know some vital secret about the murder. All of them have disappeared. It being Chip's job to find them, in a roulette-ball spin round the city, he concentrates first on a mysterious red-haired girl who has been traced to an apartment house at the corner of Pineapple and Banana.

Racing to the apartment house, Chip finds the girl gone but a corpse on the floor. He flies to a second apartment house, only to find the girl gone again and another corpse on the floor. By the time he has reached the third apartment house and the fourth corpse, he is in a spot. The police are after him, the reporters are after him, Smooth Ed Spumoni is after him, even the millionaire is after him to call him off. Chip won't be called off. He intimates, with something very like blackmail, that the old s.o.b. can't get out of it after bringing *him* in.

"All the same," says Chip, "this set-up is hopeless!"

And again we agree, since the vital secrets turn out to be innocent side-games in which everybody is chiselling everybody else, and have nothing to do with the murders. Chip, on the point of being arrested by Captain Hooligan of the Homicide Bureau, suddenly gets an inspiration -- it is never very clear how -- that the murderer is J. T. Witherspoon's wife. He confronts her; there is a gun fight all over the house; and the wife, waiting only long enough to scream out a confession, falls dead at his feet.

This is the end of the story, leaving the reader in some doubt as to just what did happen after all.

Now why, at the outset, are the adventures of Chip Hardstone so vaguely familiar? What strikes a reminiscent note? Despite the original chases and sluggings and kidnappings, we seem to have met this motiveless and clueless method somewhere before.

Don't we see that it's Inspector Brace and Reginald Du Kink all over again?

Instead of cuff-links, bus-tickets, and lace handkerchiefs which bear no relation to the problem, we have "secrets" which bear no relation to the problem either. Instead of the suspects doing their ring-around-the-rosebush outside the library, they now rush away from capture in cars and aircraft; but they still act either for no reasons at all, or for no reasons that are ever explained.

As for the fairness of the evidence, or the quality of the solution, the same test can be applied.

The American wheel, in these hard-boiled stories of the 30's, had turned full circle. We were back again among the whiskers and mothballs of an earlier era. Those very detective-story features of which the reader complained most bitterly in 1920, the features which were its essential faults, the features which craftsmen had worked so hard to eliminate ever since, were triumphantly hailed as a daring new departure from convention.

This period in America, it is true, produced its own first-raters. In 1934, with a story called *Fer-de-Lance*, Rex Stout by sheer power of characterization and plot-construction at once joined the company of Ellery Queen and S. S. Van Dine. There was Anthony Abbot, whose grim first novel *About the Murder of Geraldine Foster* -- based on a legend of Courvoisier and Lizzie Borden -- never seems to have achieved the full critical acclaim it deserves. In the front rank, or very close to it, were Clayton Rawson and C. Daly King.

But these were all practitioners in the great tradition, the clue-serpents and trap-baiters. Their narratives moved as fast as you could wish for; yet they ranged beside their British confreres of the same period, Margery Allingham and Ngaio Marsh and Nicholas Blake, in the vital business of presenting new ideas. In Nicholas Blake's first novel, *A Question of Proof*, you will find one instance of what is meant by the great tradition. The murder-knife unaccountably vanishes; and the investigators can't find it because it has been hidden, in front of their eyes, by being used as a tent-peg.

Yes; but what about the weaknesses in the English type of novel?

The fault here is just the same, though expressed in a different way. The "literary" type, like the hard-boiled, is too often apt to mistake style for substance. It imagines that with good writing, which sometimes becomes merely pretentious writing, you can disguise the lack of an original plot.

"Come, now!" the author seems to be saying. "I'm really a straight novelist, you know, indulging in this funny little medium of the detective story because nowadays it's become respectable. It's true I haven't got much of a mystery, or any very clear idea of how to handle it; but, if I give you strong characterizations and much talk-in-a-mist, you won't mind that?"

To which the answer is: Sir or madam, we do mind. Either you neglect the plot, which is bad; or else you fall off those stilts with a crash, which is worse.

So we come to the end of a survey which has covered many years and no inconsiderable number of books. And now (I confess it) I am seized by a horrible temptation. My Better Nature, seraphic with upturned eyes and halo, pleads and whispers, "No!" But the devil won't be denied; gleefully he beckons. I have enjoyed writing this introduction so much—in contrast, it is to be feared, to the labours of the weary reader—that I want to end it with a list of rules on What To Do and What Not To Do.

Admittedly, this has been done in full tabular style by Carolyn Wells, by S. S. Van Dine, by H. Douglas Thomson, by Basil Hogarth, by Howard Haycraft, and others. More cautious lines have been taken by Monsignor Knox and by Miss Sayers herself. And I think these two latter writers were wise.

Once the evidence has been fairly presented, there are very few things which are not permissible. The oath of the Detection Club, stern though it may sound, does not forbid the employment of conspiracies, gangs, death-rays, ghosts, trap-doors, mysterious

Chinese or homicidal lunatics. It is not so harsh as that. It merely enjoins the writer to preserve "a seemly moderation" in the use of them. The only thing it rules out, and rightly rules out, is the use of mysterious poisons unknown to science.

Those who nail a manifesto to the wall, saying, "The beginner will do this, and must under no circumstances do that," are in many cases quoting not rules but prejudices. That is the danger. It is prejudice, like my own prejudice against having the murder turn out to be a suicide; and should freely be indicated as such. With all due respect and admiration for those who have compiled lists, it would not be difficult to show that they were often giving dubious advice and sometimes talking arrant nonsense.

"Disguise," declares one writer—to take a single instance—"disguise, of course, went out with the bustle."

To which the answer is: "My dear sir, that is a prejudice. Furthermore, it's not true. Have the goodness to read, among other stories with whose titles half a page could be filled, G. K. Chesterton's 'The Dagger with Wings,' R. Austin Freeman's *The Mystery of Angelina Frood,* Q. Patrick's *S. S. Murder,* Ellery Queen's *The Dutch Shoe Mystery,* Philip MacDonald's *The Wraith,* E. C. Bentley and H. W. Allen's *Trent's Own Case,* Anthony Berkeley's *Top-Story Murder,* or Agatha Christie's *Three-Act Tragedy.* Disguise is one of the best weapons in the armoury. The test of a device is not whether it is new or old; there's nothing new under the sun; the test is what novel twist can be put on it."

Here, then, is my own list of Do's and Don'ts: compiled partly from those of the writers quoted above and partly from my own heart's blood.

1. The criminal shall never turn out to be the detective, or any servant, or any character whose thoughts we have been allowed to share.

2. The criminal shall never at any time be under serious suspicion until the unmasking. If you haven't the ingenuity to keep his identity a secret until the end, at least pretend you have. Even if the reader out-guesses you, and your thunderbolt-ending doesn't come off, the effect is far more satisfying than if you

apologize for your murderer by "clearing" him in an early chapter.

3. The crime shall be the work of one person. While the murderer in some instances may be allowed to have a confederate, you will ruin your story if two or three or four people are dragged in as accomplices. The essence of a detective story is that the one guilty man shall fool the seven innocent; not that the one innocent shall be fooled by the seven guilty.

4. The crime shall be clean-cut. If a character disappears and is assumed to be murdered, state frankly what has happened to him. If he hasn't been murdered it's a pity; but the reader has a right to a clear stating of the problem.

Those are four golden maxims. In each one I believe. And each one you will find shattered—shattered admirably, shattered to bits, shattered by a mighty hammer—in the "best" detective novels, while the reader wishes to do nothing but applaud. Because they are not really rules; they are only prejudices.

The greatest trap into which a critic can fall is to maintain that something is being "done" in the current year, as though there were a style in shrouds as well as in hats, or to maintain that something else has gone out of fashion. When Carolyn Wells's *The Technique of the Mystery Story* was first published in 1913, the late Miss Wells was already talking about outworn devices. But nothing ever has gone out of fashion, and nothing ever will, provided only that the old trick can be worked in a new way. Yesterday's fashion may not be today's; but it may be none the worse for that. On the contrary, it may be a devil of a sight better.

So let them write their stories, the hopeful young men and women! Let them not be frightened by that worst bogey of all, the feeling that they have got to be innovators. Let them remember that the real test of their mental skill is in the drive and nimbleness and strategy of their play; it does not consist in putting the goal-posts in the middle of the field or dashing through half the game with a ball that isn't here. And you and I, serene in our armchairs as we read a new detective story, can continue blissfully in the old game, the great game, the grandest game in the world.

Second thoughts—after 17 years

I well remember when and how the above outburst was written. It was written in London during the cold and gusty spring of 1946, and in my flat on Haverstock Hill. Despite an acute housing shortage, I had obtained that flat for reasons quite apart from my Scottish luck. When I moved into it in 1943, Adolf Hitler still walked the earth. He had yet to unleash the Little Blitz, the flying bombs, the rockets, and other drolleries from his inexhaustible sense of humour. But we were all expecting something of the sort. And nobody except your obedient servant was stupid enough to want a flat on the top floor.

If I were to write again of favourite detective novels, should I change anything above? Not one sentiment, not one author. The ensuing 17 years have produced no writers who are better, nor any (tell it not in Gath) one-half so good. It may be that for four of the authors I should choose a different novel. A. E. W. Mason, for instance, might better be represented by *The House of the Arrow*; Philip MacDonald by *The Rasp*; Ellery Queen by *The Chinese Orange Mystery*; and Dorothy L. Sayers by *Strong Poison*.

But this is a minor matter; it is the author and his detective who count. "Then you still believe all that?" will be the whisper of kindly friends. "Haven't you learned anything in all these years?" Since I have learned wisdom in no other respect, it is useless to hope for it here. And a man should always be willing to defend his prejudices. As he gets on in years, those prejudices may constitute the most satisfactory sum total of all the things he has— or is.

MORE ON AUTHOR AND SUBJECT

John Dickson Carr is well known to every lover of crime fiction as the supreme wizard of the locked-room mystery, and as the creator of Dr. Gideon Fell and (under the Carter Dickson byline) Sir Henry Merrivale. He is also (and here I offer my neck to the blade) the greatest atmospheric writer in the last forty years of crime fiction, with the possible exception of Cornell Woolrich at his best. His novels from It Walks by Night *(1930)* to The Ghosts' High Noon *(1969)* entitle him to sit among the immortals of the genre.

The preceding essay was written early in 1946 as an introduction to a mammoth anthology of mystery novels (although the project collapsed and the essay remained unpublished until 1963). In effect, though not in intent, "The Grandest Game" is a rebuttal of Raymond Chandler's equally frank polemic from the hardboiled viewpoint, "The Simple Art of Murder," which first appeared in the Atlantic Monthly *for December 1944.* Readers interested in the other side of the debate should consult Chandler's often-reprinted essay, then offer thanks that they need not stop reading either of the illustrious disputants.

†A literary genre must have certain characteristics that distinguish it from all other genres, and Jacques Barzun, the renowned historian of ideas, here attempts to isolate those features which make a detective story a detective story. Although I think his approach is a bit too Aristotelean (especially insofar as he relegates to such inferior positions the evocation of character, atmosphere and manners, and everything else that is not of "the essence" of the genre), his essay is one of the most significant sustained attempts to investigate what concepts underlie this type of fiction, and he writes with grace and wit and erudition of what he loves.

Detection and the Literary Art
by Jacques Barzun

Because detective stories, short or long, are conventionally called cheap entertainment, and yet are read and written by talented people, absurd theories have been evolved about their significance and secret function. Some have said that the spectacle of crime and punishment purges the civilized man of fear and guilt; others, that it releases by a modern myth the animal instincts of the chase and the kill. Meanwhile, among those who perceive that all this is pretentious nonsense, many conclude that detective fiction can satisfy only a juvenile and unliterary taste. It rather adds to the confusion that the holders of these various views are thinking of different kinds of stories or of several kinds at once:

they refer indiscriminately to "crime stories," "mystery stories," and "detective stories" as if they were all one.

What is morally worse—for it prevents the public from developing its own judgment—anthologists who understand the distinctions and who define the detective genre in their prefaces go on to fill their books with stories of crime and mystery absolutely devoid of detection. In the best of such books one is lucky to find four or five pieces out of fifteen or twenty that answer to the given description. No such insouciance would be tolerated elsewhere. An anthology of ghost stories is full of ghosts. A book labeled "westerns" does not include narratives of the mysterious East. A tale of love on Jones Beach would be deemed astray among sea stories.

You naturally ask, "What are the distinguishing marks of the true genre and what peculiar delights does it afford the person of literary tastes?" It is not enough that one of the characters in the story should be called a detective—nor is it necessary. What is required is that the main interest of the story should consist in finding out, from circumstances largely physical, the true order and meaning of events that have been part disclosed and part concealed. Crime is attractive but incidental. An excellent detective story could be written about the identification of an amnesia victim. The reason why murder animates most detective story-telling is that the gravity of the deed gives assured momentum. Crime, moreover, makes plausible the concealment that arouses curiosity.

Certain readers, of course, are impatient with any detection that busies itself with physical clues. They mutter against "mechanical puzzles" and say that they cannot be bothered with material facts: the mysteries of the soul are so much more—mysterious. And they conclude that detective fiction, being of the order of riddles, can have no connection with literature.

They may be right in their judgment of particular works that are dull through being mechanical, but the condemnation of riddles is unjust. Tradition itself speaks for the riddle as a compelling literary device. From the Bible and the Greek dramatists to Dickens and Henry James, the discovery of who is who and what his actions mean has been the mainspring of great narratives. The stories of Joseph and Oedipus, the plots of *Bleak House* and "In the Cage," pose questions of identification and work out puzzles in the most exact sense of these terms.

In the ancient stories a single physical fact—a ring or other object, a footprint, a lock of hair—usually suffices to disclose identity and set off the denouement. The object is symbolic and conventional rather than rationally convincing. What happens in modern detective fiction is that objects—and more than one in each tale—are taken literally and seriously. They are scanned for what they imply, studied as signs of past action and dark purpose. This search for history in things is anything but trivial. It reflects the way our civilization thinks about law and evidence, nature and knowledge. Our curiosity about objects has grown since the Greeks; we call the results science. By a parallel evolution of literature, the dominant kind of fiction is the prose narrative stuffed with material fact which we call the realistic novel. It blossomed a century and a half ago, with Scott and Balzac, and we are not surprised to find that the detective interest on the part of literary men dates from the same period of balanced rationalism and romanticism: detection is par excellence the romance of reason.

We see this new taste burgeoning in the eighteenth century in Voltaire's charming story of Zadig. We find it carried forward in a sketch by Beaumarchais about the identity of a lady at a ball.* And when Balzac follows this fictional tradition he attaches to it more than passing importance, for in an actual murder case we see him attempting to defend the accused by a memoir in which he pleads that: "Criminal investigation must retrace the dead morally *and physically,* for the proofs for and against are everywhere— *in people, places, and things.*" The emphatic italicizing is Balzac's own. A few years earlier, across the Channel, Sydney Smith had

---

*Translated by Jacques Barzun and published in EQMM, November 1956 (as "The World's Second Detective") as well as in Barzun's anthology *The Delights of Detection.* [Ed.]

attacked the custom of denying legal advice to those charged with
felony, by arguing that if "a footmark, a word, a sound, a tool
dropped. . . .are all essential to the detection of guilt," then the
"same closeness of reasoning is necessary for the establishment of
innocence."

From these and other examples it could be shown that the
literary imagination of the first half of the nineteenth century
was caught by what it understood of method in the new sciences
(especially fossil reconstruction in geology) and by its sympathy
with the new criminology, which called for the accurate use of
physical evidence. At a time when Marsh's test for arsenic was
hailed as a triumph which would eliminate the Borgias from our
midst while saving those falsely accused, Europe and America
thrilled to the descriptions of Leatherstocking's primitive way of
tracking down friends and enemies with the aid of physical clues.
Leggett's "The Rifle," published in 1830, shows how, in American
fiction, crime was first brought home to a culprit by ballistics.

It remained for a genius to take this entrancing idea of
detection and make it breed a distinctive literature by displaying
it in an appropriate form. That genius was Edgar Allan Poe and
the form was the short story, of which he was also the original
theorist. "The Murders in the Rue Morgue," published in 1841,
put an end to the episodic or casual use of detection. And when
four years later Poe had written his three other detective tales, all
the elements of the genre were in hand. What was to follow could
only be elaboration, embellishment, and complication—most of it
agreeable, some of it superior to the original in polish, but none of
it transcending the first creation.

Accordingly, I continue to think the short story the true
medium of detection. Pleasant as it is to begin a novel that
promises a crowd of actors and incidents, of clues and dis-
quisitions upon clues, the pleasure is soon marred by the apparently unavoidable drawback of a subplot and its false leads.
The poet C. Day Lewis, writing as Nicholas Blake the excellent
Minute for Murder, apologizes for this fault by having his detective refer to "the monstrous red herring" that delayed the

solution. Looking back over many a novel that is monster-ridden in this way, one cannot help thinking of the story as it was first conceived, without this artificial bustle and bulge which exists only to be deflated by a sentence or two near the end.

If this is true today when a detective novel is also a slim volume, what are we to say of the earlier phase of expansion after Poe's sober contribution? When his idea was first stretched out to fill the dominant form, the novel meant a "tangled skein" of 150,000 words. The French *romans policiers* à la Gaboriau, the milder melodramas of Anna Katherine Green, and even the best novels of the 1920's from the hand of Agatha Christie or Dorothy Sayers were massive constructions in which a great many innocent people had to behave suspiciously if the main business was to be kept long enough out of the reader's sight. Conan Doyle himself went against sound instinct, though by another route, and concocted those intolerable middle sections which pot-belly three out of four of his longer tales. The astute reader reads them once, at the age of twelve, and skips them forever after.

I grant that the short story also has its perils and defects, especially if for lack of invention it returns to the state of anecdote, that is, makes the dénouement hinge on one small point instead of on a chain of inferences drawn from several facts. Nothing is duller than the tale of the criminal who, having endured long questioning with aristocratic aplomb, turns green and claws the air because he is caught in a lie. The same holds true of the lost button, the spent match, the missing envelope—no matter how ingenious the situation or how skillfully built up the suspense, no solitary clue is good enough to satisfy the reader who knows what detection is and insists on getting it.

Ideally, the short detective story is a sequence of five parts, for which it is a pity that Greek names cannot at this late date be invented. First comes the preamble, philosophic in tone, and if possible paradoxical or otherwise arresting. It sets the mood by providing a sample of what Poe called ratiocination. However you pronounce it, ratiocination is a heart-warming prospect. The detective theorizes upon some aspect of life which the story will bear out, though he himself does not as yet know this. Next comes the predicament—mysterious, horrible, grotesque, or merely puzzling—the variation from the norm which invites inquiry. The commonplace mind, represented by the client or by some other embodiment of the *ewig-Watsonisches,* tries to assimilate the unusual and fails. But the superior mind, the detective intellect, seen through a cloud of smoke, discerns the true question and feels immortal inklings upon him—as may be gathered from the irritating silence which follows his voluble beginning.

Further events soon disconcert both the common and the superior minds, but, again, only the latter recovers. This is the signal for a little discourse on method, possibly given socratically, by questions and answers that dispose of the obvious hypothesis and leave everything in an engaging confusion. It is time for the detective to act on his still-hidden "deductions." He tests "places, people, and things." The sheep separate themselves from the goat, and the ensuing violence—confession, arrest, suicide—prepares the way for explanations.

These may of course be artfully distilled through the two or three closing sections of the tale, but if the end is not to be a wordy anticlimax, some provocation of sharp surprise must be kept to the last. We know that the culprit is the smooth solicitor with the pince-nez, but we still cannot see how he could have been in London and Buenos Aires at the same time. The final lecturette which leads up to this disclosure, far from being a rehash, is an illumination which is also an emotional peak, because it releases the tension of intelligent curiosity we have labored under from the beginning.

To be sure, "form" in narrative is rather a metaphorical guide than a commandment, and the combining of incident and ratiocination in the detective short story can be widely varied, as R. Austin Freeman proved in *The Singing Bone.* In that volume he created the two-part invention, telling first the events in forward motion, as they occurred, then once again in reverse, as the detective reconstructs their sequence and meaning. To sustain interest in such a twice-told tale requires great generalship and a faultless choice of facts, for the repetition bares the machinery to the author's own practical criticism as well as the reader's. Unless the parts are solid and well-knit, what we accepted readily on a first recital will sound feeble or improbable when served up again to match a new pattern and a diminished suspense.

All that I have been saying about the genre could be summed up in one word: the detective story is a *tale*. The pleasure it affords is that of any narrative in which the ancient riddle of who is who unravels itself to an accompaniment of worldly wisdom. In the detective tale proper there is a double satisfaction answering a double curiosity—what can the solution be? and how was the solution arrived at? But to recapture this innocent pleasure one must be sophisticated enough to abdicate other sophistications.

II

The case for the detective story cannot of course stop on this dogmatic note, for certain merits of the genre and certain objections to it are yet to be named. Among the objections is that of sameness—"read one and you have read them all." My description of the form could even be cited in support of the charge; it would be foolish to deny that detection in literature submits to very rigid canons. It is an art of symmetry, it seeks the appearance of logical necessity, like classical tragedy, and like tragedy it cherishes the unity of place—the locked room, the ship or train in motion. Its successes thus partake always of the tour de force. As Yeats rightly remarked, "The technique is *supairb.*"

But these very limitations, when appreciated, draw our eyes to the points of difference between one tale and another. Indeed, superficial sameness is a common attribute of tales, in contrast with the surface variety we expect of novels and novelistic short stories. If you read Boccaccio and Margaret of Navarre and Bandello and the *Cent Nouvelles Nouvelles* and the *Contes Drôlatiques,* you will find these tales as alike among themselves as any comparable number of detective stories. In the one group, lovers plot against husbands and are either successful or ridiculous.

In the other, the detective is confronted by the inexplicable and he reasons his way to the explanation, with or without apprehending a culprit. Fairy tales also betray a strong family likeness. There is a task set and an ogre to be conquered before the princess' hand is available; and generally everything comes in threes. Still, one can distinguish the masterpieces from the dull imitations, whatever the genre, by the art with which the formula has been vivified.

What one seems to miss in the tale is the novel's lifelike looseness, the illusion of uncontrived actuality. One is conscious of *listening to a tale,* which is why I suggest that the enjoyment of detective stories requires a superior sophistication. Again, I concede that the reader who goes to novels in order to learn something new about human character will be disappointed in detection. The tale may teach nothing but its own neatness, and its effect then is to bring a smile to the lips rather than a commotion to the soul. These are two orders of pleasure, not necessarily two degrees of it.

But if what I say is true, what becomes of the connection we observed, at least historically, between detective fiction and the realistic novel? To perceive the connection one must turn from form to substance. The raw material of detection consists of the physical objects that surround action. These become literary substance when the detective imagination has chosen and arranged them so that some are clues while others produce atmosphere, verisimilitude, suspense. In detection details are numerous and must be instantly convincing. We are ready to swallow long descriptions of houses and their furnishings, we are greedy for the contents of posthumous pockets, we long to master time tables, speeds of vehicles, and procedures for collecting evidence, provided always that these records of matter moving through time and space conform to the common standards of credibility. That is the reason why many years ago Father Ronald Knox laid down as one of the laws of detective fiction: "There must be no Chinamen." For this cryptic rule, which its author said he could not explain, is in fact the principle of the realistic novel: the world of magic and mystery yields to a sense of reality based on the persuasiveness of things. To be sure, the great novels of the realistic school portray character even more painstakingly than things, whereas detection rightly keeps character subordinate. But detection makes up for this neglect by giving intelligence a place which it has in no other literary form. Only in the detective tale is the hero demonstrably as bright as the author says he is.

Some readers of course are by temperament impatient with small details. Trollope tells us that he did not like stories in which he had to remember what happened at a given hour on the Tuesday, or how many yards from the milestone the lady was abducted. But in so saying he is telling us about himself rather than criticizing the genre. His own work is full of little points to remember about people, church politics, and county snobbery. We follow him because, as we say, we gain an understanding of English life as well as of humankind. What do we gain from the details of detection? An understanding, first, of the silent life of things, and next, of the spectacle of mind at work. This is no doubt why detective feats have been, since Voltaire and Poe, the delight of intellectuals. The emotion called forth is that of seeing order grow out of confusion. This is no mean or despicable emotion: it can match in intensity the light of recognition which Aristotle declared the strongest effect of tragedy.

To experience this pleasure of discovery one must be willing to explore, as minutely and lovingly as the author desires, the nature and connections of the inanimate—including the corpse. One must be attentive to the interlinked traces of human action upon the material world. No doubt this is an acquired taste, like the taste for reading the history of the earth in rocks and rivers. But a generation reared on Proust's crumb of cake in the teacup should readily concede that bits of matter matter.

To those who acknowledge this, the attempt to "improve" the detective story and make it "a real novel" seems a sign of bad judgment. Replacing clues with "psychology" and intelligible plot with dubious suspense is childish tinkering. Far from "maturing" detection and giving us genuine novels with "real" characters, the so-called stories of suspense have only obscured a true genre and further muddled the criticism of it. The name itself is meaningless. Any good tale is a "story of suspense." What we are in fact given in the new mongrel form is "stories of anxiety," which cater for the contemporary wish to feel vaguely disturbed. I do not question the pleasure derived from this sort of self-abuse. I merely decline to call it superior to another pleasure which is totally different. And I hope I need not add that I enjoy and admire, each in its own kind, a great many of the tales now confused with detection, from Dashiell Hammett's *Red Harvest* to Stanley Ellin's "Broker's Special" and from Agatha Christie's "Witness for the Prosecution" to Anthony Boucher's "Elsewhen."

The truth remains that it cannot improve a genre to drain out its essence, fill the void with second-hand soul-searching and arty verbal tricks, and pretend that the result is at once the classic article and something loftier. When I hunger for "real characters," I am satisfied by nothing less than Stendhal, Balzac, Meredith, James, Dickens, Hardy, or Joyce. When I want to read about "the psychology of a murderer," I go to Dostoevsky, Buchner, Victor Hugo, Stevenson, or Shakespeare: I do not want it from Miss Mary Limpet or Mr. Sterling Brass, who write in the *I Did It* and *I Done It* manners respectively.

Again, the detective tale is not the place to make us appreciate the moral burdens of the times by presenting a detective who (I am quoting a review) is "middle-aged, humane, and embittered," so that his detection gives "glimpses of man's callous indifference to man." Finally, detective fiction has more to offer the reader than an incomplete Baedeker to some unfamiliar region of the world. All these novelties are but inferior substitutes for detection, the genius of which, conceivably, is played out. All forms eventually die. Yet if we are to believe the late Anthony Boucher, a most alert observer of the tendencies affecting the genre, "there seems to be something of an upswing in the pure basic detective story, the logical and well-clued whodunit." (*New York Times,* June 12, 1960)

Meanwhile, from the modern deviations one can reason back-

ward to certain critical conclusions. If you ask the ordinary reader which of the Sherlock Holmes short stories he likes best, the
chances are that he will say: "The Speckled Band." The vision of
the snake coming down the bell pull is the utmost thrill he expects
from detection. To the connoisseur, however, the tale is one of
Doyle's weaker efforts. It stands far below, say, "The Six
Napoleons." The point of the contrast is not that "sensationalism" is out of place because detection is "intellectual." Think
of Ernest Bramah's "Brookbend Cottage" and you will see how
compatible detection can be with thrills and fireworks. The
point is rather that in any combination of the detective interest
with anything else, the something else must remain the junior
partner.

By this principle we can see why it is so rare that a detective
tale of French or German authorship is true to its name. The old
roman policier tradition hangs over it and makes one groan. Fanciful "reconstructions" of the crime, inane accusations, a vicious
love of coincidence, a smug acceptance of chance solutions—all
this, saturated with the unhealthy flavor of the secret police, generally spoils the dish. Simenon's long-winded irrelevancies are the
same thing modern style, that is, with morbid coloring added.
What shall one say of the Oriental adaptation of our genre? To
believe, among other things, that a criminal can for professional
purposes conceal himself inside the upholstery of an armchair
demands an effort of nonvisualization that few Western readers
will be willing to make. The fact that the author of such inventions has taken the pseudonym of Edogawa Rampo only adds a
touch of resentment to our dismay.

Yet strict naturalism is not enough, either, as we see in the
so-called novels of police routine. These works are a little too
conscientiously instructive and sociological. They should be taken
in moderation, unless one is a salesman and able to find a narcissistic pleasure in seeing other patient men ring doorbells. I repeat:
nothing less than the play of the detective intelligence upon the
physical world will give us a detective tale. It might seem at first
sight as if Mr. Kemelman's admirable "Nine-Mile Walk" destroyed

the rule: what is his story but a few words overheard and analyzed? This is mere appearance. The detection is genuinely of the
physical conditions surrounding the deed and implied by the one
short sentence—an exemplary work as well as a tour de force.

III

But am I not still a good way from showing that detective fiction
is a branch of literature in the honorific sense of belles-lettres? Is
not detection perhaps a frivolous by-product of legal and scientific
writing, a *jeu d'esprit* for tired professional men who lack the
energy to tackle poetry? Behind these questions lurks a general
suspicion about style. The literary conscience demands that anything called literature show mastery not only of structure but also
of tone and diction. The manner of these is not prescribed, but
the commonplace will degrade a narrative, however ingenious, to
the rank of popular journalism.

Detective stories have been written, certainly, which show
complete indifference to the felicities of feeling and expression.
But this is true in equal measure of every type of story. Nick Carter has his counterparts in all genres, and we must judge detective
fiction as we do other kinds, by the best examples. It is no con-
cession to admit that there would be no genre to speak of and no
art to criticize if detective stories gave us but stock situations
interlarded with footprints and tobacco ash. It is the shuttling between the infinity of possible human actions and their equally
varied physical setting that gives the detective story-teller the
chance to be original, adroit, revelatory. And success here as elsewhere calls for the fundamental literary powers.

The supreme quality in our special genre is of course invention, which is to say imagination. Because the light shines on
all the material circumstances, these must seem fresh, at least in
function, and yet sufficiently common to be plausible—streets and
moors and stairs and potting sheds must be recognizable and in no
way fanciful. Incidents, likewise, must show a studious regard for
the norms and conventions of life and yet avoid that predict-

ability which is the mark of journalism in the derogatory sense.
Only art, the art of words, will support a writer who tries to walk
this narrow path. It is style that in the fictions of Dorothy Sayers
or Rex Stout, of E. C. Bentley or G. K. Chesterton, makes their
works at once worthy of belief and pleasurable to read. Here
again, as in classical tragedy, the illusion works, artificiality disappears, thanks to a scrupulous attention to language. And as in
Racine, a few clichés must be accepted as part of the convention:
when "tangled skeins" are out of date we must tolerate the detective's happy thought that his work resembles "the fitting together
of a jigsaw puzzle."

Nor is literature in abeyance because we consent to character
drawing being in detective fiction a secondary concern. For in
these tales characters must none the less move and talk agreeably
to their role—and to ourselves. We must know them at least as
well as we know the many people, not our intimates, with whom
we deal in daily life. By a right use of the Jamesian "point of
view" the writer of detection allows us to see into his actors far
enough to recognize their type and judge their ostensible motives.
Were we to go farther we would see too much: the writer would
have given away what it is his business to keep hidden until circumstances speak. In this half-concealment lies an art which is
none other than literary.

The one exception to this deliberate superficiality is the portrait of the detective, and here too the literature can show some
triumphs. Sherlock Holmes is as fully a character as Mr. Pickwick.
And by virtue of Doyle's almost unique success in giving a soul to
the detective's partner—the common man—we have in the two a
companion pair to Don Quixote and Sancho Panza, a contrast and
concert capable of occupying our imaginations apart from the
tales in which the two figure. Similarly in Nero Wolfe and Archie
Goodwin this old pattern of the knight and his squire, which is as
old as the *Iliad,* is repeated with conspicuous success in the American idiom.

It does not of course take such a partnership to prove that
writers of detective tales can animate their heroes with a pictur-

esque variety. From Father Brown to Peter Wimsey the range is wide. There is in fact but one limit that must not be transgressed; the detective cannot be a fool. I have no use for those ineffectual little men who are always mislaying their belongings and nursing a head cold, yet manage to track down desperate murderers. An all-embracing awareness of physical surroundings and great powers of ratiocination being the spectacle we look for, we are cheated when amiable bumblers hold the stage and succeed by accident at the last minute. They are as unconstitutional in their way as the "poison unknown to science" which kills before the cork is out of the bottle. And my objection to ineffectuality goes for the same paradox in any other form—the great Cointreau, let us say, who is always drinking and hiccuping, and who ends his cases snoring face down on the table while the prisoner is led away in a whiskey-scented haze. Poe decided once for all that the detective should be a man of independent mind, an eccentric possibly, something of an artist even in his "scientific" work, and in any case a crea-ture of will and scope superior to the crowd. He is, in short, the last of the heroes. It follows that to produce him the author must be at least his equal in observation and vocabulary: wit, learning, and repartee constitute the hallmark of detective literature.

The final grace of the perfect tale is its ornamentation. I mean by this the small touches which, while they fit the working parts of the plot, give them a characteristic coloring. Beyond this, an exact measure of levity in detection shows the master's hand, for as Arthur Machen pointed out long ago, the true tone of the genre springs from the alliance of murder and mirth. The laughter is a touch sardonic and must never degenerate into hilarity. The joke of death is on us. Conan Doyle and Dorothy Sayers, among the classics, understood this better than anyone else. What finer-humored critique of detection itself, and at the same time what more brilliant invention, than the casual reference in the Holmes story to the case which hinged on "how far the parsley had sunk into the butter upon a hot day"?

A muffled irony is perhaps as much as our later sensibility will stand, but some such injection of butter and parsley is needed if we are to preserve our proper distance from what is after all ugly business. Murder and detection in real life can give pleasure to very few. The one evokes anger and misery, the other boredom. Only when transmuted into literature by the artificial light of reason and the arbitrary rearrangement of parts do these social and anti-social realities begin to afford delight: after a time, the horrors perpetrated by Burke and Hare become the stuff of De-Quincey's *Murder Considered as One of the Fine Arts*—the first model of still another genre. But since Poe's great feat, we need no longer depend on Burke and Hare and DeQuincey, nor on the four or five disciples of the last-named who have reshaped for us the incidents of actual crime. We have for our solace and edification the literary genre I have tried to describe—abundant, variegated, illustrious, classical—the detective story.

MORE ON AUTHOR AND SUBJECT

Jacques Barzun is the University Professor at Columbia University and one of the most distinguished historians of ideas of our times. His long series of volumes on various aspects of Romanticism and other currents of nineteenth-century thought is not unrelated to his long and deep devotion to the last century's magnificent contribution to our lives, the detective story—"the romance of reason."

In another essay, "From Phèdre to Sherlock Holmes" (in his collection The Energies of Art, *Harper 1956), Barzun traces the intellectual attitudes underlying the detective story from Balzac and Voltaire through the 1930's. The essay is directly related to his later article which you have just read, and is well worth your careful attention.*

†My experience with Frank McSherry has been that he has never written about a story, even in the most casual letter, without making me want to drop whatever I'm doing, dash out and find and read the tale he has described so warmly and infectiously. Here he discusses a topic at the center of his many literary interests: the relation between the mystery story and occult fiction, and the little subgenre to which the fusion of the two forms has given birth.

The Janus Resolution
by Frank D. McSherry, Jr.

When an author puzzles a reader by asking if the mysterious or criminal events that make up the plot are caused by natural forces or by supernatural, there are two obvious ways in which he can resolve the question. The crimes may be the work of supernatural forces, in which case the story falls into the occult or fantasy classification; or the crimes may not be supernaturally caused at all, chance or the villain having made them seem so. However, the author has a third option: he may deliberately leave the question open. He may skillfully and cleverly plot his story in such a way that a natural explanation and a supernatural one account equally well for all the facts. Making the weight of the evidence on one

side as equal as possible to that on the other, and deliberately failing to state which explanation he considers or intends to be correct, the author leaves the reader to decide for himself.[1]

Let us call this device of leaving the plot open-ended and facing both ways the Janus Resolution.

As far as I can determine, this resolution that combines the
detective story with the tale of the supernatural was created by
pulp writer-novelist-movie producer Richard Sale, in a series of
short stories featuring police captain McGrail that appeared in
Argosy and *Detective Fiction Weekly* beginning in 1938. In the
first story of the series, "Perseus Had a Helmet" (*Argosy*, February 5, 1938), McGrail is faced with a problem he never succeeds in
solving: did the killer have, as he claimed, the legendary helmet of
Perseus that makes its wearer invisible, or was he just lucky in slip-
ping past the police cordon guarding his victim's apartment?
Other stories followed in *Argosy*, including "The Pig Was in the
Parlor" (August 6, 1938) and "Death Had a Pencil" (October 8,
1938), and still others appeared in *Detective Fiction Weekly*, such
as "The Old Oaken Eight-Ball" (February 15, 1941). These clever,
entertaining and fast-moving stories have unfortunately never been
collected in one volume.

One of the most impressive and frightening examples of this
subgenre is L. Ron Hubbard's novella "Fear" (*Unknown*, July
1940). A university professor denies the existence and sneers at
the mere possibility of demons; are the terrors and crimes that
later strike around him the work of vengeful devils, or the result
of his growing mental illness? After its appearance in *Unknown*,
splendidly and eerily illustrated by Edd Cartier, the story was
later published in book form in Hubbard's *Two Science Fantasy
Novels: Typewriter in the Sky and Fear* (Gnome Press, 1951.
"Typewriter," also a novella, is a straight fantasy.)

Lester Dent, who under the pen-name Kenneth Robeson
wrote most of the two hundred-odd novels for *Doc Savage* magazine, tried the Janus approach in at least two of those novels. In
"The Black, Black Witch" (*Doc Savage*, March 1943), Doc and
two of his men parachute by night into occupied France, seeking

to rescuc a scholar who has, so he claims, found a vitally important military secret: the ability to look into the future. Has he really found a chemical formula for the mind-expanding drug used by Nostradamus and created by Nostradamus' teacher, Peterpence? Or are his accurate predictions the result of common-sense deduction and one wildly lucky guess? In the end, even the highly intelligent Man of Bronze is not sure if the secret for which he risked his life and for which many men died ever existed, as he, his men, the French Resistance, the dreaded Gestapo, and several equally vicious American gangs battle in a furious two-continent struggle for the secret of Peterpence.

One of the few Janus stories not written by an American is Nicholas Monsarrat's novella "The Ship That Died of Shame" (*Saturday Evening Post,* October 18, 1952, as "The Last Days of MGB 1087"; reprinted in Monsarrat's *The Ship That Died of Shame and Other Stories,* William Sloane, 1959). Throughout World War II, Motor Gun Boat 1087 and her crew had fought with courage and gallantry beyond the call of duty to defend England's life. Honored, decorated, tired, the crewmen return to a gray and exhausted postwar England that is fighting a war for economic survival that is every bit as savage and relentless as the war just ended; there are many taxes and no jobs for those with only the skill to kill. No legal jobs, that is—and finally the broke and desperate crew refit their ship and begin a sordid smuggling career of secret high-speed runs across the Channel by night. First they take gold out of England, knowing and not caring that its loss wounds the country they formerly fought to protect; then they turn to transporting drugs; on their last trip they carry a psychopathic child-molester and killer. But a strange thing happens—as the jobs become increasingly dirty, the ship increasingly breaks down, even though her equipment is the latest and best available and is run by an experienced crew. An eerie idea enters the captain's mind: can a ship have pride and a soul to be torn? Can a ship, like a man, be ashamed of what it is doing? Has a ship a heart that can be broken? Surely that's a ridiculous idea, the breakdowns are accidental; but why do the breakdowns only occur at times and places that put them all in danger of arrest?

The second of Lester Dent's Doc Savage tales to make use of the Janus Resolution, "Up from Earth's Center," appeared in the magazine's last issue (*Doc Savage*, Summer 1949). Geologist Sullivan, lost for two weeks while cave exploring, returns with a wild story. Has his mind been affected by hallucinogenic volcanic gases trapped underground, or has he actually found a secret entrance into hell itself? Or has Sullivan found a multimillion-dollar uranium deposit, and is his story an attempt to keep the location secret from two criminals who are pursuing him? Are these men criminals, or are they low-ranking, limited-power devils sent from hell to bring the escaped Sullivan back? Despite some eerie touches and a couple of effective scenes, this is a weak, confusing and disappointing work, a dying swansong for the Savage series.

In striking contrast, Helen McCloy's novel *Through a Glass, Darkly* (Random House, 1950) is perhaps the classic of the whole subgenre. Panic runs like a forest fire through a girls' school as a lady teacher is discovered apparently to have the weird power to create and send forth a psychic double to kill for her. Is Dr. Basil Willing, psychiatric consultant to the New York District Attorney's office, faced with a clever killer trying to frame the innocent teacher, or is there really such a thing as that frightening occult being, the doppelgänger? The book can be read with equal plausibility and effectiveness either as a novel of the supernatural or as a detective story set in the classic mold; either way, it is superb.

Two years later Anthony Boucher successfully tried this form in his short story "The Anomaly of the Empty Man" (*The Magazine of Fantasy and Science Fiction*, April 1952). A sleuth named Dr. Horace Verner tackles an eerie case that his cousin and rival, a famous consulting detective of Victorian London, failed to solve. Men vanish in an incredible way, almost as if magically sucked from the clothes they wore and left so neatly behind them, buttoned shirts tucked into belted pants, socks still inside tied shoes. All they seem to have in common is

their last action: they have, accidentally, played backwards a
rare record of the Lord's Prayer, sung by the diabolically beautiful
and notorious late opera singer Carima—a woman whose lovers
all died violently; a singer of such inhuman perfection that she
was rumored to have had the aid of black magic.   Did the empty
men vanish by a clever trick in order to avoid such personal
problems as creditors and jealous husbands, or did they disappear
because the most powerful black magic spell possible is the Lord's
Prayer recited backwards?   The police have one opinion; Dr.
Verner has another; the reader may choose either for himself.
This fine, often reprinted story[2] was supposed to be the first of a
series about Dr. Verner; regrettably, no others ever appeared.

Edward D. Hoch's first published story, "Village of the
Dead" (*Famous Detective*, December 1955), marked the debut of
detective Simon Ark and another specimen of the Janus Resolution.   The entire population of a small isolated community has
apparently committed suicide by calmly walking off a cliff. Is the
man responsible a clever criminal seeking large financial gain, or is
he really the returned Axidus, leader of the cult of suicide-
worshipping Circumcellions who roamed North Africa centuries
ago, killing all the Catholics they could find?

Three times in their long career, Solar Pons and his associate
Dr. Lyndon Parker have felt the disturbing touch of the inexplicable.   "The Adventure of the Snitch in Time," by August
Derleth and Mack Reynolds, appeared in *The Magazine of Fantasy
and Science Fiction* for July 1953. The tedium of a foggy London day is relieved for Pons and Parker when an oddly-dressed
visitor arrives, claiming to be a government agent from an alternate universe where history took a different path—where the
sinister Professor Moriarty survived the struggle at the Reichen-
bach Falls and, armed with the alternate world's immensely
advanced weapons, plans to invade less advanced worlds, such as
Pons' London of the 1920's, that cannot possibly stand against
him. How can he be stopped? Amused, Pons solves the problem
for the visitor, but wonders later how, if the man was an escaped
lunatic as Pons had assumed, he found his way to Pons' flat

through the thickest fog London has seen in years.

In Derleth and Reynolds' "The Adventure of the Ball of Nostradamus" (*The Magazine of Fantasy and Science Fiction,* June 1955), Scotland Yard brings the famous consulting detective a horrifying problem: someone is hiring thugs to kill small boys, first in Berlin, Rome and Paris, and now in London. Pons finds the killer and learns his strange motive: he claims to have found the magic ball in which Nostradamus saw the future, and, seeing dictators murdering millions in concentration camps years from now, he decided, he says, to kill the dictators while they are still boys and prevent the mass murders later.. Someone in the case is a mad dog; but is it the killer or his victim? Pons cannot be sure. Both this story and the earlier collaboration appear, as "Off-Trail Tales," in Derleth's collection *A Praed Street Dossier* (Mycroft and Moran, 1968).

Derleth tried the form alone with equal success in "The Adventure of the Blind Clairaudient" (*Saint Mystery Magazine,* September 1961). Mysterious voices tell blind Lily McLain of the future, enabling her to make a very good living as a fortune-teller. Now they tell her she is going to be murdered soon, and she engages Pons to solve her murder. Male readers must decide whether her accuracy is due to feminine intuition or to genuine extra-sensory perception. The story appears in book form in *The Reminiscences of Solar Pons* (Mycroft and Moran, 1961).

Science-fiction writer James Blish employed the Janus Resolution with a new twist in *The Frozen Year* (Ballantine, 1958). The novel tells of a scientific expedition to the North Pole which faces sabotage and death after uncovering evidence of Martian criminal activity in the remote past. Is the saboteur a madman, or a Martian intent on hiding that evidence? Blish never tells us, and the facts he presents are consistent with either interpretation.

Blish used the Resolution again later that same year in *A Case of Conscience* (Ballantine, 1958). In the far future a Catholic priest returns from another planet, bringing a monstrous alien with him. Riots and wars break out, and civilization itself soon threatens to totter. Are these crimes committed by the alien with the aid of advanced scientific devices, or (as the priest believes) is the alien Satan himself, achieving these horrible results by the use of black magic? Again, the author does not say. The facts are consistent with an explanation based on modern science and equally consistent with one based on orthodox Christianity. The reader must choose for himself.

One of the most unusual mystery novels of the Sixties continues the use of a Christian motif within the Janus Resolution. Turn left past the End of the World store, and you will find the Valley of Quenan, an oasis in the western desert, where a small religious sect endeavors to live, morally and physically, as in Biblical times. Overtired from war work, Ellery Queen arrives here in 1944 by what is, as far as he knows, pure accident; yet his coming is expected and foretold. Are religious fanatics confusing his name with the Biblical name "Elroi," or is some vast Power moving humanity like pawns in the re-enactment of an ancient drama? For Ellery's detective talents suddenly become badly needed when, after fifty years without a single crime, theft and murder strike in this valley of innocence. *And On The Eighth Day* (Random House, 1964) is in many ways the ever-innovative Queen's most unusual work, and his only effort in this subgenre. It is a permanent reminder to mystery readers that the word "mystery" has not lost its supernatural connotations.

In George Lanning's *The Pedestal* (Harper and Row, 1966), a man released from a mental institution as cured returns to his home town. As he becomes convinced that a tall heavy pedestal in his home moves at night with evil intent, a series of murders begins in the town. Are the crimes the work of supernatural forces acting through the pedestal, or is the man not quite as cured as his doctors thought?

Leslie H. Whitten's *Progeny of the Adder* (Doubleday, 1967) is a sober, quietly convincing story of the police procedural school—with one difference. It details the efforts of the Washington, D. C. Police to deal with a murderer who either (a) is so insane he believes himself to be a vampire, and is thus compelled to act exactly like one, or (b) is the undeluded and genuine article. Which alternative is correct the author keeps to himself, up to and including the last sentence, which can be read in either of two ways.

Whitten's next novel, *Moon of the Wolf* (Doubleday, 1968), written in the same quiet gripping style as its predecessor, tells of the horror that sweeps the Depression-era town of Stanley, Mississippi, as a series of ghastly murders occurs, the bodies torn and ripped as by the attacks of a giant wolf. Are these crimes the work of a werewolf, or of a man driven insane by a rare form of encephalitis that alters his physical appearance? Again, the author leaves the answer entirely up to the reader.

From the days of Dupin to date, the detective story has been the epitome of the rational. It is strange to see this type of story—which traditionally stresses science, careful observations, facts and logically reasoned deduction from those facts—suddenly walking hand-in-hand with its exact opposite, the tale of irrationality and superstition, of ghosts and hobgoblins and things that go bump in the night. Why, in the most scientifically advanced era the world has ever known, has this strange alliance come about?

Let me hazard a suggestion. Science has replaced many of our previous guesses and wishes about the nature of reality with accurate, mathematically precise and experimentally provable facts. But in the process of doing so it has shown how much of what we once fervently believed to be unquestionably true was actually false, and it has done this so decisively that we cannot help wondering what else we believe to be true may not also in fact be false. And from the darkness outside the light we may hear a nasty little voice whispering: Are you sure of your rational explanations? Are you sure there are no vampires, werewolves, demons. . .? Out of this doubt has arisen the combination of the tale of rationality with that of irrationality. Science has increased our certainty and our uncertainty at the same time; the brighter the light, the darker the shadows it must cast.

NOTES

[1]This definition would exclude such well-known works as John Dickson Carr's *The Burning Court* (Harper, 1937), in which the author clearly indicates which of the two explanations is correct, the false one being put forward to conceal the true one.

[2]The reprinted version of the story is revised from the original magazine text. Boucher explains why in his Introduction to the story in the MWA anthology *Crooks' Tour*, (ed.) Bruno Fischer (Dodd Mead, 1953).

MORE ON AUTHOR AND SUBJECT

Frank D. McSherry, Jr., was born in 1927 in McAlester, Oklahoma, served in the Air Force during World War II, lived for a while after the war in Manila and Vienna, then returned to his native state. He received a Bachelor of Fine Arts degree from the University of Oklahoma in 1953, and has done commercial art work since that time, specializing in book jackets and illustrations. There are very few mysteries or science fiction stories that he has not read, and very few facts in either field that he does not know.

Although there do not appear to be any other essays on the subject of Janus resolutions, several of Mr. McSherry's other articles for The Armchair Detective *may be of interest to the reader. I especially recommend his "Who-Really-Dun-It?: Two Sub-Branches of the Detective Story" (January 1969) and "Under Two Flags: The Detective Story in Science Fiction" (April 1969). And by all means don't overlook his "The Shape of Crimes to Come," later in this volume.*

I have argued elsewhere that the central ritual of detective fiction is the process whereby the inexplicable, the absurd, the nightmarish are fused by the power of human intelligence into a rationally harmonious mosaic. If that view is correct, it is no wonder that the locked-room problem, in which the impossible is evoked and then dispelled with a maximum of intellectual intensity and excitement, is one of the favorite subgenres of so many distinguished writers and readers in the field. Prof. Yates in his paean to the locked room communicates a measure of the wonderment and delight that this type of fiction provides.

An Essay on Locked Rooms
by Donald A. Yates

Dorothy Sayers once observed that man has long delighted in tormenting himself with puzzles, riddles, conundrums and the like, apparently for the sole purpose of experiencing the subsequent pleasure of discovering their answer or solution. While this is, admittedly, a form of torment, it is also a form of entertainment. And it is within this category that most detective fiction can be classified; it is essentially "entertainment" fiction. ("Detective fiction," let us hasten to say, consists of prose narratives that deal primarily with detectives whose principal activity is to detect.) The "whodunit" is also the novel of formal limitations *par excellence*. The fact of the matter is that should its traditional requirements be abandoned, the *genre* would cease to exist.

Several members of the first generation of detective fiction critics, attracted by this rigid aspect of the novel of detection, set for themselves, individually, the task of listing what seemed to them to be the most important of these requirements. Among such literary investigators are recorded the names of S. S. Van Dine (Willard Huntington Wright), Father Ronald Knox, Dorothy L. Sayers, and (a group effort) the London Detection Club.

It must be admitted, however, that on review some of these listings suffer from a lack of objectivity, and serve little purpose other than that of recording the particular peeves and fancies of their compilers. However, there is an observation to be made from the mere existence of such lists: they suggest a general awareness that the detective novel does, in effect, impose an unwritten yet widely respected set of what we might appropriately term "rules of the game."

Within the bounds proscribed by these rules there are roughly a dozen "patterns" or "plot themes" under which virtually the entire body of detective literature can be organized: the unbreakable alibi, the disappearing corpse, the series of murders *a clef*, etc. But there is among these themes one in particular which most perfectly embodies the special generic characteristic of strict limitations. It is the problem that makes the purest appeal to logic for its solution. It highlights the "closed" nature of the detective tale and is, unquestionably, its most traditional expression. I am speaking of what has come to be referred to as "the locked room mystery." There is yet another interesting feature about the locked room tale: it is unique among detective story gambits in that it would seem to possess, at one and the same time, not only the most glorious past of any detective fiction theme but also the most dubious future.

Dubious, indeed! Actually, you know, they've condemned the locked room story to death. Rather I should say they've tried to prognosticate it out of existence.

This can't be done, of course. But let's look first at the long and colorful history of the locked room mystery. A brief glimpse backward over the milestones allows us to review its development at the hands of a number of the countless writers who, at different times during the past century, directed their ingenuity and talent to it.

There is a temptation to place the origin of the locked room story far back in the Apocryphal Scriptures wherein the History of Bel is related. The "detective" of the episode was Daniel, who accomplished a neat bit of debunking of the pagan idol Bel. The Babylonian king Astyages was convinced of the sanctity of the stone god, and demanded that the prophet Daniel disprove Bel's powers or forfeit his life for having blasphemously questioned them. Daniel, faced with the mystery of a stone image who by night devoured prodigious meals that had been set out for it behind locked and sealed doors, secretly scattered ashes on the temple floor in the presence of the king after the customary feast had been prepared. He witnessed the affixing of the king's seal on the temple door and then retired until the following morning.

With the break of day, Daniel accompanied the king back into Bel's chamber and had the untouched seal opened. The dozens of footprints left among the ashes on the floor attested to the habitual practise of the deceitful temple priests and their families who, it was shown, entered and left their nightly banquet hall by a secret passage. Through such shrewd methods, therefore, Daniel saved his own skin and another idol bit the dust.

It certainly makes a nice little story. But if we adhere to the generally accepted definition, we must agree that there was no true detective story until there was a true detective.

Thus it is that we honor as the creator of the formal locked room tale no less a personage than the father of the detective story itself—Edgar Allan Poe. Moreover, the first detective story and the first locked room story were one and the same: "The Murders in the Rue Morgue," which appeared in *Graham's Magazine* for April, 1841 in Philadelphia.

The brutal and bloody murders of Madame L'Espanaye and her daughter in that story were committed in a locked room where, Poe's C. Auguste Dupin determines, no human could have entered or left. But, unquestionably, violence by some outside agent had been done. Poe makes the most out of the ingenious and original device he had come upon; and there ensues a full-scale, detailed investigation that eventually brings out the grisly truth. One of the memorable moments of detective fiction occurs when Dupin unravels the bizarre account of the errant and terrified ourang-outang and his horror-struck keeper.

Many persons do not realize the great debt that Sir Arthur Conan Doyle owed to Poe and his Dupin. The truth is that the man who gave Sherlock Holmes to the world was indebted to the American for many of the characteristics of the London detective as well as for numerous plot ideas which were developed into the Holmes stories. In no instance is this latter debt more apparent than in Doyle's wonderful tale, "The Adventures of the Speckled Band," from *The Adventures of Sherlock Holmes* (1892). To be sure, the atmosphere of the story was completely Doyle's. (Atmosphere, with him, was a forte; cf. *The Hound of the Baskervilles*.) The type of problem, however, (essentially a locked room story), was originally of Poe's design. Now it belonged to the world. Doyle expressed the familiar circumstances with model economy:

> "The medical examiner investigated the case with great care but he was unable to find any satisfactory cause of death. My evidence showed that the door had been fastened upon the inner side, and the windows were blocked by old-fashioned shutters with broad iron bars, which were secured every night. The walls were carefully sounded and were shown to be quite solid all around, and the flooring was also thoroughly examined, with the same result. The chimney is wide, but is barred up by four large staples. It is certain, therefore, that my sister was quite alone when she met her end."

One specific characteristic Doyle gave Holmes that sets him apart from Dupin was the degree of active participation his detective took in the solution of the crime. Dupin was the original sit-at-home-detective who solved cases from his armchair; whereas Holmes is fondly recalled for grabbing a passing hansom and projecting himself (and faithful Watson) into the thick of things. Doyle thereby gained much in suspense and reader identification that was absent in the clear, logical, precise tales of ratiocination of Poe.

Yet, in the method of commission of the crime in Doyle's "Speckled Band," there still sounds the echo of Poe. Sherlock Holmes solves the problem by hiding in the fatal room and waiting for the murderer to strike again. He promptly does so and, as in Poe, the agent of death turns out to be of the animal world. The "speckled band" the dying victim referred to had been introduced into the room through a ventilator. It was a deadly Indian swamp adder.

*   *   *   *

The year 1895 saw the publication of a tremendously popular though now virtually forgotten detective novel by Israel Zangwill. It was titled *The Big Bow Mystery*. The author, a successful journalist of the time, first wrote the tale in serial form for a daily newspaper. His original and imaginative resolution of the locked room problem made of the story a brilliant *tour de force*.

So appealing, in fact, was his solution to the problem of a man apparently murdered in an inaccessible room that it has been employed with considerable success in numerous detective tales since—by John Dickson Carr, G. K. Chesterton, and James Yaffe, to mention only those that come immediately to mind.

Following the appearance of *The Big Bow Mystery*, Zangwill, in a coy mood, made a public statement to the effect that when he began to write the commissioned story he had no idea who the murderer might be, but that as the readers of the serial began to send in their unsolicited premature solutions identifying the killer, he automatically began to eliminate from possible guilt every character the readers named. When the time came for the denouement to be written, Zangwill claimed, he had only one unsuspected character left. Therefore, he made *that* person the murderer.

It was a charming exposition on the author's part, but we know better. The plot, its solution, and its culprit were firmly fixed in Zangwill's mind long before he wrote the final scene. We have his own words on the truth of the matter.

> "Long before [*The Big Bow Mystery*] was written, I said to myself one night that no mystery monger had ever murdered a man in a room to which there was no possible access. The puzzle was scarcely propounded ere the solution flew up."

This was the solution that made *The Big Bow Mystery* such a popular success. Zangwill had posed, then ingeniously circumvented the challenge of the locked room. For in that novel, the drugged victim was killed *after* the sealed room had been forced open and the "corpse" discovered.

*   *   *   *

A dozen years later, another journalist, this time in France, turned his imagination loose on the intriguing problem and came up with what has been termed "the most brilliant of all locked room novels" by none other than the chief historian of the detective story, Howard Haycraft. Mystery author John Dickson Carr has stated categorically that the novel is "the best detective tale ever written." The latter is high praise indeed, coming from today's undisputed master of the locked room mystery.

The book was Gaston Leroux's *The Mystery of the Yellow Room*. The date, 1907. In the Frenchman's treatment, an *accident* occurs behind the locked doors: an accident that offers all outward characteristics of murder. Here, then, is still another solution to the enigma of the corpse in the sealed room. However, the novel's outcome is not nearly so simple nor anticlimactic as it might seem. The "locked room accident" is proved;

but, in the cleverly handled denouement a criminal is trapped as well.

Even at this date, 1907, with the tradition already well-established and moving confidently into the second half of its first century, the possibilities of the locked room had scarcely been tapped. In 1918, back in America, Melville Davisson Post, creator of the too-little-known rural, God-fearing detective, Uncle Abner, gave the concept another twist in the genuinely memorable short story entitled "The Doomdorf Mystery."

Old Doomdorf, a profane, liquor-brewing trouble-maker, is found in his bedroom with his breast split open by a gunshot wound. He is locked inside the room, alone, with the gun which killed him hanging on the wall. Abner triumphed by demonstrat-ine that the sealed room *had* been penetrated; the rays of the sun had come through the closed window, passed through a jug of the bootlegger's raw liquor and focussed on the cap of his gun where it hung between two dogwood forks on the wall. Thus, as he lay asleep on his bed, the weapon had discharged and his evil life was ended.

Authors whose names are far better known to reading audiences of today than those of Zangwill, Leroux, and Post have also made contributions to locked room literature. S. S. Van Dine, creator of Philo Vance, in 1927 brought forth *The "Canary" Murder Case*, in which a body is discovered behind a door locked and bolted on the inside. Vance, seldom at a loss to explain anything, comes up with an answer to the locked room puzzle which demonstrates what seeming miracles can be accomplished by a murderer with some ingenuity and a length of wire. In short, he shows how the door of a room containing a corpse can be locked and bolted from the *outside*. Edgar Wallace, a prolific mystery novelist, pulled off the same trick some years before Van Dine, in *The Clue of the New Pin* (1923). But the Vance adventure seems by far the superior of the two.

*   *   *   *

The name of Ellery Queen cannot long be excluded from any discussion of American detective fiction. Predictably, one of his most celebrated cases is an admirable locked room novel: *The Chinese Orange Mystery.* Published in 1934, it enjoyed a phenomenal success and ended up being sold in condensed form out of vending machines like gum. Essentially, Queen's treatment of the locked room situation is similar to that of Van Dine. But here we have the corpse itself performing macabre gyrations in the process of getting the critical door bolted from the inside.

Should this strike you as being an absurd and perhaps exaggerated expression of the locked room puzzle, I would like to recommend to you a report on a real life murder case in which a Chinese laundryman was murdered in his New York shop, under authentic locked room circumstances. Alan Hynd has given a good account of the baffling crime in the January 1933 issue of *Mystery* Magazine. And in *Actor's Blood* (1936) writer-journalist Ben Hecht gives his colorful fictionization of the same incident in the story "The Mystery of the Fabulous Laundryman." In Hecht's bizarre case, the murderer, as if to stress the beauty of his crime and reduce suspicion of suicide, lopped off the unfortunate laundryman's hands and carried them away.

Ellery Queen's last word on the locked room was by no means spoken in 1934. In 1937, in *The Door Between,* he constructed a new solution—equally brilliant and completely original. A successful woman novelist is discovered stabbed to death behind the locked doors of her study. The death weapon, a scissors half, is missing. For this reason murder is immediately suspected, and the official investigation is off in a cloud of dust—which is also how it ends up. It takes Ellery, in one of his neatest reasoning performances, to deduce finally that the novelist had committed suicide. His main problem was, of course, to explain the disappearance of the fatal blade. The Queen deductions are so dazzling that they satisfy where lurking disappointment might have arisen. But not only that: Ellery goes on to put his damning finger on the woman's actual murderer!

*   *   *   *

The name of John Dickson Carr has already appeared in this discussion linked with his well-deserved title of present day "undisputed master" of the locked room tale. An essay on the treatment accorded the locked room puzzle at the hands of Mr. Carr (oftentimes imperfectly concealed behind the pseudonym of Carter Dickson) would occupy many, many pages and, come to think of it, would probably result in a completely fascinating monograph.

It is enough to say here that Carr-Dickson specializes in making the seemingly impossible possible; and that he solves many a knotty fictional problem by doing so. He delights in having a victim walk out into the middle of a tennis court, leaving distinct footprints, and there vanish into thin air. He takes similar enjoyment from having a man dive into an ordinary backyard swimming pool and disappear from sight. But his favorite and most entertaining pastime is creating and solving one locked room puzzle after another. His methods are infinite and varied, for it is apparent that he has given more than offhand attention to the problem and the possibilities it offers.

As far back as 1935 Carr made a careful analysis of the possible solutions to the locked room puzzle and published his findings in a chapter titled "The Locked Room Lecture" in his novel of that type, *The Three Coffins*. Even so openly showing his hand to his audience, he has not diminished his extraordinary ability to puzzle the reader. Proof of this is that today, more than three decades and some forty novels later, his resourcefulness continues to perplex us as before.

Worthy of special mention among these highly entertaining Carr-Dickson novels is *He Wouldn't Kill Patience* (1944), in which the author carries the "hermetically sealed" aspect of the locked room mystery to its *n*th degree. This time the victim is situated within a perfectly sealed room. The windows, the doors, every possible point of access to the room have been sealed with tape from the inside.

How, one wonders, could a murderer (and there *was* a murderer) conceivably have accomplished this? Really very simple, as Carr demonstrates at the end of the story. All the murderer had to do was kill his man, then tape up all the windows and other exits with tape, save for the principal mode of exit, the inside door. This he edged with tape all along its border, leaving an inch or so protruding beyond the margin of the door. He then calmly closed the door on the murder scene, sought out the vacuum cleaner and from outside the murder room sucked the overhanging flap of tape on the inside edge of the door tightly against the inside jamb—by means of the cleaner's suction! Now *that* one's hard to top.

Mr. John Dickson Carr's title would seem secure for some time to come.

*　　*　　*　　*

All of which brings us more or less up to the present— comfortably into the second century of the locked room's history—and face to face with the question of its future.

With so extensive and varied a development behind it, the temptation exists, does it not, to conclude that the locked room *genre* is "written-out," exhausted, depleted, no longer capable of novelty or surprise? Such a conclusion seems reasonable, and one would not need to look far to find this attitude echoed in the words of a responsible critic and authority on the subject. The truth in the matter is, as we have already indicated, that its decline has been prophesied over and again in the past. While S. S. Van Dine put thumbs down on one particular type of locked room gambit in his 1928 listing of "Twenty Rules for Writing Detective Stories," no more sober judgment of its fate has been pronounced than that of the respected detective fiction critic and historian, Howard Haycraft. In his volume, *Murder For Pleasure: The Life and Times of the Detective Story* (1941), Haycraft makes a saddening choice for "don't" number one on a list of "random *do's* and *don'ts* for the beginner concerning (detective story) device and general technique." Item number one reads as follows:

"Avoid the Locked Room puzzle. Only a genius can invest it with novelty or interest to-day."

Apparently, some thirty years ago, Mr. Haycraft felt that the last significant variation had been accomplished within the tradition of locked room mysteries. His warning seemed to imply that, in 1941, its days were numbered.

Curiously, however, a number of beginning writers have doggedly devised twists on the formula for their maiden murders. Judson Philips (perhaps more widely known as Hugh Pentecost) published his first story, a "locked room" entitled "Room Number 23," in the fondly remembered *Flynn's* magazine. James Yaffe made his debut (at age 15) in *Ellery Queen's Mystery Magazine* with his version of a classic locked room puzzle. And—ah, fondly gazing back!—I wrote my own first detective story when I was thirteen and under the pervasive spell of Ellery Queen, offering what still seems to me to be a unique solution to the locked room situation and applying to it the designation of the only problem that ever stumped Ellery—"The Case of the Wounded Tyrolean." (At least that's what I read in a footnote to Queen's *The Spanish Cape Mystery.)*

Thus, with young blood periodically pumped into it, the locked room adventure has managed to survive up to our day in short stories. And even after so definitive a going-over as it received in Carr's classic tape-sealed sanctuary, the plot idea has continued to be developed and function successfully in one detective novel after another. On occasion it has served as the major plot device, other times as a minor puzzle element (as in Frederick C. Davis' 1955 novel, *Night Drop).* We simply cannot ignore the obvious truth that, despite Mr. Haycraft's warning, the time-honored detective story device is still fresh and. very much with us.

Hans Stefan Santesson, detective fiction critic and former managing editor of the *Saint Detective Magazine,* has lent considerable stature to the concept with his recent anthology, *The Locked Room Reader* (1968). Over the years I had put together my own imaginary anthology of favorite locked room stories and somewhere around the house I have the list. My anthology was to sport the same title as this essay and it was a purist's delight. Santesson, by contrast, has opened the door a little wider and subtitles his collection "Stories of Impossible Crimes and Escapes." I must admit he scooped me and I confess admiration for the genius stroke of including the entire text of Zangwill's *Big Bow Mystery,* so long out of print. My coup would have been the inclusion of Carr's "Locked Room Lecture" from his 1935 novel, *The Three Coffins.* Also, my anthology drew much more generously from the past. Of the sixteen tales brought together by Santesson, thirteen have been published since 1942. (What was that somebody said in 1941?)

In final perspective, the remarkable hardiness of the locked room device is explained in large part, I think, by the fact that the detective story normally attracts a sizeable proportion of the cleverest and most ingenious writers practicing at any given time. The limitations of the locked room puzzle offer a challenge that is plainly difficult to reject. New expressions continue to appear with constant shifting of emphasis from character to atmosphere to incident and, of course, to "gimmick." For it seems that in hand with every new advance in the field of human knowledge and technology there comes a new way to polish someone off inside that irresistibly appealing locked cubicle. Poe had no vacuum cleaner; we have no ray gun. But that might be next.

MORE ON AUTHOR AND SUBJECT

Donald A. Yates teaches in the Department of Romance Languages at Michigan State University, his specialty being Latin American literature. He has translated mystery stories from the Spanish and Portuguese for Ellery Queen's Mystery Magazine *and other periodicals, and his own crime fiction has been published in* Saint Mystery Magazine, *notably "Inspector's Lunch" (May 1959) and "Proof Positive" (February 1962). He is presently working on an anthology of crime-fiction scholarship of his own, tentatively titled* Detectives in Fiction.

As J. R. Christopher pointed out earlier in this book, the three seminal documents on locked-room theory are Chapter XVII of John Dickson Carr's The Three Coffins *(Harper, 1935), Chapter 13 of Clayton Rawson's* Death from a Top Hat *(Putnam, 1938), and Chapter 14 of H. H. Holmes' (Anthony Boucher's)* Nine Times Nine *(Duell, Sloan & Pearce, 1940). For a monumental recent collection of relevant fiction, see the anthology discussed at the end of the above essay, Hans Stefan Santesson's* The Locked Room Reader *(Random House, 1968).*

PART III

SPECULATION AND CRITIQUE

†We tend to think of the detective figure in fiction as the epitome of reason and optimism and cool-headedness, but there is a nightside to him as to every other figure. Prof. Gilbert here turns the coin over and finds something less reassuring but no less intriguing on the other side.

The Detective as Metaphor in
The Nineteenth Century

by Elliot L. Gilbert

Recently, interest in detective fiction has been running high among book collectors. At the famous London auction house of Sotheby's, hard-to-obtain copies of mystery novels and short story anthologies have, according to the *Times Literary Supplement*,[1] been bringing up to a hundred pounds each; and in the same number of *TLS* appears a review of *Victorian Detective Fiction*, a catalogue of the "small, choice collection" of nineteenth-century detective stories made by Dorothy Glover and Graham Greene. Thus, bibliographically speaking, the detective is booming these days. There is no sign, however, that he is also being "rediscovered" as a significant literary figure or even as a sociological phenomenon. Indeed, the anonymous reviewer of the Glover-Greene catalogue makes this point directly. "We find no hint," he writes, "either in Graham Greene's preface or John Carter's introduction, that these early detective stories are worth *reading,* or even—not that we should expect it in such company— that they throw an interesting sociological light on, etc. . ."[2] Yet it would surely be strange if the detective, so ubiquitous in our literature since his first appearance there in the middle of the nineteenth century, should have nothing at all to tell us about our civilization. One question, for example, inevitably suggests itself: if there is no meaningful connection between the detective as a literary figure and the century which gave him birth, why were there no detective stories—that is, no stories whose main subject is the professional detection of crime—before the nineteenth century?

Howard Haycraft, in his book *Murder for Pleasure,* suggests, in answer to this question, that "there could be no detective stories until there were detectives," and he further points out that "professional detectives did not appear in history until the nineteenth century."[3] But why then were there no detectives before the nineteenth century? Haycraft's answer to this is to associate the sudden appearance of professional detectives in this period with the rapid development of democracy, and in particular with the growing acceptance of the rule of reason which democracy implies. " 'Detectives,' " Haycraft writes, " 'cannot flourish until the public has an idea [of] what constitutes proof' . . . And of all the democratic heritages, none has been more stubbornly defended. . .than the right of a fair trial safeguarded by known, just, and logical rules."[4] Thus, the critic sees the detective as a function of all that is most rational and progressive in nineteenth-century society.

It is, of course, extremely satisfying to view the detective— that apostle of pure reason—as the product and even the symbol of a reasonable age. But if reason had its triumphs in the nineteenth century, it also had its failures, and the detective was a product of these as well. To be sure, reason had discovered the laws which made men masters of the physical universe. But, as if to testify to the intransigence of chaos, these same laws also gave rise to the dark, satanic mills and sprawling slums that blighted industrial Europe and America during this period. Man's shaping mind, which had set out to build Jerusalem in England's green and pleasant land, had built Tom-all-Alone's instead. And from the dark and terrible slums of Tom-all-Alone's there sprang a new kind of crime—impersonal, anonymous—that required for the first time great hordes of impersonal, anonymous policemen for its detection, policemen who, simply by undertaking to solve these crimes, became themselves unwilling dwellers in the slums that reason had built. If, then, the detective was a metaphor for the nineteenth century's faith in man's problem-solving abilities, he was just as importantly a symbol of growing nineteenth-century disillusionment with reason as a meaningful response to the human condition.

Nothing, for example, could more perfectly epitomize both the possibilities and the limitations of human reason than the life history of Edgar Allan Poe, author of the first detective story. The details of Poe's biography are too familiar to require elaboration here: a painful childhood and adolescence, increasing loss of control, and, by 1840, complete collapse and delirium; and then, suddenly, the possibility of regeneration, one last chance— so to speak—for the mind to master the dark.

Poe was offered the editorship of *Graham's Magazine* on the condition that he give up his "irregular" behavior, and for a time his efforts in this way were successful. Through the sheer force of a fine intellect kept under precise control, he shaped the world to his own design, making of *Graham's* the first mass circulation magazine in America and at the same time writing the tales of ratiocination which were to be the basis of all future detective fiction. It is surely no coincidence that Poe wrote these stories during the months when he was struggling successfully against an impending dissolution no less terrible than M. Valdemar's. As

Joseph Wood Krutch has put it, "Poe invented the detective story that he might not go mad."

It was, then, the ape of insanity in man that the writer was after, the murderous ape of the Rue Morgue which, in one ingenious disguise or another, had prowled unchallenged through dozens of the earlier nightmare tales. And now at last the ape had met its match in the author's super-intellectual alter ego, Auguste Dupin. The mind had triumphed. But was the victory final? Unhappily for Poe, the period of perfect lucidity which produced the detective stories was all too brief. Soon the writer had slipped back into the old ways and into the old stories. He produced no more tales of ratiocination, for the detective had been given his chance and had been found wanting. The descent was a precipitate one back into the familiar maelstrom of "waking dread" from which not even Auguste Dupin could rescue him.

Poe's disillusionment with reason as the key to man's salvation was, of course, merely the accident of his private life. The fact, however, that during this same period other writers, in the deliberateness of their art, chose to express this same disillusionment, and chose to do so in stories about detectives, is more suggestive. Charles Dickens, for one, in creating in *Bleak House* the first detective in an English novel, deliberately refrained from portraying, through this character, the complete triumph of reason.[5] Indeed, the police force in *Bleak House*, like the Court of Chancery and the great mills and factories in the book, is shown by Dickens to be just one more potentially disastrous product of man's intellect. The courts, created to dispense justice, are instead the great centers of injustice; the factories, dedicated to the elimination of human discomfort, only make men more uncomfortable; the police force, designed to drive out crime with the pure strength of reason, merely corrupts reason with the terrible vitality of crime.

For it is clear from *Bleak House* that just as a jailer becomes a prisoner of the men he guards, so Inspector Bucket is as much the *creature* of crime as he is its nemesis. The machinery of detection must wait, in the first place, upon the commission of the crime. Thus, crime is passionate, self-starting, independent, while detection is initially powerless, nearly always fighting its battles on the enemy's ground, and in the end often obliged to become a part of what it seeks to destroy. Bucket, for example, succeeds in avenging the inhumanity of murder only by coldly perverting the human obligations of friendship and sympathy.[6]

In this respect, Dickens' detective is very much like Hugo's Javert in *Les Misérables,* another mechanical man, fated, in his pursuit of the sewer-dwellers, to plunge into the sewers himself. Nor did the nineteenth century exhaust this metaphor of the detective as a slave rather than a master of darkness. In his recent play, *Victims of Duty*, Eugene Ionesco has a detective sum up his life with these words: "My duty, you know, my dear sir, is simply to apply the system." And when one of the other characters protests, saying, "You're not just a civil servant, you're a *thinking being* (emphasis mine)," the detective dismisses the suggestion. "I am only a soldier, monsieur," he says.

This preoccupation of the nineteenth and twentieth centuries with detectives as thinking beings whose intellects cannot cope with the disorder of the world may in part account for the period's great interest in two other literary figures—Hamlet and Oedipus. Both these characters are, as has frequently been noticed, detectives of a sort; that is, they are both obliged to solve murder mysteries, and at first glance they both seem ideally suited for the job.

Hamlet, just home from the university, is called upon to restore order to his dissolute country by bringing the murderer of his father to justice. Though the prince knows the importance of his mission, and though he recognizes that if no action is taken to root out the corruption in Denmark the whole court may well be destroyed, he nevertheless cannot manage to put off the final massacre. Why he could not do so has fascinated generations of playgoers and readers, and each generation has sought its own answer to the question. Significantly, the answer which the early nineteenth century (and in particular Coleridge) found was that Hamlet's undoing was precisely that instrument which was supposed to save him—his mind. In the end, according to this explanation, reason was no match for the rottenness in Denmark.

As Hamlet was an obsession in the first years of the nine-teenth century, so Oedipus, through the imagination of Freud, began to be an obsession in the last. Like Hamlet, Oedipus is also well-suited to the role of detective. He has gained his throne by solving the riddle of the Sphinx, and he is therefore, highly quali-fied to investigate the murder of Laius. But once again the mind is no match for the horror; indeed, by a grim irony, it is the very act of investigation, the very application of reason, which brings on the tragedy. In the same way, Oedipus' success in answering the riddle of the Sphinx does not really lift the curse from Thebes as it appears to do, it simply shifts the curse to another quarter just as the nineteenth century's application of the new physical laws to its problems only succeeded—nightmare-like—in creating new and more serious problems.

The man who, more than anyone else, gave Oedipus to the nineteenth and twentieth centuries—Sigmund Freud—was himself, as Stanley Edgar Hyman has noted in *The Tangled Bank*, a "great detective."[7] Hyman remarks that a number of exchanges of dialogue between doctor and patient in Freud's case histories read like passages from Sherlock Holmes stories, nor is this surprising when we recall that Conan Doyle based the character of Holmes on Dr. Joseph Bell, a teacher of his at medical school. Conversely, the detective Porfiry in Dostoevsky's *Crime and Punishment* is, in his sensitive investigation of Raskolnikov, as much a psychoanalyst as he is a policeman, there being, however, an important distinc-tion between him and a real-life doctor. For where the psychoan-alyst-detective in the novel manages to rescue his prisoner-patient from the darkness—though not, to everyone's taste, convincingly—the real-life psychoanalyst was not always so successful. Some-times, Freud would encounter a patient whose hysterical lameness, for example, would vanish after deep probing into the victim's un-conscious. But often the same patient would return only a few months later, this time with hysterical paralysis of some other limb or perhaps with symptoms of hysterical blindness. The

Sphinx had not been killed after all; her destructive energies had only been displaced a little and would never finally be overcome.

Even in his own life, Freud was helpless to forestall the famous prophecy of the oracle which had come both to Oedipus and to Laius; that is, he could not himself avoid growing from Oedipus into Laius, from son into father, from heir presumptive into king. Nor, when the time came, could he keep himself from violently dismissing most of his disciples—his professional sons—just as if, for all his knowledge and understanding, there still rang in his ears the dread and not-to-be-ignored warning: "If you have a son, he will kill you."

Of course, in spite of Bucket and Javert, in spite of Hamlet and Oedipus and Freud, detectives were not universally ineffectual in nineteenth-century literature and experience. In popular mystery fiction, for example, they were almost invariably triumphant spokesmen for human reason. Indeed, during the century and a quarter that have passed since Poe created the detective story, the genre has spawned literally thousands of detective-geniuses from whom nothing can be hidden and who always succeed in restoring order to a murderous world. But even as the mystery story industry has been grinding out these optimistic tales for readers who would certainly not devour them so eagerly if they were not aware of the stubborn persistence of evil in the real world, that real world has been encroaching on the fictional one. Among the more recent popular literary detectives, for instance, such figures as Raymond Chandler's Philip Marlowe and Dashiell Hammett's Sam Spade begin, realistically, to blur the distinctions between detective and criminal. Then there is a character like Mickey Spillane's Mike Hammer, who neither in actions nor in values differs in the least from the people he pursues.

It may be objected, of course, that Mike Hammer was never intended to be an apostle of reason and that therefore his surrender to the violence he is supposed to eliminate is not meaningful. But even about Sherlock Holmes, that very type of the perfect intellect triumphing over a chaotic universe, it is possible to raise disquieting questions. All of those successful cases which

permit us to flatter ourselves that man's mind is indeed in control
of the world—do they not, according to Watson, constitute only a
portion of the mysteries which Holmes investigated? Do we not
hear with alarming frequency of cases which trailed off inconclu-
sively or, even more astonishing, of cases which in the end left
Holmes baffled? And with the introduction of the sinister Professor Moriarty and his complex network of world crime, do not even
Holmes' greatest successes—successes with lost jewels and curious
cyphers and ingenious bank robbers—come to seem rather pallid
and, in the long run, insignificant?

The story called "His Last Bow" makes this point most inci-
sively. Time and again in the early days, Holmes, by the simple
expedient of discovering the hiding place of the top-secret plans
or of revealing the activities of international spies, had single-
handedly kept Europe from going to war. Now, however, it is
August, 1914, and though the great man has come out of retirement to do battle once more with the forces of darkness, and
though his mind seems as quick as ever, this time the darkness is
not to be denied. To be sure, Holmes foils the German agent, but
World War I, the ultimate symbol of irrationality, cannot so easily
be put off. It has a vitality too terrible even for the great detective, who withdraws once more to the Sussex Downs and to his
bees, never again to appear in the world.

Can it be that in the end even Sherlock Holmes, whose creator—Conan Doyle—was himself to move from the realm of reason
to the world of the occult, had come to doubt the efficacy of
intellect, had come to see that if the detective was a metaphor for
the nineteenth century's faith in ratiocination, he was also symbolic of the age's profound disillusionment with human reason?
We have the evidence of his own words at the end of "The Adventure of the Cardboard Box," where Holmes asks solemnly,

What is the meaning of it, Watson? What object
is served by this circle of misery, violence and fear?
It must tend to some end, or else our universe is
ruled by chance, which is unthinkable, But what

end? *There* is the great standing perennial problem to which human reason is as far from an answer as ever.

NOTES

[1] December 8, 1966, p. 1160.

[2] *Ibid.,* p. 1145.

[3] Howard Haycraft, *Murder for Pleasure* (New York, 1941), p. 5.

[4] *Ibid.,* p. 313. Haycraft here quotes from E. M. Wrong's Introduction to *Crime and Detection* (New York, 1926).

[5] And this, despite the fact that the book's Inspector Bucket is said to have been modeled on the author's personal friend, Inspector Field of the London Metropolitan Police Force.

[6] Moreover, even where the detective succeeds, his triumph is frequently trivial in the face of the criminal's victory; the murderer may be undone but never the murder.   Consider Mlle. Hortense's baiting of Bucket in *Bleak House* moments after the detective has exposed the woman as Tulkinghorn's killer.   " 'Listen then, my angel,' says she, after several sarcastic nods. 'You are very spiritual.   But can you restore him back to life?'   Mr. Bucket answers 'Not exactly.' "

[7] Stanley Edgar Hyman, *The Tangled Bank* (New York, 1962), p. 309, 313.

MORE ON AUTHOR AND SUBJECT

Elliot L. Gilbert teaches English at the University of California, Davis.   He is a specialist in nineteenth-century English literature, and is presently preparing a critical biography of Rudyard Kipling, to be published by the St. Martin's Press.   His own crime fiction has appeared in Ellery Queen's Mystery Magazine, *notably*

"Death Wore a Beard" (June 1966) and "Link in the Chain" (July 1969). The latter story has been included in Allen J. Hubin's anthology of Best Detective Stories of the Year (Dutton, 1970).

Readers with a further interest in the subject of the preceding essay will be happy to learn that Prof. Gilbert is at work on its expansion into a full-length study.

Mystery fiction has sometimes been accused of being a sterile and artificial genre, in which an author cannot give form or expression to his deepest concerns or his inmost views on the nature of man and the world. In reality, the accusation is simply not true of a goodly number of the foremost names in the field, such as Hammett, Chandler, Woolrich, Hitchcock, and Ross Macdonald. In the following essay the creator of Lew Archer indicates how the figure of the detective can function for a writer who does put himself on the line in his crime fiction.

The Writer as Detective Hero
by Ross Macdonald

A producer who last year was toying with the idea of making a television series featuring my private detective Lew Archer asked me over lunch at Perino's if Archer was based on any actual person. "Yes," I said. "Myself." He gave me a semi-pitying Hollywood look. I tried to explain that while I had known some excellent detectives and watched them work, Archer was created from the inside out. I wasn't Archer, exactly, but Archer was me.

The conversation went downhill from there, as if I had made a damaging admission. But I believe most detective-story writers would give the same answer. A close paternal or fraternal relationship between writer and detective is a marked peculiarity of the form. Throughout its history, from Poe to Chandler and beyond, the detective hero has represented his creator and carried his values into action in society.

Poe, who invented the modern detective story, and his detective Dupin, are good examples. Poe's was a first-rate but guilt-haunted mind painfully at odds with the realities of pre-Civil-War America. Dupin is a declassed aristocrat, as Poe's heroes tend to be, an obvious equivalent for the artist-intellectual who has lost his place in society and his foothold in tradition. Dupin has no social life, only one friend. He is set apart from other people by his superiority of mind.

In his creation of Dupin, Poe was surely compensating for his failure to become what his extraordinary mental powers seemed to fit him for. He had dreamed of an intellectual hierarchy governing the cultural life of the nation, himself at its head. Dupin's outwitting of an unscrupulous politician in "The Purloined Letter," his "solution" of an actual New York case in "Marie Roget," his repeated trumping of the cards held by the Prefect of Police, are Poe's vicarious demonstrations of superiority to an indifferent society and its officials.

Of course Poe's detective stories gave the writer, and give the reader, something deeper than such obvious satisfactions. He devised them as a means of exorcising or controlling guilt and horror. The late William Carlos Williams, in a profound essay, related Poe's sense of guilt and horror to the terrible awareness of a hyperconscious man standing naked and shivering on a new continent. The guilt was doubled by Poe's anguished insight into the unconscious. It had to be controlled by some rational pattern, and the detective story, "the tale of ratiocination," provided such a pattern.

The tale of the bloody murders in the Rue Morgue, Poe's first detective story (1841), is a very hymn to analytic reason intended, as Poe wrote later, "to depict some very remarkable features in the mental character of my friend, the Chevalier C. Auguste Dupin." Dupin clearly represents the reason, which was Poe's mainstay against the nightmare forces of the mind. These latter are acted out by the murderous ape: "Gnashing its teeth, and flashing fire from its eyes, it flew upon the body of the girl and embedded its fearful talons in her throat, retaining its grasp until she expired."

Dupin's reason masters the ape and explains the inexplicable—the wrecked apartment behind the locked door, the corpse of a young woman thrust up the chimney—but not without leaving a residue of horror. The nightmare can't quite be explained away, and persists in the teeth of reason. An unstable balance between reason and more primitive human qualities is characteristic of the detective story. For both writer and reader it is an imaginative arena where such conflicts can be worked out safely, under artistic controls.

The first detective story has other archetypal features, particularly in the way it is told. The "I" who narrates it is not the detective Dupin. The splitting of the protagonist into a narrator and a detective has certain advantages: it helps to eliminate the inessential, and to postpone the solution. More important, the author can present his self-hero, the detective, without undue embarrassment, and can handle dangerous emotional material at two or more removes from himself as Poe does in "Rue Morgue."

The disadvantages of the split protagonist emerge more clearly in the saga of Dupin's successor, Sherlock Holmes. One projection of the author, the narrator, is made to assume a posture of rather blind admiration before another projection of the author, the detective hero, and the reader is invited to share Dr. Watson's adoration of the great man. An element of narcissistic fantasy, impatient with the limits of the self, seems to be built into this traditional form of the detective story.

I'm not forgetting that Holmes' *modus operandi* was based on that of an actual man, Conan Doyle's friend and teacher, Dr. Joseph Bell. Although his "science" usually boils down to careful observation, which was Dr. Bell's forte, Holmes is very much the scientific criminologist. This hero of scientism may be in fact the dominant culture hero of our technological society.

Though Holmes is a physical scientist specializing in chemistry and anatomy, and Dupin went in for literary and psychological analysis, Holmes can easily be recognized as Dupin's direct descendent. His most conspicuous feature, his ability to read thoughts on the basis of associative clues, is a direct borrowing from Dupin. And like Dupin, he is a projection of the author, who at the time of Holmes' creation was a not very busy young doctor. According to his son Adrian, Conan Doyle admitted when he was dying: "If anyone is Sherlock Holmes, then I confess it is myself."

Holmes had other ancestors and collateral relations which reinforce the idea that he was a portrait of the artist as a great detective. His drugs, his secrecy and solitude, his moods of depression (which he shared with Dupin) are earmarks of the Romantic rebel then and now. Behind Holmes lurk the figures of nineteenth-century poets, Byron certainly, probably Baudelaire, who translated Poe and pressed Poe's guilty knowledge to new limits. I once made a case for the theory (and Anthony Boucher didn't disagree) that much of the modern development of the detective story stems from Baudelaire, his "dandyism" and his vision of the city as inferno. Conan Doyle's London, which influenced Eliot's "Wasteland," has something of this quality.

But Holmes' Romantic excesses aren't central to his character. His Baudelairean spleen and drug addiction are merely the idiosyncrasies of genius. Holmes is given the best of both worlds, and remains an English gentleman, accepted on the highest social levels. Permeating the thought and language of Conan Doyle's stories is an air of blithe satisfaction with a social system based on privilege.

This obvious characteristic is worth mentioning because it was frozen into one branch of the form. Nostalgia for a privileged society accounts for one of the prime attractions of the traditional English detective story and its innumerable American counterparts. Neither wars nor the dissolution of governments and societies interrupt that long weekend in the country house which is often, with more or less unconscious symbolism, cut off by a failure in communications from the outside world.

The contemporary world is the special province of the American hardboiled detective story. Dashiell Hammett, Raymond Chandler, and the other writers for *Black Mask* who developed it, were in conscious reaction against the Anglo-American school which, in the work of S. S. Van Dine for example, had lost contact with contemporary life and language. Chandler's dedication, to the editor of *Black Mask,* of a collection of his early stories (1944), describes the kind of fiction they had been trying to supplant: "For Joseph Thompson Shaw with affection and respect, and in memory of the time when we were trying to get murder away from the upper classes, the week-end house party and the vicar's rose-garden, and back to the people who are really good at it." While Chandler's novels swarm with plutocrats as well as criminals, and even with what pass in Southern California for aristocrats, the *Black Mask* revolution was a real one. From it emerged a new kind of detective hero, the classless, restless man of American democracy, who spoke the language of the street.

Hammett, who created the most powerful of these new heroes in Sam Spade, had been a private detective and knew the corrupt inner workings of American cities. But Sam Spade was a less obvious projection of Hammett than detective heroes usually are of their authors. Hammett had got his early romanticism under strict ironic control. He could see Spade from outside, without affection, perhaps with some bleak compassion. In this as in other respects Spade marks a sharp break with the Holmes tradition. He possesses the virtues and follows the code of a frontier male. Thrust for his sins into the urban inferno, he pits his courage and cunning against its denizens, plays for the highest stakes available, love and money, and loses nearly everything in the end. His lover is guilty of murder; his narrow, bitter code forces Spade to turn her over to the police. The Maltese falcon has been stripped of jewels.

Perhaps the stakes and implied losses are higher than I have suggested. The worthless falcon may symbolize a lost tradition, the great cultures of the Mediterranean past which have become inaccessible to Spade and his generation. Perhaps the bird stands for the Holy Ghost itself, or for its absence.

The ferocious intensity of the work, the rigorous spelling-out of Sam Spade's deprivation of his full human heritage, seem to me to make his story tragedy, if there is such a thing as dead-pan tragedy. Hammett was the first American writer to use the detective-story for the purposes of a major novelist, to present a vision, blazing if disenchanted, of our lives. Sam Spade was the product and reflection of a mind which was not at home in Zion, or in Zenith.

Chandler's vision is disenchanted, too, but in spite of its hallucinated brilliance of detail it lacks the tragic unity of Hammett's. In his essay on "The Simple Art of Murder," an excitingly written piece of not very illuminating criticism, Chandler offers a prescription for the detective hero which suggests a central weakness in his vision:

> In everything that can be called art there is a quality of redemption. . . .But down these mean streets a man must go who is not himself mean, who is neither tarnished nor afraid. . . .The detective in this kind of story must be such a man. He is the hero, he is everything. . . . He must be the best man in his world and a good enough man for any world.

While there may be "a quality of redemption" in a good novel, it belongs to the whole work and is not the private property of one of the characters. No hero of serious fiction could act within a moral straitjacket requiring him to be consistently virtuous and unafraid. Sam Spade was submerged and struggling in tragic life. The detective-as-redeemer is a backward step in the direction of sentimental romance, and an over-simplified world of good guys and bad guys. The people of Chandler's early novels, though they include chivalrous gangsters and gangsters' molls with hearts of gold, are divided into two groups by an angry puritanical morality. The goats are usually separated from the sheep by sexual promiscuity or perversion. Such a strong and overt moral-

istic bias actually interferes with the broader moral effects a novelist aims at.

Fortunately in the writing of his books Chandler toned down
his Watsonian enthusiasm for his detective's moral superiority.
The detective Marlowe, who tells his own stories in the first person, and sometimes admits to being afraid, has a self-deflating wit
which takes the curse off his knight-errantry:

> I wasn't wearing a gun . . . I doubted if it
> would do me any good. The big man would prob-
> ably take it away from me and eat it. (*Farewell,
> My Lovely*, 1940)

The Chandler-Marlowe prose is a highly charged blend of
laconic wit and imagistic poetry set to breakneck rhythms. Its
strong colloquial vein reaffirms the fact that the *Black Mask* revolution was a revolution in language as well as subject matter. It is
worth noticing that H. L. Mencken, the great lexicographer of our
vernacular, was an early editor of *Black Mask*. His protegé James
M. Cain once said that his discovery of the western roughneck
made it possible for him to write fiction. Marlowe and his predecessors performed a similar function for Chandler, whose English
education put a special edge on his passion for our new language,
and a special edge on his feelings against privilege. Socially mobile
and essentially classless (he went to college but has a working-
class bias), Marlowe liberated his author's imagination into an
overheard democratic prose which is one of the most effective
narrative instruments in our recent literature.

Under the obligatorily "tough" surface of the writing, Marlowe is interestingly different from the standard hardboiled hero
who came out of *Black Mask*. Chandler's novels focus in his hero's
sensibility, and could almost be described as novels of sensibility.
Their constant theme is big-city loneliness, and the wry pain of a
sensitive man coping with the roughest elements of a corrupt
society.

It is Marlowe's doubleness that makes him interesting: the

hard-boiled mask half-concealing Chandler's poetic and satiric
mind. Part of our pleasure derives from the interplay between
the mind of Chandler and the voice of Marlowe. The recognized
difference between them is part of the dynamics of the narrative,
setting up bipolar tensions in the prose. The marvelous opening
paragraph of *The Big Sleep* (1939) will illustrate some of this:

> It was about eleven o'clock in the morning,
> mid October, with the sun not shining and a look
> of hard wet rain in the clearness of the foothills.
> I was wearing my powder-blue suit, with dark blue
> shirt, tie and display handkerchief, black brogues,
> black wool socks with dark blue clocks on them.
> I was neat, clean, shaved and sober, and I didn't
> care who knew it. I was everything the well-
> dressed private detective ought to be. I was calling
> on four million dollars.

Marlowe is making fun of himself, and of Chandler in the
rôle of brash young detective. There is pathos, too, in the idea
that a man who can write like a fallen angel should be a mere
private eye; and Socratic irony. The gifted writer conceals himself behind Marlowe's cheerful mindlessness. At the same time the
retiring, middle-aged, scholarly author acquires a durable mask,
forever 38, which allows him to face the dangers of society high
and low.

Chandler's conception of Marlowe, and his relationship with
his character, deepened as his mind penetrated the romantic fantasy, and the overbright self-consciousness, that limited his vision.
At the end of *The Long Goodbye* (1953) there is a significant
confrontation between Marlowe and a friend who had betrayed
him and apparently gone homosexual. In place of the righteous
anger which Marlowe would have indulged in in one of the earlier
novels he now feels grief and disquiet, as if the confrontation
might be with a part of himself.

The friend, the ex-friend, tries to explain his moral breakdown: "I was in the commandos, bud. They don't take you if you're just a piece of fluff. I got badly hurt and it wasn't any fun with those Nazi doctors. It did something to me." That is all we are told. At the roaring heart of Chandler's maze there is a horror which even at the end of his least evasive novel remains unspeakable. Whatever its hidden meaning, this scene was written by a man of tender and romantic sensibility who had been injured. Chandler used Marlowe to shield while half-expressing his sensibility, and to act out the mild paranoia which often goes with this kind of sensibility and its private hurts, and which seems to be virtually endemic among contemporary writers.

I can make this judgment with some assurance because it applies with a vengeance to some of my earlier books, particularly *Blue City* (1947). A decade later, in *The Doomsters*, I made my detective Archer criticize himself as "a slightly earthbound Tarzan in a slightly paranoid jungle." This novel marked a fairly clean break with the Chandler tradition, which it had taken me some years to digest, and freed me to make my own approach to the crimes and sorrows of life.

I learned a great deal from Chandler—any writer can—but there had always been basic differences between us. One was in our attitude to plot. Chandler described a good plot as one that made for good scenes, as if the parts were greater than the whole. I see plot as a vehicle of meaning. It should be as complex as contemporary life, but balanced enough to say true things about it. The surprise with which a detective novel concludes should set up tragic vibrations which run backward through the entire structure. Which means that the structure must be single, and *intended.*

Another difference between Chandler and me is in our use of language. My narrator Archer's wider and less rigidly stylized range of expression, at least in more recent novels, is related to a central difference between him and Marlowe. Marlowe's voice is limited by his role as the hardboiled hero. He must speak within his limits as a character, and these limits are quite narrowly conceived. Chandler tried to relax them in *The Long Goodbye*, but he was old and the language failed to respond. He was trapped like the late Hemingway in an unnecessarily limiting idea of self, hero, and language.

I could never write of Archer: "He is the hero, he is everything." It is true that his actions carry the story, his comments on it reflect my attitudes (but deeper attitudes remain implicit), and Archer or a narrator like him is indispensable to the kind of books I write. But he is not their emotional center. And in spite of what I said at the beginning, Archer has developed away from his early status as a fantasy projection of myself and my personal needs. Cool, I think, is the word for our mature relationship. Archer himself has what New Englanders call "weaned affections."

An author's heavy emotional investment in a narrator-hero can get in the way of the story and blur its meanings, as some of Chandler's books demonstrate. A less encumbered narrator permits greater flexibility, and fidelity to the intricate truths of life. I don't have to celebrate Archer's physical or sexual prowess, or work at making him consistently funny and charming. He can be self-forgetful, almost transparent at times, and concentrate as good detectives (and good writers) do, on the people whose problems he is investigating. These other people are for me the main thing: they are often more intimately related to me and my life than Lew Archer is. He is the obvious self-projection which holds the eye (my eye as well as the reader's) while more secret selves creep out of the woodwork behind the locked door. Remember how the reassuring presence of Dupin permitted Poe's mind to face the nightmare of the homicidal ape and the two dead women.

Archer is a hero who sometimes verges on being an anti-hero. While he is a man of action, his actions are largely directed to putting together the stories of other people's lives and discovering their significance. He is less a doer than a questioner, a consciousness in which the meanings of other lives emerge. This gradually developed conception of the detective hero as the mind of the novel is not new, but is probably my main contribution to this special branch of fiction. Some such refinement of the conception of the detective hero was needed, to bring this kind of novel closer to the purposes and range of the mainstream novel.

It may be that internal realism, a quality of mind, is one of the most convincing attributes a character can have. Policemen and lawyers have surprised me with the opinion that Archer is quite true to life. The two best private detectives I personally know resemble him in their internal qualities: their intelligent humaneness, an interest in other people transcending their interest in themselves, and a toughness of mind which enables them to face human weaknesses, including their own, with open eyes. Both of them dearly love to tell a story.

MORE ON AUTHOR AND SUBJECT

Ross Macdonald (Kenneth Millar in private life) was born near San Francisco in 1915 and educated in Canada and at the University of Michigan. In 1938 he married a Canadian girl who went on to fame in her own right as mystery novelist Margaret Millar. It was not long before, in Ellery Queen's words, he "became infected with the detective-story virus by exposure to his wife," and his own first mystery, the superb (but today almost unobtainable) The Dark Tunnel, *was published in 1944. In 1949 he took up the name of Macdonald (first John, then John Ross, finally just Ross) and the exploits of private detective Lew Archer, which, like the private-eye stories of Hammett and Chandler before him, have become the province of literary critics as well as discriminating readers. His current Archer novel,* **The** Goodbye Look, *has been on the best-seller list for almost four months as of this writing.*

In a later essay, "A Preface to the Galton Case" (in **After**words: Novelists on Their Novels, *ed. Thomas McCormack, Harper & Row 1969), Macdonald discusses in detail the relation between his personal and artistic conflicts and the shaping of one of his crime novels. That essay no less than the preceding one is indispensable to the serious student of mystery fiction.*

Intelligent critiques of detective fiction are rare indeed (witness the Edmund Wilson fiasco of a quarter century ago), but Prof. Aydelotte's is one of the best. I don't agree with everything he says, and I wish he had discussed even one specific detective story at sufficient length to show how it supported his contentions; but he raises issues that need a good long look.

The Detective Story as a Historical Source
by William O. Aydelotte

One would hardly go to the detective story for an accurate picture of modern life. If a historian five hundred years hence were to base a reconstruction of our twentieth-century civilization solely on the evidence contained in detective stories, he might reach strange conclusions. He would probably infer that the most prominent features of our culture were inefficient or corrupt police forces, a multitude of private detectives, sometimes urbane and sometimes hard-boiled, and a constant series of domestic crimes occuring principally in large country houses and committed exclusively by people of the most harmless and respectable outward appearance. What little realism detective stories possess lies on the surface and does not extend to the characters or to the action.   The notion that they give a literal representation of modern society may be rejected at the outset.   Far from being realistic, they constitute one of the most conventionalized of literary forms, being exceeded in this respect perhaps only by the comic strip.

This does not argue, however, that detective novels are completely dissociated from the age in which they are written. On the contrary, their immense popularity—it is alleged that one out of every four new works of fiction published in the English language belongs to this category—suggests that they are an impressive portent of our cultures. Their popularity is not likely to be accidental. If we can ascertain the reason for it, we may be able to grasp the link between detective literature and the society of which it forms a part.

I suggest that the widespread and sustained popularity of detective stories is principally due to the very elements which make them unrealistic, to their conventions. These conventions (which will be analysed at length in the course of this essay) have been fairly constant in the century-long history of the *genre,* amid all the variations of setting and technique. A substantial number of them appear even in the stories of Poe. The long persistence and regular recurrence of these stereotypes afford at least a presumption that they are essential to the detective story's continued vogue. Their role is of course clear. They are wish-fulfillment fantasies designed to produce certain agreeable sensations in the reader, to foist upon him illusions he wants to entertain and which he goes to this literature to find.

The charm of detective stories lies neither in originality nor in artistic merit, though they may possess both these qualities. It consists rather in the repetition of a formula that through trial and error has been found pleasing. We read these books, not to have a new experience, but to repeat in slightly different form an experience we have had already. Thus, for example, the "surprise" ending is not really a surprise. It is the ending we expect and demand, and we would feel outraged if any other kind of ending were offered to us. It is true that many of these works introduce elements of novelty in the background and setting, and that the best of them unquestionably show considerable skill in writing and construction. Such amenities, however, serve not so much to change the formula as to render it more palatable to the highbrow. The educated part of the detective-story audience shows no unwillingness to accept the formula but merely a fastidious distaste for its cruder expressions.

The interest of detective stories to the historian is that they shed light on the people who read them. By studying the fantasies contained in this literature, one may gather a description of its readers, in terms of their unsatisfied motivational drives. Thus these books are the more illuminating the more unrealistic and inaccurate they are. It is precisely by their inaccuracies that they reveal attitudes and emotions of the audience to which they cater. To the historian concerned with popular opinion, this audience is of particular interest for two reasons. In the first place it is large—the detective story is a mass medium—and in the second place it is extremely varied. Detective novels appeal to different types of readers, highbrows as well as lowbrows. They are read with avidity by intellectuals who despise soap operas and are repelled by the success stories in popular magazines. Some critics even assert that they are written primarily for intellectuals, a claim which is of course invalid in view of the breadth and extent of their circulation. The reading of this literature is, rather, a widespread habit to which the educated also adhere.

The extent and variety of the detective-story audience argue a surprising degree of unity in our culture, at least in respect to the demand for the particular fantasies which this literature purveys. Since these books appeal, not only to many people, but to many different kinds of people, they presumably reflect attitudes and needs that are widely distributed. A study of the stereotypes in the detective story may, therefore, reveal to us attitudes and opinions which, if not universal, at least occur in our age with significant frequency..

Primarily, the detective story presents a view of life which is agreeable and reassuring. By ingenious and long-tested devices, it persuades the reader that the world it describes is simple and understandable, that it is meaningful, and that it is secure.

(1)   In place of the complex issues of modern existence, people in a detective story have very simple problems. Life goes along well except for the single point that some crime, usually, in modern stories, a murder, has been committed. (There are some exceptions, particularly among the Sherlock Holmes stories, which are not wholly typical of the modern form of the *genre*: many of these contain no murder, and some involve no crime at all, merely a puzzle.)   From this act follow most of the troubles which the sympathetic characters must endure: they may, for example, come under temporary suspicion of murder, or they may have a misunderstanding with their loved ones. Troubles are objectively caused by an external circumstance, the murder, which can and will be resolved, whereupon the troubles will disappear. Once the solution has been reached, most of the other difficulties are ended and the characters go away happy, never apparently to be vexed by the minor worries and neuroses of modern man. The mess, confusion, and frustration of life have been reduced to a simple issue between good and evil, virtue and wickedness. And virtue triumphs.

To carry the argument to the next stage, the simplification of the problem is matched by a corresponding simplification of the solution. Here we come to one of the most universal conventions in the *genre*, the essential clue, the unique significant detail that unlocks the mystery. The detective story makes a distinction between essential and non-essential facts. As Sherlock Holmes puts it, "It is of the highest importance in the art of detection to be able to recognize, out of a number of facts, which are incidental and which vital. Otherwise your energy and attention must be dissipated instead of being concentrated." ("The Reigate Puzzle.") In the unreal world of the detective story, we depart from the intricate currents of causation in life as we know it, and find instead that a whole elaborate plot may be unravelled by discovering the one relevant detail. Furthermore, the factual nature of this detail lends an air of concreteness to the solution:

we are led to feel it is the only solution, inevitable, unique, completely certain.

(2) By other commonly used devices the detective story makes life more meaningful and endows the events it describes with significance, even with glamor. To say that detective stories provide a thrill which compensates for the dullness of their readers' lives is only the beginning of the story. It is true that they offer the excitement of adventure, and also capitalize on popular indignations or fetishes in the manner of other types of sensation literature. But they do more than this. In many subtle ways they help their readers to believe in the existence of a richer and fuller world.

Even the sordid surroundings of crime make their contribution to the atmosphere of richness and meaning. As G. K. Chesterton says, this form of literature succeeds often in getting the romance and poetry of the city, and "the investigator crosses London with something of the loneliness and liberty of a prince in a tale of elfland."

Comparable effects are achieved in other ways. Consider, for example, the following quotation, in which Sherlock Holmes is explaining one of his solutions: "I am only, of course, giving you the leading results now of my examination of the paper. There were twenty-three other deductions which would be of more interest to experts than to you." ("The Reigate Puzzle.")

This is one of many passages in which Conan Doyle contrives to suggest there is a great world of intellectual phenomena, beyond the range of the average man, but really existent for all that and within the competence of the superior mind. Thus, for other illustrations, Holmes deduces a whole life-history from the appearance of a hat or a watch. ("The Blue Carbuncle," "The Sign of Four.") The implication is that life is not the simple and drab affair we ordinarily encounter, but something more extensive and more interesting.

To add further to the reader's sense of new frontiers of meaning and significance, the detective story manages in various ways to cast a glamor on its characters and to convey to the reader that these people count, that they matter in the world. Such an illusion is achieved, for example, when the action takes place in the classical setting of the large English country-house with its atmosphere of butlers and scullery-maids, lawns and shrubberies, French windows and guest-wings, and large house parties of elegant guests.

(3)   Finally, the detective story introduces us to a secure universe. We find here an ordered world obedient to fixed laws. The outcome is certain and the criminal will without fail be beaten by the detective. In this world man has power to control his own affairs and the problems of life can be mastered by human agency.

Even the handling of the theme of death contributes to this feeling of security. One might not at first expect a form of literature which deals with death by violence to have the cheerful and encouraging effect I have attributed to the detective story. Yet murder is an almost universal feature of these books. From the point of view of literary construction, of course, a murder is useful for the plot and provides the suitable starting-point for an investigation. But there is another reason for including it.

This is that the detective story, by its peculiar treatment of death, contrives to minimize the fear of it. Death is always presented in a rather special way. It is something that happens to somebody else, not to anyone we like or identify ourselves with. The victim, though he is ultimately avenged, is not allowed to be a sympathetic character. The reader's emotions must not become engaged on his behalf. At the least the victim is killed off before his personality has been developed far enough for the reader to take an interest in him or to like him. More often the victim is clearly unattractive, a man who has been injuring the lives of a number of the other characters (which also helps the plot by increasing the list of possible suspects), and his death is good riddance. In many cases, the murder turns out to be the best thing that could have happened. After everything has been straightened out, the lovers, if any, are brought together, the detective has had a chance to prove his worth, all the other characters are now freed from the guilt of his murder, since this guilt has now been thrown on an acceptable scapegoat, and everyone is set for a cheerful future.

The detective story uses crime not to make life more horrible but to make it more cheerful. The despair and horror it seems to offer the reader are presented in a very manageable form and really subserve, not a pessimistic view of life, but a view that is exactly the opposite. Its concern with crime and the seamy side of life misleads the observer as to its true impact. Its message is essentially agreeable, almost to the point of being saccharine.

The agreeable view of life presented in the detective story is deepened and enlarged by the actions of its two most important characters, the criminal and the detective. Each plays a standardized role that affords a special kind of satisfaction to the reader. We will consider the criminal first.

The criminal is a scapegoat. He is the cause of and can justly be blamed for all the troubles of the detective-story world, the murder and everything that follows from it. The detective story evades the complex issues of life and saves us the effort of analysing the sources of our difficulties and frustrations by presenting every problem as one of personal morality. The criminal therefore must be a single individual, who can eventually be identified. A detective novel where the murder was due to "conditions" of some sort, and where no individual was responsible, would be quite unsatisfactory.

But the criminal is not only a scapegoat, he is also something more deeply gratifying, a scapegoat that can be beaten. His great charm is that he is conquerable and will infallibly be conquered. He appears for most of the story as a colossus, formidable in his cunning and power. But his strength, though great, is futile, only sham strength. His position is actually unreal, for he has no place nor meaning in an ordered world. If you look closely, the criminal is a miserable creature. He can do little ultimately against organized society which is rapidly closing in on him. If we are terrified of him for a while, because of his apparent cunning and dexterity, that simply enhances the relief we feel when he gets beaten, and also the satisfaction we have in knowing all the time, in our inmost hearts, that he is going to be beaten.

Besides this, I believe the criminal also fulfills another and more subtle purpose. He relieves our feelings of aggression, not only by becoming an object of them himself, but also in a second and quite different way, by committing the murder. As I tried to show earlier, it not infrequently happens that the murder is a good thing; the victim is a menace to the sympathetic characters and the murder starts off the train of events that leads finally to the happy ending. In novels where this is the case, the criminal, by killing the victim, performs a service to society, a service we would not wish, however, to have performed by any sympathetic character because of the penalty that must ensue. The criminal, though he is made to act from selfish and unworthy motives and must therefore be punished, still gratifies us by committing the act we are glad to see done. He shares something of the ambiguous character of the scapegoat of mythology who is both a friend and enemy to society, who commits the act of sin or disobedience that helps us all and then removes the taint or penalty attached thereto by himself undergoing the punishment, a punishment that is occasionally even inflicted by the beneficiaries.

Perhaps the most gratifying function of the detective story, and one that is also achieved through the agency of the criminal, is the illusion the reader obtains of being released from guilt and dissociated from the murderer. This illusion is achieved by bringing a number of the most prominent characters, including any with whom the reader might perhaps identify himself, temporarily under suspicion. For this purpose, the criminal must be a member of the closed circle, the small group affected by or concerned with the crime, so that the possibility of an outside murderer will be excluded and any member of this little society may therefore conceivably be guilty. (Here again the Holmes stories constitute a partial exception to the convention that has crystallized in our own day: in very few cases are there several suspects, and in some cases the criminal is an outsider who does not appear till caught.) The criminal must also be the least likely person, revealed only in the surprise ending, so that, since the identity of the murderer is kept a secret until the end, no single character in the closed circle can be assumed to be assuredly free from guilt. By such means the fear of guilt is temporarily intensified and the reader's relief at the identification of the criminal is increased.

Once the criminal is discovered, everyone else is at once freed from the burden of possible guilt. The suspicious actions of the other characters now turn out to have a perfectly innocent explanation. Yet the temporary suspicion directed against them was in a sense justified, for many of them benefited from the crime and would perhaps have liked to commit it if they could have escaped the consequences. For that reason, their relief is the greater. The satisfaction of the "innocent" characters and the reader at being released from guilt is all the more poignant because they do not deserve it; in thought and feeling, if not in action, they are also guilty. Therefore our gratification when the murder is committed does not conflict with our satisfaction at being ultimately freed from guilt, but on the contrary enhances it.

Besides all this, the criminal has one additional function. He contributes to the illusion of the power of the detective. His crime is thought out in great detail, is indeed perfect except for the single flaw discernible only to the detective's penetrating eye. The botched crime of real life is unknown to the detective story. The criminal shows incredible self-possession and address, and conducts himself with such poise and assurance that he is not suspected until the end. In all this he is a worthy antagonist and gives the detective full scope to demonstrate his talents. However, though the crime is so difficult that it can be solved only by the detective, the detective almost invariably does succeed in solving it. He always has the particular bit of esoteric knowledge or the particular type of intuition that turns out to be just what is needed, the one and only thing that will clear up this particular mystery. The point, as we may now perceive, is that the crime is tailored to fit the detective. It finally proves to be exactly the kind of crime that is best suited to his peculiar and unique talents. The criminal actually serves the detective by offering him just the kind of problem that he is best equipped to deal with. Though a skilful writer seeks to maintain the illusion, the crime is really a setup, and the detective solves it because the author has contrived everything to that end.

The detective contributes even more than the criminal to the good view of life set forth in these books. He makes the world simple, comprehensible, and orderly by discovering the essential clue and solving the murder. He understands the meanings and possibilities of life and reveals its vistas to us. He gives us security, certainty and protection. By unearthing the criminal he sets in motion the scapegoat mechanism which shifts the burden of guilt from our shoulders. He can do all these things because he has control over the world we know and the destinies of men in it.

The most prominent feature of the detective is his power and strength. The fact that he is also represented as an intellectual need not lead us astray about this. He is not the feckless intellectual of popular culture, the absent-minded professor, the man who is cloistered, impractical and ineffective. On the contrary, his talents are used for a concrete practical end, the apprehension of the murderer. Intellect is for him simply a path to power, a means of controlling the external world.

Furthermore, his power is not solely intellectual. There is a tradition that he must be physically as well as mentally competent. Detectives in American stories of the hard-boiled school are supposed to be handy with their fists. Sherlock Holmes, though to some extent a recluse and at times a drug-addict, is an expert singlestick player, boxer, and swordsman. Peter Wimsey, no he-man, is still a famous athlete whose proficiency as a cricketer gives away his identity in "Murder Must Advertise." Even the effeminate Poirot shows a courage and alertness in ticklish situations which fit him a little bit into the type of the hero of adventure. Besides this, the detective works not just by intellect and logic but also by intuition. He often senses something wrong in a situation, and this sense prevents him from acting mistakenly or making a fool of himself, even though the whole truth is not yet revealed to his intellect. He plays his hunches, and they are apt to be right.

To make the detective appear a figure of power the police, like the criminal, are drummed into his service. By their very inadequacy or opposition to him they do more to display his qualities than they could by giving him the most efficient cooperation. The convention of the inept police force helps to establish the unique excellence of the detective, his ability to do things nobody else can do. Thus the superiority of the detective to the police has been a common feature of detective literature from Poe's Dupin to Gardner's Perry Mason. It has become especially prominent in recent books, especially American ones such as those of Geoffrey Homes or Dashiell Hammett. Despite some notable exceptions like Inspector Alleyn or Inspector French, there have been relatively few policeman-heroes, and a substantial number of these are police officers only in name who in practice perform something like the role of a private detective. Ellery Queen plays a lone hand and summons in his father's cohorts only for special tasks; the solution is his work and not theirs. Maigret, too, works mostly alone and excites the enmity or disapproval of his colleagues. In one of the latest of the series, he has retired from the Sûreté.

Since our present interest in the detective story is its impact on the reader, the important question to ask about the detective is what kind of fantasy he evokes in the reader's mind. At first glance the issue might seem to be whether the reader's relation to the detective is one of identification or dependence. We might attempt, as Louise Bogan suggests would be possible, to divide detective stories into those written for sadists and those written for masochists. Yet this first and most obvious way of putting the question does violence to the complexity of the reader's emotions and reactions, which for any book are likely to be not simple but ambiguous and multiple. As a matter of fact, identification and dependence do not exclude each other; each refers to a different aspect of the reader's reaction, and both are possible at the same time.

I suggest that the reader probably does identify himself with the detective, make the detective an extension of his ego, but only

THE DETECTIVE STORY AS A HISTORICAL SOURCE 317

in very general terms. The detective is on our side. His actions are beneficial to us, and we feel ourselves in some degree represented in them. On the other hand, this representation occurs at a distance. The reader may identify himself with the detective to the extent that he gets a vicarious thrill of power when the detective solves the mystery. But I doubt that he identifies himself with the detective to the larger extent of trying to solve the murder himself. The reader is audience. He is like the spectator at a football game, identifying himself with his team, feeling a personal triumph if they win, yet always aware that it is the players and not himself who do the work on which his satisfaction is based. Though the reader both identifies and depends, the emphasis is on the latter, the significant relationship is dependence.

I would argue, to support this, that the reader does not generally compete intellectually with the detective. A detective story is not an invitation to intellectual exercise or exertion, not a puzzle to which the reader must guess the answer. On the contrary, the claim of detective stories to be puzzle literature is in large part a fraud, and the reader, far from attempting to solve the mystery himself, depends on the detective to do it for him.

This is an extremely controversial point. Many detective stories claim to put all the clues in the reader's hands, to show him everything the detective sees, so that the reader has an equal chance to make something out of it. This is the so-called "gentlemen's agreement," the supposedly best modern practice, according to which, says Miss Sayers, readers demand to be put "on an equal footing with the detective himself, as regards all clues and discoveries." Mr. R. Austin Freeman, who also insists that the satisfaction a detective story offers the reader is primarily an intellectual one, argues that the principal connoisseurs of this literature are theologians, scholars and lawyers. To please this audience of subtle and skilled dialecticians, he thinks a good detective story must have above all two things: accuracy as to external facts, and freedom from fallacies of reasoning.

Unfortunately many detective stories, including some of the best-known ones, have neither one nor the other. Critics have

amused themselves for some time now by pointing out errors of
fact and deduction in the Sherlock Holmes tales. And the same
weaknesses can be found in many other works. If we applied to
detective stories the critical attention we give to serious literature,
we would find a surprising number that simply do not hang
together intellectually. This point is the theme of an important
article by Raymond Chandler in the December, 1944, issue of
the "Atlantic." Mr. Chandler examines a number of the most
famous detective novels of all time, "The Red House Mystery,"
"Trent's Last Case," "Busman's Honeymoon," "Murder in the
Calais Coach," and demonstrates conclusively that none of them
is free from important fallacies of reasoning, and that they will
not stand up for a moment under strict analysis.

The point should not, however, be pushed too far, for there
is a certain amount to be said on the other side. It might be
argued that the four stories selected by Mr. Chandler for comment
are not a fair sample of the best writing in the *genre*. Furthermore, the very fact that the detective story is popularly regarded
as puzzle literature has no doubt influenced writers to try to
create puzzles that are fair. Some of these books, particularly
including Mr. Freeman's, are well written and articulated, and in
fact detective literature at its best demands a good deal in the
way of strict construction and technical proficiency, and is not
easy to write. Also, I have found a number of readers who insist
that they read detective stories as puzzles, and are often able to
determine the identity of the murderer in the middle of the story
by logical deduction from the clues. And yet, without going into
the question of the extent to which these readers may be deceiv-
ing themselves, I would doubt that the majority of readers discover the murderer by logical processes of thought before the
denouement, and I would doubt that this is even possible in a
large number, perhaps the majority, of detective stories.

Any writer of detective fiction who tries to adhere to the
"gentlemen's agreement" faces the problem well put by Miss
Sayers, "How can we at the same time show the reader everything

and yet legitimately obfuscate him as to its meaning?" I submit that what this "legitimate obfuscation" often amounts to is that either the clues are *not* all given to the reader or, if they are, this is not done in a significant way that will enable him to determine their meaning.

The reader, if he guesses correctly at all, does so not by reasoning from the evidence, but rather by selecting the least probable character, the person the evidence does not point to. The reader's solution is a guess and not a deduction. It is on the level of the speculations of the woman in the Thurber story who knew that, whoever might have murdered Duncan, the deed could not possibly have been done by Macbeth because he was too obvious a suspect, a patent red herring.

For the detective story to have a solution that could readily be guessed by the majority of readers would go clean against the whole nature and character of the *genre*. The solution has to come as a surprise. A story has no punch when the reader can guess the murderer before the denouement. Furthermore, the purpose of the detective novel, as we saw from other evidence, is to comfort the reader, create agreeable illusions for him. If these books described themselves primarily as tests of the reader's intelligence, which the reader would flunk if he did not guess the murderer before the end, many readers would scarcely find detective stories comforting. For, if the puzzles are so difficult that they can be worked out by the most intelligent readers only with some effort, they would be far beyond the less intelligent but more numerous remainder of the audience.

Detective stories are not a test of the reader's intelligence but, at the most, a means of creating in the reader a delusion that he is intelligent and that, by following the steps in the analysis, he has somehow displayed intellectual proficiency. All too often, the "gentlemen's agreement" means in practice nothing more than that the *appearance* of fair play is to be maintained. The good writing, if any, helps to create and maintain this illusion.

This effort to maintain the illusion of the reader's intelligence is simply a device to keep decently concealed what I consider to be the basic feature of the detective story, the reader's dependence on the detective. Our attitude toward dependence is apt to be ambivalent: we may need it, and at the same time resent having to confess this need or having it called to our attention. The pretense that the detective story is an intellectual puzzle helps to hide the feeling of dependence which the reader goes to these books to find but which he hates to acknowledge.

In any case, there seems little doubt about the dependence of the reader, as of all the characters in the story, upon the detective-hero. The attraction of this literature is that, though the problem may be beyond the powers of the reader or of any of the characters in the story, we can always depend on the detective to step in and solve it. We get satisfaction from seeing him do this even before we know how he is going to bring it off, for the interest lies not in the steps of the analysis but in the certainty of the solution. Thus the reader may get a little bored in the middle of the book when one theory after another is tried and discarded, but when Dr. Fell says he now pretty well knows who the murderer was, when Poirot says he of course identified the murderer two days ago and is only waiting to settle the details, when Holmes says the crime is simple and obvious and presents no difficulty—the reader's interest is quickened by a thrill of excitement.

The characters in the book, like the reader, prove to be passive under the detective's control. By the end they sometimes become his puppets, doing what he planned without knowing he meant them to. In the denouement scene, a character will make an important statement, or act in a particular manner, or even commit suicide, and after it is all over people will realize that the detective planned it just that way. The detective's interference with the lives of the other characters is almost as self-confident as that of a deity, and the reader is supposed to love it.

The passiveness of the reader is underlined by one of the most famous devices of all, the narration of the story by a confidant, a foil to the detective, of which Dr. Watson is the outstanding example. The reader sees the story through the eyes

of Watson or Hastings or whoever it may be, and also shares the
confidant's sense of security and stability which comes from his
dependence on the detective.

The confidant, though he may be of various types, is generally somewhat stupid, inferior to the detective, and the detective
pokes fun at his blunders and obtuseness.   But the confidant
doesn't object to this.   Even Dr. Watson, though he does at times
rebel against Holmes' superior manner, shows an almost maso-
chistic streak.   He doesn't mind being ordered around by Holmes
without explanation; in fact, he gets a thrill out of it.   He is
delighted to be proved wrong and to have his stupidity shown up.
For all this enhances his belief in the infallibility of the detective.
The detective becomes a kind of father-image to whom the
narrator is occasionally opposed but in general submissive.   The
Watson-Holmes relationship gives an opening for the instincts of
hero-worship.

But what is the historical importance of this? How can such
a description as I have attempted here of fantasies and the motivations to which they correspond, even if it is made much more
accurate and extensive, be translated into terms of society and
politics? The answer to this question, suggested at the beginning
of this paper, may now be given more fully. The point of all I
have been saying is that the detective story is hokum, a means of
arousing in the reader a belief in contrary-to-fact conditions, an
opiate and a drug, which protects the reader from the facts of life
by covering him with veils upon veils of illusions. The historical
value of the detective story is that it describes day-dreams, and describes them with a wealth of documentation extending into innumerable volumes. A knowledge of people's day-dreams may enable us to progress to an understanding of their desires. In this
way, a careful study of literature of this kind may reveal popular
attitudes which shed a flood of light on the motivation behind
political, social, and economic history.

The method can be illustrated on the basis of the preliminary
survey attempted here, and I will now, finally, indicate by a
couple of suggestions how it might work. To take a negative
point first, even this cursory examination will enable us to dismiss

as uncritical and altogether false the thesis, which has been hazarded by not a few writers, that the detective story is in some fashion a flower of democracy and an embodiment of the democratic way of life. The argument used to support this view is that these books have appeared almost exclusively in democratic countries, chiefly England and America, while by contrast the writings of Agatha Christie and Edgar Wallace were banned by Hitler as "decadent." The reason alleged is that this kind of literature can flourish only in a society where there is due process of law, a non-faulty procedure for handling evidence, public sympathy on the side of order, and an effective police dedicated to finding the truth by objective means.

This argument, in the light of what has so far been said, is obviously nonsense. It is not true, incidentally, that detective literature has appeared solely in democratic societies, for Vidocq published his "Memoirs" in the age of Louis Philippe and Gaboriau wrote mostly under the Second Empire. Nor does the development of effective police forces seem relevant, since the fictional detective works separately from or even against the police, who are represented as anything but effective.

Even if we grant, what is for the most part true, that the *genre* has flourished mainly in England and the United States, it does not follow that it is an illustration of democratic sentiment or a symbol of democratic culture. Our analysis of the detective story would lead to a somewhat less reassuring view. The whole tenor of these books appears to be that they show an enormous demand for gratification, on the level of fantasy, of basic drives which apparently cannot be satisfied in our western society on the level of ordinary reality, and which have an application going rather beyond democratic institutions. The resemblance of the fantasies of dependence and aggression in the detective novel to the two principal political figures of totalitarianism, the dictator and the scapegoat, has been pointed out before this.

Though the detective story appears non-political on the surface, the roles of its two protagonists are saturated with political meanings. The criminal, by the very fact that he is the least likely person, justifies the reader's suspicion that all men, including those who appear most innocent, are really his potential enemies. The reader gets a tremendous vicarious satisfaction when the criminal is identified, for this denouement confirms to the reader that he is right to suspect everybody. The criminal is a fantasy developing out of a competitive, uncohesive society. He is a personalization of our grievances, as we like to personalize them in the atmosphere of political or social crisis in real life. We have toward the criminal the same or comparable feelings that we have toward any one of the commonly accepted scapegoats of our day, the Jew, the labor agitator, Wall Street, the "radical," the capitalist, or whatever other image we have formed the habit of using. And we like to attribute to these bogeymen, as we do to the criminal, sham strength instead of real strength, and to think of them as major threats which, however, we will somehow always be able to counter.

The detective, on the other hand, has many characteristics in common with the modern political leader or agitator. He simplifies life, makes sense out of it and gives it meaning. His strength is real, unlike the criminal's pseudo-strength, for it is based not just on externals but on intuition and a sense of community with the right things in the universe. Like the agitator in Professor Lowenthal's article (in "The Public Opinion Quarterly," Fall, 1948), he is conservative and objects not to the system but to certain people, the criminal or criminals, who seem to be endangering it. And yet the detective is not really a part of the established framework of society, for he neither belongs to the police, the official guardians of the law, nor is he a member of the closed circle or group within which the plot develops. Thus, though he moves in an ordered universe, the order is not that of the police or other regular authorities, but an order that is discovered and imposed by him. The detective may have a kind of democratic aura, for he frequently rises from the ranks and is not distinguished by birth, and although he moves unperturbed among the highly placed he is not one of them. Yet he is indispensable, for he alone can solve the riddle.   Therefore the authorities (the family or the police) perforce surrender the controls to him, sometimes reluctantly and occasionally with sharp protest. One could argue that all these qualities add up to a dictator, that the detective is the extra-legal superman who is called in to accomplish by extraordinary measures what is impossible within the traditional organization of society.

Thus a case could be made to show that the detective story is no monument to the strength of democracy but rather a symptom revealing its weaknesses, the insupportable burdens it places on the individual. The detective story does not reflect order, but expresses on the fantasy level a yearning for order; it suggests, then, a disordered world, and its roots are to be sought in social disintegration rather than in social cohesion.

All this is not to suggest that the impulses catered to in this literature made their first appearance in history in the nineteenth century, and never existed before. On the contrary, the fantasies of the detective story appear in recognizable form in the popular culture of other ages, in folklore for example, and the drives they reveal are therefore by no means recent in origin but might rather be regarded as traditional elements of the human character as it has developed in our civilization. Nostalgia for the dependent relationships of childhood is hardly a novelty of our own age. The significant thing is rather that so many people of our age, roughly the era of democratic liberalism, have seemingly come to depend on an enormous literature for the development and even the artificial stimulation of these fantasies. This literature offers disturbing evidence of psychological tensions, and of the prevalence in our modern western culture of elements of character-structure which do not provide adequate support for democratic institutions. The hypothesis toward which a study of these books might tend is that the political arrangements in a democracy, in contrast to the political arrangements in more authoritarian types of government, are simply not adequate to take up this strain.

But perhaps we should beware of taking evidence of this sort too tragically, or of deducing from detective stories nothing but a pessimistic moral. The condemnation of detective stories as drugs or cheap escapism may be pedantic. For, if they are a symptom, they can also be a cure. If we credit the Freudian view that socially dangerous impulses can be got rid of by removing them to the level of fantasy, then detective stories could be described as a harmless safety valve, a wholesome therapy serving a desirable social purpose. And yet one may wonder if this commonly accepted view is entirely correct, if fantasy and real life are actually so unrelated. To some extent we may build our real life around our fantasy and, if this is so, sensation literature may not so much rid us of dangerous drives as reinforce and reshape them.

In any case, if detective stories are not so sinister as they at first appear from analysis, neither are they as frivolous as some critics have judged them. The drives they cater to are compelling and basic, and relate ultimately to the struggle for self-preservation. It is the universal nature of their theme which explains the size and variety of their reading audience. The intellectual, who scorns the cheap fantasies of the popular magazines, is not likely to be able to forgo the fantasies which give him hope for his survival in an alien world. Detective stories deal, in their own way and on their own level, with the most essential and urgent problems in the human situation.

MORE ON AUTHOR AND SUBJECT

William O. Aydelotte was born in Bloomington, Indiana in 1910, received his A.B. from Harvard in 1931 and his Ph.D. from Cambridge in 1934. He joined the History Department of the University of Iowa in 1947, was associate editor of the Journal of Modern History *from 1949 to 1952, and has been a full professor at Iowa since 1950.*

I know of no other critique of crime fiction that takes the same line of approach as Prof. Aydelotte's.

†If an award is ever created for the most horizon-broadening commentator on crime fiction, it will have to go to Frank McSherry. His essay on the concept of crime in stories of the future, which you are about to read, is the most speculative piece in this book, and its relevance extends to students of science fiction, and of science, and of society, as well as to devotees of crime fiction.

The Shape of Crimes to Come
by Frank D. McSherry, Jr.

Are you doing anything today that may be declared a crime tomorrow?

The detective-crime story deals with the commission and detection of criminal acts and with the circumstances surrounding such acts. A criminal act is any act that any society decides to call criminal. Under this empirical and pragmatic definition, we need not bother our heads about the fact that what may be branded a crime at one time and place may not be so labelled at another. Detective-crime stories set in the Roaring Twenties and dealing with the crime of bootlegging are still detective-crime stories despite the fact that the open sale and use of intoxicants is not now a crime and was not before Prohibition.

The category of detective-crime story therefore includes stories in which the crime involved is not a crime now, and may even be an admirable moral act now, but is a crime in the imagined future in which a given story is set. The stories which fall within this description are completely new to most mystery readers, who have tended to classify such tales (correctly) as science fiction and (incorrectly) as science fiction only. But it would be unfortunate if lovers of mystery fiction continued to overlook these works; for, quite apart from their often high qualities as fiction, they offer more food for thought than do most detective-crime stories, especially about the legal, social and philosophical problems that are marching toward us from the future with a grim inevitability. The sooner we begin thinking about some of these problems the better; and if we get a first-rate story thrown into the bargain as well, we are that much better off.

Of all the situations approaching us in the future with which society may attempt to deal by imposing criminal sanctions, first and foremost is the population explosion.

Daniel Boone left his Kentucky valley home in disgust because another family moved into the other end of the valley twenty miles away: by God, it's gitting so a feller can't sit on his own front porch no more without a whole passel of people breathing down the back of his neck! That wasn't so long ago, either, as time goes in the life of nations; but things have changed immensely in the short time since then.

Tried to cross the street—or highway—lately? It takes longer with every year that goes by. Every year there are more cars, because every year there are more people to be transported and supplied.

Have your taxes gone up lately? There are many reasons why, but one of them is the rising number of people. Twice as many people in a given area need twice as many schools, hospitals, policemen, etc.

Have prices gone up at the supermarket lately? If you have twice as many people, you need twice as many trucks to supply them with food. Twice as many trucks means so much more traffic (and traffic jams), and so many more man-hours required to deliver the food, which means that the distributor must increase his prices proportionally or go out of business.

The problems created by the population explosion seem to be increasing all over the world. If the trend continues society may decide to deal with it by passing new criminal laws. The imposition of birth controls by law is a controversial subject as every newspaper reader knows. Does any government have the right to tell you how many children you can have? Should it be given that right? Several authors have written stories postulating that government will be given or take upon itself such a power.

In Harry Harrison's "A Criminal Act" (*Analog,* January 1967), our society takes a fairly simple and obvious course. The Criminal Birth Act of 1993 forbids married couples to have more than the legal limit of two children per couple. Though the law and the crime are new, the punishment is a secular version of an old one: excommunication. The police power of the state will no longer protect Benedict Vernall, criminal, whose wife is going to have a third child. Any public-spirited citizen who volunteers to kill Vernall will be given a license and twenty-four hours in which to do so without fear of punishment. However, since the purpose of the law is to limit the population, the charge against Vernall will be dropped if he can kill his assassin. Harrison's story tells excitingly of the twenty-four hours during which Vernall is hunted down in his own apartment by an experienced professional killer-for-thrills.

Editor John W. Campbell's introduction to the story is sharply pointed and thought-provoking, especially for those who take a blindly literal view of law-and-order. "A criminal act is, by definition, something that's against the law. George Washington was a criminal, Hitler was not. . .because he passed laws before he acted. That a thing is legal doesn't guarantee that it's good or evil." It is true that Vernall is fighting for his new baby's right to survive, but what about the right of us others to survive? There's only so much food, water and land available. Which side are you on?

Harrison's method may be accused of giving an unfair edge to any criminal who is fast with a gun. A more democratic method of solving the population problem is presented in Frederik Pohl's "The Census Takers" (*The Magazine of Fantasy and Science Fiction,* February 1956). The titular officials count the population once a year; all people over the count of 300 found in any census team's area are executed by the team on the spot. "Jumping"—that is, packing with intent to move when a census team is in the area—is a capital crime in this society. Encountering a family of five that is guilty of this offense, the Enumerator mercifully has only the father executed.

Where the supply of food has not increased and the supply of people has, intense emotions can be generated. As Pohl's narrator recounts: ". . .I couldn't help telling him: 'I've met your kind before, mister. Five kids! If it wasn't for people like you we wouldn't *have* any Overs, did you ever think of that? Sure you didn't—you people never think of anything but yourself! Five kids, and then when the Census comes around, you think you can get smart and Jump.' I tell you, I was shaking."

Society devises a third method of dealing with the consequences of a shortage of food and a surplus of people in H. Ken Bulmer's novelette "Sunset," published in the now-deceased Scottish magazine *Nebula Science Fiction* (November 1955). In this world, not too long from now, it is a capital crime to be too ill or old to work. Society simply does not have the surplus of goods to support any person who cannot support himself. Any person who fails to pass the periodic medical checkup required of everyone is given three days' warning by the State so that he may hold and attend his own funeral, at the conclusion of which he is tastefully and painlessly put to death. Those who attempt to evade this law and practice are criminals to be executed by the police on sight and without trial.

Anton Rand, foreman at Interplanetary Shipbuilders and helping the firm to finish a new automatic rocketship for travel to settlements on Mars and Venus, has been brought up under this system and approves of it. "I don't remember the old days. . . . It must have been rather terrible to see cripples and old helpless people on the streets, and to know that somewhere in the world other people were starving for the food those useless mouths were eating. We do things decently today." He approves of the system, that is, until his father fails to pass the routine checkup and is given the customary three days' warning.   Rand then turns criminal and plots to smuggle his sick father aboard the new rocket to safety on another world.

Though its writing is generally undistinguished, the story is memorable for its point of view. With grim and realistic honesty, Bulmer points out that Rand is not a hero but a villain. In the future society Bulmer postulates, Rand's attempt to save his sick father from execution is not just a technical crime but a genuinely criminal act, injurious to other human beings and to society in general. In a world so short of food that no one gets more than the bare minimum necessary to survive, the feeding of any extra person means that the amount available for the rest of us must be cut below subsistence level by just that much. Rand's act would today be admirable and moral, not criminal; but in the society of tomorrow that we are fast approaching—a society of too many people and too little food that we with our overproduction of people and our waste of natural resources are even now creating—Rand's act is, unpleasant though the fact may be to a reader of today, both illegal and immoral. Or do you prefer to defend him?

An ingenious new law that not only keeps the population down but solves the problem of the Generation Gap at the same time is shown in operation in William F. Nolan and George Clayton Johnson's novel *Logan's Run* (Dial Press, 1968). In this future world it is a capital crime to be over twenty-one.

A colored flower is indelibly imprinted on the palm of every child at birth. The color automatically changes every five years, and flickers throughout the day preceding one's twenty-first birthday. The citizen must then report promptly to the Deep Sleep factories, where he will be painlessly killed. On his twenty-first birthday the flower turns black, automatically alerting the Sandmen, or Deep Sleep police, that someone has not reported to the factories and is trying to run for his life. The police will then hunt the hated Runner down. Locating him through their many TV spy eyes throughout the city, they will kill him on sight. It is rumored, however, that some Runners have succeeded in escaping the Sandmen, that there is an underground route to safety and to the man rumored to be the oldest human now alive, almost forty years old.

Sandman Logan supports the system, hunting and killing the criminal Runners with ruthless efficiency, until the flower on his own palm begins to flicker. He fails to report to the Deep Sleep factories, telling himself he is doing so only in order to locate and destroy the underground route and die in a blaze of suicidal glory while doing his duty. Logan begins his run from the police, using his thorough knowledge of their own techniques against them.

Logan's run takes him through a world of nightmarish garishness, a world slowly breaking down and incapable of progress, since no one lives long enough to acquire the experience needed to make advances in any area of endeavor. There is time only to perform an insufficient number of repairs on the old machines. From a dying city miles under the sea, from state-owned nurseries where children are brought up entirely by machines, to the giant computer that governs the world though its parts are slowly running down and its lights slowly going out as no one comes to repair it, and to the jungle growing over the ruins of atom-bombed Washington, Logan runs into and from a nightmare world devoted entirely to the young.

Nolan and Johnson do not say that these things will happen, let alone that they ought to happen; the legal and moral problems they raise are kept in the background and implied rather than expressly dealt with. Their primary concern is to write a suspenseful chase story, filled with images of beauty and horror. *Logan's Run* is intense, almost poetic, and hard to forget. But again, whose side are you on?

Charles Beaumont provides an even more nightmarish answer to the population problem in his well-known "The Crooked Man" (*Playboy,* August 1955; *The Hunger and Other Stories,* Putnam 1957). Here society attempts to control the phenomenon of heterosexual attraction and its resultant overabundance of babies (the story was of course written before the Pill) by structuring its legal and educational system so as to turn its citizens into sexual perverts and making heterosexual relations a crime. Adding to the grim force of this memorable and horrifying tale is the reader's feeling that, in view of what atrocities governments have committed within our lifetime, Beaumont's nightmare vision is far from impossible.

Another method of keeping the population low is adopted by the future society of Philip K. Dick's novelette "Time Pawn" (*Thrilling Wonder Stories,* Summer 1954; later revised and expanded into a novel, *Dr. Futurity,* Ace 1960). When some strange force hurls young Dr. Parsons from his safe world of 1998 onto a night hillside, one look at the changed shapes of the stars tells him he has been thrown into the far future. But Parsons, an intelligent man, isn't especially worried. He is a trained doctor, his brain full of the race's most advanced medical knowledge, his bag full of the most advanced medical discoveries science has yet made. Surely he will be able to get along wherever he is; every society needs doctors.

Entering a city, he finds a girl dying after a vicious and unprovoked attack by a band of armed, uniformed and apparently government-supported band of juveniles. Parsons confidently goes to work, performing major surgery in a hotel lobby, removing the girl's damaged heart and replacing it with a mechanical one operated by an atomic battery. For a doctor of 1998 this is a routine and almost boring operation; the girl lives—and Parsons is promptly arrested by horrified onlookers. The charges: saving a human life and practicing medicine, both capital crimes. The next morning the girl herself signs the charges against him, then commits suicide.

Society's way of controlling the number of people is to make the teaching and practice of medicine illegal, and to authorize extra-legal killings by armed juvenile gangs. Every male is sterilized at puberty and samples of his gametes are kept in frozen form in sperm banks. The only ones allowed to reproduce are those few who win the world-wide games and tests society has devised to locate superior specimens of humanity. The death of one person automatically authorizes the birth of another from the frozen sperm of the ideal specimens, so that each newborn baby is far superior to the dead person he replaces; a man's death does not diminish mankind but advances and improves it. Naturally, therefore, a doctor, a man whose vocation is to prevent death, is a criminal.

The court mercifully takes cognizance of Parsons' unusual background and sentences him not to death but to life-long exile on Mars. But in every society there are groups that can use the services of a professional criminal. Indeed, it is one such group, armed with an imperfect knowledge of time travel, that brought Parsons to the future in the first place. For reasons of their own, they need a doctor badly; so they rescue Parsons. The plots and counterplots thus set in motion keep Parsons on the run, taking him far forward in time to a deserted Earth where he finds a giant stone monolith with his name carved in it; back to the past to see Sir Francis Drake and his *Golden Hind* stop over in California on a round-the-world trip; and back to the world he was thrust into, where he becomes involved with a radical student society that advocates the open teaching of medicine and is viciously hunted by the police as a consequence.

Dr. Futurity is a fine fast-moving novel, full of action and counterplots. It is interesting to note that in the novel one side wins whereas in the earlier short version "Time Pawn" the other side comes out on top. You pays your money, you takes your pick.

In our own time we have seen medical science improve to the point where successful transplants of the heart and other vital organs have been accomplished. As long as man can replace his worn-out organs with brand-new ones in fine condition, he may live virtually forever. In his short novel "The Organ leggers" (*Galaxy*, January 1969), Larry Niven points out some unpleasant legal and social consequences of this new scientific advance.

Since there are many more people with damaged organs needing to be replaced than there are people with good organs they are willing to part with, the demand for hearts and limbs and so on will inevitably exceed the supply. How can the supply be increased? Niven suggests two ways. One is legal: society restores the death penalty, applies it to more and more offenses, and finally imposes it automatically on anyone found guilty of exceeding the speed limit three times. A surgical team carries out the sentence, removing the victim's vital organs and quick-freezing them for storage in organ banks until they are called for. (Doubtless you believe yourself to be a kindly person, but would you vote to abolish the death penalty, even for such an offense as speeding, if it meant that you might lose your chance for centuries of extra life?)

The second way is illegal. New scientific advances often bring new crimes with them. Where demand of a commodity exceeds supply, as in Prohibition, criminal organizations arise to fill that demand, as in Prohibition. The new criminal, the organlegger, supplies hearts, legs, lungs etc. in brand-new condition to those who are rich enough to pay his fees and desperate enough not to care whether those organs were given up willingly and legally. The protagonist in Niven's story is Gil Hamilton, a member of ARM, which is a branch of the UN Police Force organized expressly to track down this new breed of criminal. For some time Gil has been trying to nail a new group of organleggers who somewhere have found a large supply of untraceable victims. When a friend of his dies in a particularly gruesome way, Gil slowly realizes that the man was murdered and that the organlegger group is involved.

Another problem area with which the law may attempt to deal in the future is the prevention of nuclear war. In John Wyndham's short story "The Wheel" (*Startling Stories*, January 1952), a five-year-old boy commits a capital crime: he rediscovers the wheel. In the wake of an all-out atomic war, the terrified few survivors had outlawed all discovery. They have made science the scapegoat for their own failures, and the wheel the symbol of science. Wyndham's point of course is that it is not knowledge, but what man does with his knowledge, that is good or evil.

Even in the Dark Ages some research went on, though only in narrowly circumscribed areas. In Lewis Padgett's (Henry Kuttner's) "Tomorrow and Tomorrow" (*Astounding Science Fiction,* January-February 1947; *Tomorrow and Tomorrow and The Fairy Chessmen,* Gnome Press 1951), all scientific research is made illegal. In this future, an appalling third world war has been stopped before it has killed more than a few million people. Riots of unparalleled violence break out, for "When a man is in an ammunition dump that is on fire, he will have less hesitancy in firing a gun." No government survives the riots, and the UN's successor, the Global Peace Commission, takes over control of the world by default. Its solution to the problem of war is to make any scientific advance in any field illegal. Dedicated fanatically to the status quo, it places a murderous stranglehold on human progress for a hundred years. No one starves, no one is fired, but there is no cure for cancer or any other yet-uncured disease, nor will there be as long as that stranglehold exists.

It is not surprising that a criminal group arises that wants to restart World War III and play it through to the finish, believing that full-scale nuclear war is preferable to the slow death by strangulation that the GPC is imposing on the human race. The malcontents feel that the GPC's grip is so strong that only an atomic war can break it. They ask atomic physicist Joseph Breden, monitor of Uranium Pile One, to join them. In addition to deciding whether to join the revolutionaries, Breden has personal problems to wrestle with: lately he has been having bad dreams in which he cuts off all protective devices against sabotage on the pile, pulls out the cadmium control rods and detonates the pile, setting off an atomic explosion that will destroy not only the pile but civilization as well.

Kuttner's story, full of excitement and suspense, poses a

problem not only for its protagonist but for the reader as well. Would you prefer a society where perfect safety and security is achieved for you at the price of permanent stagnation and the almost certain death of the whole race centuries later, or a society that achieves constant progress in all areas though it runs a risk of destruction in atomic holocaust?

We have seen that new advances in science may bring new crimes with them. Let us assume that psychology and genetics will have developed so far in a future time that inheritable diseases such as color-blindness, bad eyesight and rheumatic hearts can be bred out of the race entirely if its members will marry only people with the correct genes, and that one can be psychologically treated so that he will fall genuinely in love with another who possesses the proper genes. In such a world it will be a crime to marry anyone whose genes combined with yours will produce a physically or mentally defective child. Do you have the right to marry whom you please, if it can be scientifically proved that the children of that union will be defective? Should you have such a right? And when a characteristic is judged "defective," how do you judge that judgment?

The Population Control Board tells artist Aies Marlan on her twenty-first birthday whom she will marry, so that she and her chosen husband will be certain to produce children without defects. But Aies is in love with Paul, whose genes are not right for her. To escape the psychological conditioning that will destroy her love for Paul and force her to love the man the Board has chosen for her, Aies steals a plane and with Paul beside her attempts "The Escape" in John W. Campbell's short story (*Astounding Science Fiction*, May 1935; in book form, *Cloak of Aesir*, Shasta Press 1952.)

We today would tend to regard Aies and Paul as heroic revolutionaries against a vicious tyranny; but, given the advances in psychology and genetics that Campbell postulates, the reader must consider the painful question whether they are not in reality a pair of selfish, antisocial immoralists. Behind its excellent writing and action and suspense, the story poses two basic questions. One, how much power should the government have over you? Two, may not the advance of science make the right answer to question one today a wrong answer tomorrow?

A society that has solved all its problems may well be in trouble just as deep as one with too many problems, as the British author S. Fowler Wright suggests in his novel *The Adventure of Wyndham Smith* (London: Jenkins, 1938), in which the protagonists commit the capital crime of failing to commit suicide.

A scientific experiment sends Wyndham Smith into a far distant future where the human race has solved all the problems facing us now. It is a quiet and peaceful world, without war, want or crime. And that is the ironic catch: having solved all problems, the people have nothing left to do, and are bored to death. The governing council decides that the only logical solution to the quandary is mass suicide. The people agree, and happily go off one by one to a painless death in the great suicide chambers; that is, all but Smith, the man from the past, and the beautiful girl he has fallen in love with. They become criminals, evading the mass-suicide law, and thus become the last people alive. But the dead are not fools; they have made provision for the contingency that someone, somewhere, might actually wish to go on living. They have designed and left behind them a deadly mechanical bloodhound, like a small tank, that is set to find any living thing and kill it on sight. Smith and the girl flee for their lives through an abandoned world whose superscientific devices have been permanently turned off, a world sunk in a moment to the level of the stone age.

Wright's grim, slow-moving novel asks: What is the goal of human life; and what happens after that goal is achieved? What can the human race do after all its problems are solved, all its passions spent, the Utopia it claims to want made real at last? Where can you go from the top? The novel is written in a dry, matter-of-fact pedestrian style which would kill most stories but which surprisingly makes this one immensely convincing. Incidentally, Wright used the same concept a little later for his short story "Original Sin," published in England in his collection *The Witchfinder* (Books of Today Ltd., n.d.) and in the United States in *The Throne of Saturn* (Arkham House, 1949). Again two criminals disobey the law of mass suicide. The story has a sting at the end that remains in the mind long after.

Most of the stories dealing with crimes of the future are fast-moving and full of action and suspense. Their authors are writers first, intent on telling a good story well. They do not suggest that the events, laws and solutions in their stories will happen or should happen. They are aware of the many moral, philosophical and legal problems they are raising, but they use these problems to forward the plot and make the story interesting, to provide a background for the action in the foreground. Nevertheless, they do raise the problems. Someday you and I will have to decide these problems, perhaps sooner than we wish to; and the earlier we begin to think about them the more time we will have to consider our decisions. If we are spurred to hard thinking on these topics, we will have derived more than the excitement of a rousing good story from these tales of the shape of crimes to come.

MORE ON AUTHOR AND SUBJECT

A brief biography of Frank McSherry appears at the end of his "The Janus Resolution," earlier in this book.

I know of no other work of non-fiction on the precise topic of "The Shape of Crimes to Come," but a recent and relevant anthology of the kind of stories McSherry has analyzed, Hans Stefan Santesson's Crime Prevention in the 30th Century *(Walker, 1969), may be consulted with profit. And in another essay, "Under Two Flags: The Detective Story in Science Fiction" (The* Armchair Detective, *April 1969), McSherry treats the relations between the two genres from an entirely different perspective.*